Metric Conversion Table

Inches (in.)	1/64	1/32	1/25	1/16	1/8	1/4	3/8	2/5	1/2	5/8	3/4	7/8	1	2	3	4	5	6	7	8						
Feet (ft.)																										
Yards (yd.)																									1	1 1/10[†]
Millimeters* (mm.)	0.40	0.79	1	1.59	3.18	6.35	9.53	10	12.7	15.9	19.1	22.2	25.4	50.8	76.2	101.6	127	152	178	203	229	254	279	305	914	1,000
Centimeters* (cm.)							0.95	1	1.27	1.59	1.91	2.22	2.54	5.08	7.62	10.16	12.7	15.2	17.8	20.3	22.9	25.4	27.9	30.5	91.4	100
Meters* (m.)																								.30	.91	1.00

To find the metric equivalent of quantities not in this table, add together the appropriate entries. For example, to convert 2 5/8 inches to centimeters, add the figure given for the centimeter equivalent of 2 inches, 5.08, and the equivalent of 5/8 inch, 1.59, to obtain 6.67 centimeters.

Metric values are rounded off.
†*Approximate fractions.*

Conversion Factors

To change:	Into:	Multiply by:
Inches	Millimeters	25.4
Inches	Centimeters	2.54
Feet	Meters	0.305
Yards	Meters	0.914
Miles	Kilometers	1.609
Square Inches	Square Centimeters	6.45
Square Feet	Square Meters	0.093
Square Yards	Square Meters	0.836
Cubic Inches	Cubic Centimeters	16.4
Cubic Feet	Cubic Meters	0.0283
Cubic Yards	Cubic Meters	0.765
Pints (U.S.)	Liters	0.473 (Imp. 0.568)
Quarts (U.S.)	Liters	0.946 (Imp. 1.136)
Gallons (U.S.)	Liters	3.785 (Imp. 4.546)
Ounces	Grams	28.4
Pounds	Kilograms	0.454
Tons	Metric Tons	0.907

To change:	Into:	Multiply by:
Millimeters	Inches	0.039
Centimeters	Inches	0.394
Meters	Feet	3.28
Meters	Yards	1.09
Kilometers	Miles	0.621
Square Centimeters	Square Inches	0.155
Square Meters	Square Feet	10.8
Square Meters	Square Yards	1.2
Cubic Centimeters	Cubic Inches	0.061
Cubic Meters	Cubic Feet	35.3
Cubic Meters	Cubic Yards	1.31
Liters	Pints (U.S.)	2.114 (Imp. 1.76)
Liters	Quarts (U.S.)	1.057 (Imp. 0.88)
Liters	Gallons (U.S.)	0.264 (Imp. 0.22)
Grams	Ounces	0.035
Kilograms	Pounds	2.2
Metric Tons	Tons	1.1

THE FAMILY
Handyman®

Weekend Improvements

THE FAMILY Handyman®

Weekend Improvements

Over 30 Do-it-yourself Projects for the Home

Reader's Digest

THE READER'S DIGEST ASSOCIATION, INC.
Pleasantville, New York / Montreal

A READER'S DIGEST BOOK

Produced by Roundtable Press, Inc.
Directors: Susan E. Meyer, Marsha Melnick
Executive Editor: Amy T. Jonak
Project Editor: William Broecker
Editor: Thomas Neven
Assistant Editor: Megan Keiler
Design: Sisco & Evans, New York
Production: Phil Fabian, Steven Rosen

For The Family Handyman
Editor: Gary Havens
Senior Editor: Ken Collier
Associate Editor: Spike Carlsen

For Reader's Digest
Executive Editor: James Wagenvoord
Editorial Director: John Sullivan
Design Director: Michele Italiano-Perla
Managing Editors: Diane Shanley, Christine Moltzen
Editorial Associate: Daniela Marchetti

Library of Congress Cataloging in Publication Data
The family handyman weekend improvements: over 30 do-it-yourself
    projects for the home.
        p.   cm.
    Includes index.
    ISBN 0-89577-685-5
    1. Dwellings—Remodeling—Amateurs' manuals.   I. Reader's Digest
    Association.   II. Title: Weekend Improvements.
    TH4816.F354   1995
    643'.7—dc20   94-46623

A Note from the Editor

Every project in this book has been adapted from the pages of *The Family Handyman* magazine, which has been published continuously since 1951. Today, more than four million do-it-yourselfers read it ten times each year. More important to you, every project in the book was actually built by a member of the magazine staff. Long before we began writing and producing how-to articles for the magazine, every one of us made our living with our hands. That is, we are carpenters, plumbers, electricians, painters, and cabinetmakers who are expert in our chosen fields.

This wasn't always so. At one time we were all beginners. We knew we didn't know a lot, but it was a shock to discover we knew even less than we thought! Our own masters and teachers told us that. But we learned, and now we'd like to do our part to make things easier, more enjoyable, and less scary for you.

As editor, my job is to ask questions. "Where's the warm, helpful human voice in this?" I'll scrawl on an early draft of a magazine article. Or, "Wouldn't this be better shown with a colorful illustration, rather than explained in words?" Or, "You're using insider talk here. Will the reader know what it is? Explain it in plain English!" Or, "Where might this project NOT work? In some regions of the country, or in a certain type of structure? Let's be clear with the reader!"

We try to anticipate and resolve problems that do-it-yourselfers usually don't even know are on the way. We also help with the problems you do know about, and give clear directions that—we hope—keep difficulties to a minimum. I hope you'll enjoy these projects.

Gary Havens, Editor
The Family Handyman

Contents

Introduction

Few things are as satisfying as making your home a more pleasant place to live and increasing its value at the same time. When you do it yourself, not only do you save money but you can take great personal pride in the results.

The over 30 projects in *The Family Handyman Weekend Improvements* show you how to upgrade, repair, and redecorate the interior of your home. Each project has been developed by experienced professionals to be well within the capabilities of the nonprofessional do-it-yourselfer. No special tools are required, and the instructions are written so that you are sure to get excellent results even without previous experience. New and unfamiliar techniques are clearly explained. The construction diagrams and photographs use colors to show each important part distinctly, to help you understand and avoid mistakes. In addition, helpful tips tell you how to save time, work, and money and still get professional-looking results.

Perhaps the most important part of any DIY project is doing it safely. Wear safety glasses whenever you hammer, saw, drill, or do overhead work. Wear a cap, long sleeves, and gloves when painting, handling insulation, or doing any demolition. Use hearing protection when working with noisy power tools. Make sure your tools are clean and sharp, and that the work area is clear. Check the labels of all materials you use for specific handling instructions, and follow the safety recommendations in the text carefully. These precautions will make your work safe—and a great deal more enjoyable.

Windows

Blinds and Shades

There's a great array of choices for dressing up your windows. All are quick and easy to install. Here's how.

12

Interior Shutters

Good-looking indoor shutters give you both light control and adjustable ventilation. They can go in any room of the house.

18

Install a Glass Block Window

For increased privacy and security without a loss of light, replace a conventional window with a glass block panel.

22

Install a Skylight

A skylight can flood a room with beautiful natural light. Here are clear, step-by-step instructions for installing one in your home.

26

The light, view, and air provided by windows can turn into too much of a good thing. Too much bright sunlight, too much view of your bedroom from the street, too much cold draft.

Blinds and Shades

That's when blinds and shades come to the rescue, tempering the sunlight, giving privacy, and making a window a better insulator.

These window treatments can do it beautifully, too, adding color, shape, and texture to a room.

Here's a look at what you can buy, the advantages and disadvantages of different blinds and shades, and how to install them.

CHOICES

You can choose from among four major kinds of adjustable window coverings: miniblinds, pleated shades, vertical blinds, and roller shades. There are many different styles, colors, and materials within each type; all are easy to install. Base your choice on appearance, convenience of operation, and the degree of light blocking or privacy you want. Following are more details about each kind of window covering to help you choose.

Miniblinds

Miniblinds are venetian blinds with narrower, more graceful slats than those in typical office and schoolroom blinds. They offer variable amounts of light control and privacy, and let you see out the window while they block the sun. They have a sleek, clean look that works well in contemporary homes, and they are offered in an array of colors.

However, miniblinds tend to accumulate dust, they don't block all the light the way shades do, and their straight-line, modern look may not fit the style of your room.

You have several options in choosing miniblinds for your windows.

Stock miniblinds range in quality from lightweight vinyl blinds to heavy vinyl and aluminum versions. They come in 1- to 2-inch intervals of width and are generally 64 inches long. You can easily shorten them to fit windows throughout your house.

Stock blinds are low in cost and you can take them home immediately, but they offer fewer color choices and may not fit as precisely as made-to-measure custom blinds.

Custom miniblinds are available from shade shops, paint and decorating stores, and some home centers. They are usually made of aluminum for durability, they come in a wide range of colors, and they are built to fit the width and height of your window exactly.

Microblinds have slats that are 1/2 inch wide instead of the usual 1 inch, for a sleeker, more delicate look. They are custom-made. Microblinds have many applications and are especially well suited for glass-paneled hinged doors and for sidelights, the narrow windows alongside an entry door, because they are less bulky than other blinds.

Wood miniblinds have slats made of stained or painted wood. They give a warm, traditional look. Wood miniblinds offer all the practical advantages of blinds, but at significantly greater cost than vinyl or aluminum.

Pleated shades

These are pull-up shades that rise on cords and fold in single or double accordion pleats, rather than wrapping around a roller. They have a more textured appearance than mini-blinds, and the permanently pleated fabric is available in different degrees of translucence and a wide variety of muted colors.

Pleated shades give a warm, filtered quality to the light, they insulate the window fairly well, and they don't show dust the way miniblinds do. They can also be custom-made to fit triangular, trapezoidal, or semicircular windows. They are an excellent choice for French doors because they fold up very compactly at the top, allowing the door to open.

However, pleated shades don't provide as much variability in light control as blinds, and when positioned to cut off the light they also cut off the view out the window.

A new style is the Duette shade, which has a honeycomb appearance and folds like a pleated shade. The honeycomb creates a dead air space that acts as insulation. The disadvantage of this style is its higher cost.

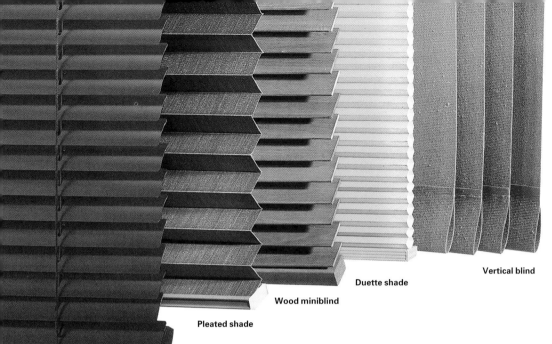

Vertical blind

Duette shade

Wood miniblind

Pleated shade

Miniblind

Pull-operated blinds and shades come in many different types, each in a variety of colors and sizes.

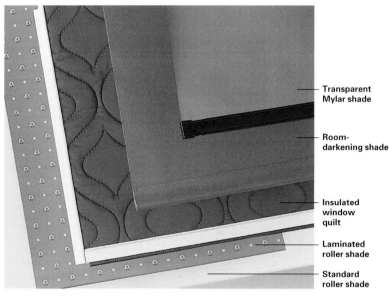

Transparent Mylar shade

Room-darkening shade

Insulated window quilt

Laminated roller shade

Standard roller shade

Roller shades are suitable for windows throughout the house, in any season, at any time of day.

Vertical blinds

Vertical blinds have wide, overlapping slats, or vanes, that hang vertically from an overhead track and rotate 180 degrees to admit or block light. This style is the usual choice for patio doors and full-length windows. The entire blind pulls to one or both sides to uncover a door fully. The wide vanes allow good visibility while controlling the light, and they close tightly, cutting down on drafts. They come in a wide variety of fabric and vinyl materials, and they don't collect dust nearly as much as horizontal slats do. Their strong vertical lines make a room with low ceilings look taller and more expansive. However, vertical blinds protrude from the wall quite a bit, they're fairly expensive, and they tend to dominate a room, especially if used in strong colors.

Roller shades

The familiar roll-up shade mounted on a spring-driven roller may seem old fashioned, but it can be a great problem solver.

Standard roller shades are economical and unobtrusive, and they fit easily behind curtains. Your hardware store probably will have only white and off-white, but a shade shop or mail-order supplier will have a wide variety of colors and fabrics to choose from. Although inexpensive and easy to install, roller shades don't give the variability in light control that blinds do, and they can block the view.

Room-darkening shades are made of a special laminated material that totally blocks the light—the best choice for bedrooms.

Mylar shades filter the light while giving you a perfectly clear view out the window.

Quilted shades are very good insulators but are also quite bulky. They fit in vertical tracks mounted to the window trim, so they block drafts almost completely.

Laminated shades are made up from a fabric of your choice, glued to an ordinary roller shade material. This gives you a tremendous range of decorating possibilities.

HOW TO MEASURE

Once you decide on the kind of window covering you want, you must measure each window. How you measure depends on whether you want to mount the blinds or shades inside or outside the window frame.

Inside mounting

This is the most common way to install all window coverings except vertical blinds. The shade or blind must fit inside the frame and clear all cranks and other window parts. Inside mounting doesn't obscure the trim, and does the best job of insulating the window.

▲ For inside installations, measure the width between the frame pieces to which the mounting brackets will attach.

▲ For blinds, measure the width at three points—top, middle, and bottom of the opening (Figure 1)—and then use the narrowest of these measurements.

▲ For roller shades, measure the width at the inside top of the frame (or the bottom—see Installing Roller Shades, page 17), where the roller will be located.

▲ For both blinds and shades, measure the length from the surface of the stool (interior sill) to the surface of the frame piece at the top of the opening. Your dealer will use these inside measurements to order the shade or blind to fit with enough clearance for proper operation.

Outside mounting

To install a shade or blind outside the frame, you can mount it to the window trim, to the wall above the trim, or to the ceiling. The mounting hardware supplied with blinds and pleated shades is designed to be used in all positions. Outside mounting can be used for odd-shaped windows, when there isn't enough room inside the frame, to cover up unattractive trim, or to achieve a special decorating effect.

Hire a Pro

Two measurement and installation situations are very difficult for the DIYer and are best left to a professional: outside mounts on corner windows and bay windows. This is especially true for vertical blinds, because they protrude so far from the wall.

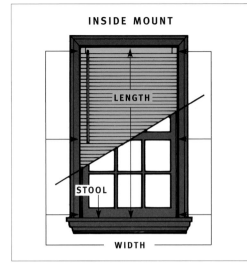

Figure 1. For blinds, measure inside width at top, middle, and bottom of opening; use the narrowest measurement. For shades, measure just at the top (or bottom, for bottom mounting). Measure length from the stool to the top of the opening.

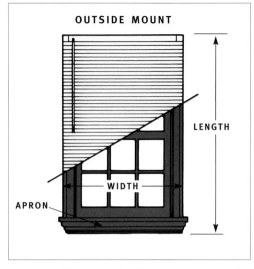

Figure 2. Measure width from outside edges of the casing. Add 0–3 in. according to taste. Measure length from bottom of apron to outside top of casing, or to wall or ceiling position of the top of the mounting brackets.

▲ Measure for an outside mount from wood to wood on the outside (Figure 2) and add 0 to 3 inches, depending on how much of the wall you want to cover.

▲ Measure width for vertical blinds, which are almost always outside mounts, from the outside edges of the wood trim (casing). Your window-blind dealer will add 3 inches or more to the width on each side.

▲ Depending on the placement you plan to use, measure length for outside mounting:

    (a) from the top edge of the window casing,
    (b) from the point on the wall where the
    tops of the brackets will be, or
    (c) from the ceiling.

Measure down to the bottom of the apron—the molding under the stool—or to the floor for French doors, patio doors, and floor-length picture windows.

CONSIDER BEFORE YOU BUY

Before purchasing blinds or shades, consider the following additional options.

▲ You can order blinds with the tilting wand and pull cord on either side, or both on the same side. This is useful where one end of a window is difficult to reach, or to avoid having controls in the middle of a pair of blinds that cover a large window.

▲ For extra-wide windows and French doors, you can order double or even triple sets of blinds or shades that have a single headrail. This looks better than two or three blinds with individual headrails butted end to end.

▲ You can inside-mount a shade at the bottom of the window frame so that it pulls up to cover the opening. This is particularly useful for skylights and for windows where you want privacy without blocking the light entirely.

INSTALLING MINIBLINDS: INSIDE MOUNTING

It's easy to install blinds and pull-up window coverings such as pleated and Duette shades. In most cases you simply mount the brackets securely and then slip the headrail of the covering into place. The basic steps for inside mounting are shown below (Figures 3, 4, 5). Outside mountings and steps for adjusting blinds are shown on the next page.

Use screws, not nails, to install brackets for blinds and pull-up shades. Use two screws per bracket to inside-mount miniblinds. Wood blinds are heavier, so use more screws. Pleated shades usually require just one screw per bracket for inside mounting. For outside mounting of any window covering, use at least two screws per bracket.

Be careful to avoid splitting hardwood trim or window parts. Drill pilot holes for all screws, and keep screws at least 1/4 inch away from the edge of the frame or trim.

Often, the hardware supplied with blinds and shades includes hex-head slotted screws. Use a nutdriver on these screws; it works much better and is faster than a screwdriver.

INSTALLING MINIBLINDS: INSIDE MOUNTING

Figure 3. Attach brackets for inside mounting as shown, one on each side. Use screws and predrill holes to avoid splitting wood.

Figure 4. Minimum mounting surface is about 1/2 in. On crank-out windows the blind must not interfere with the screen or operating crank.

Figure 5. Install a blind by snapping the headrail into the brackets. Then attach valance strips, supplied with the blind, to the front of the headrail.

Tools You Need

Drill

Screwdriver

Nutdriver

Level

Scissors or sharp knife

INSTALLING MINIBLINDS: OUTSIDE MOUNTING

For outside mounting, you can attach brackets to the window trim or to the adjacent wall. Figures 6 and 7 show how to attach brackets to the window casing for installing both miniblinds and pull-up shades.

For a window covering that extends past the edges of the window casing, you may need to attach brackets to the wall. In that case, you must first install mounting blocks that are the same thickness as the casing, so the blind will clear the window frame. Attach blocks with screws into studs, or with expansion bolts into drywall if there is no stud. Paint the blocks, then fasten the mounting brackets to them.

ADJUSTING BLINDS AND PULL-UP SHADES

If you need to shorten a blind, cut the ladders and pull cords. You may find the pull cords tied off at separate holes at each end of the bottom rail. Or the cord may run through the rail so that both ends tie off at a single hole. Either way, follow Figures 8 and 9 to change the length.

If the bottom of a blind or pull-up shade isn't level, loosen the clip or knot that holds the two pull cords together. Then use the pull cords individually to make the necessary adjustment. When the bottom of the blind or shade is level, clip the two cords back together.

If you have small children in your house, screw a cup hook or tie-off cleat high up on the window frame to hang the control cords out of reach. This eliminates the possibility of injury—even strangulation—from getting tangled up in the cords.

For installation on doors or whenever you don't want the bottom bar to flap around, purchase bottom hold-down hardware from your shade and blind dealer.

Figure 6. Attach brackets for outside mounting to the upper corners of the window casing. For wall mounting, shim each bracket with a block the same thickness as the casing.

Figure 7. Pleated and Duette shades are held by brackets into which the headrail clips. A nutdriver can speed up driving hex-head screws. Measure for these shades as for miniblinds.

ADJUSTING BLINDS

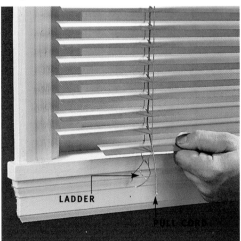

Figure 8. Adjust the length of stock blinds by cutting the ladders and pull cord 3 in. below the stool (inside mount) or apron (outside mount). Slide out the extra slats and bottom rail.

Figure 9. Insert the bottom rail in the shortened ladder, thread the pull cord through the hole and plug, and tie a knot. Stuff excess ladder into the hole and seal it with the plug.

INSTALLING ROLLER SHADES

Roller shades have a blade tip at one end of the roller, a pin tip at the other end. A set of mounting brackets correspondingly has one slotted and one round-hole bracket. For bottom-mounting (Figure 10)—ideal for skylight or basement window application––install the brackets so the blade end will be at the right, the pin end at the left. For the more usual mounting with the roller at the top of the window, the blade end will be at the left (Figure 11). Use footless brackets where necessary (Figure 12).

Be sure to install roller shades level for proper operation. The brackets have oblong mounting holes so you can make adjustments. Brackets often come packaged with nails. It is better to use 1/2- or 3/4-inch pan-head screws. Over the years, nails almost invariably pull loose. Be sure to drill pilot holes for the screws.

INSTALLING ROLLER SHADES: BOTTOM MOUNTING

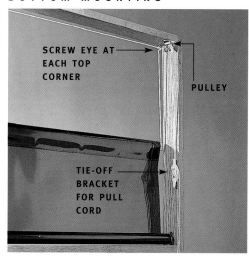

Figure 10. Place brackets for bottom mounting at the sill. Attach pull cords to ends of shade rod; run them through screw eyes and a pulley at the top. Mount a tie-off bracket wherever convenient.

INSTALLING VERTICAL BLINDS

Brackets for vertical blinds usually mount directly on the wall. Install at least two brackets with screws into wall studs (Figure 13). Use expansion bolts where there is no stud. Follow the instructions supplied with the blind for bracket spacing. For strength, the two brackets at the pull cord end are spaced more closely than the others.

Install the headrail for full-length vertical blinds either level or parallel with the ceiling, whichever looks best.

Hang vertical blinds with at least 1/2 inch clearance at the floor so the vanes can pivot freely and the blind can be pulled easily.

INSTALLING ROLLER SHADES: TOP MOUNTING

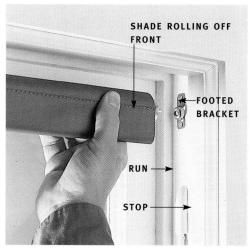

Figure 11. Attach footed brackets for roller shades in the run, as shown here, or on the stop. Install run-mounted shades to roll off the front of the roller, stop-mounted shades off the back.

Figure 12. Use footless brackets to mount roller shades on crank-out and other windows with neither a run nor a stop. Blade-end bracket goes at left, pin-end bracket at the right of the window.

INSTALLING VERTICAL BLINDS

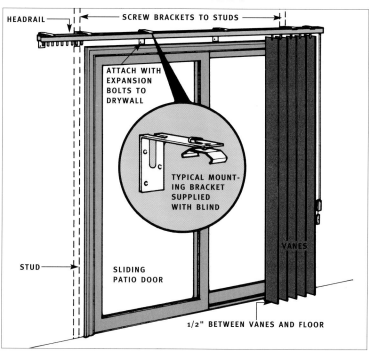

Figure 13. Install brackets for vertical blinds with screws into wall studs or expansion bolts into drywall. Space brackets according to the instructions supplied with the blind. Cut off vanes if necessary for proper clearance at the floor.

Few interior window treatments are as classically beautiful as wooden shutters with movable louvers.

Interior Shutters

You can open the shutters for full light, or close them and adjust the louvers to admit only as much light as you want. And if the window sash is open, shutters will admit fresh air without sacrificing privacy.

Installing interior shutters is an easy project that can transform the appearance of a room or stairway with little effort and only basic skills.

Easy-to-install wide-louver shutters provide both a handsome appearance and versatile light control. Installation should take about half a day per window.

CHOOSING SHUTTERS

Fixed- and movable-louver shutters are usually sold as unfinished pine panels in stock sizes. You install the hardware—hinges and closures—after trimming the shutters to size and finishing them. For adjustable light control, you need shutters with movable louvers.

Traditional shutters have louvers just 3/4 inch wide. Usually, they can be mounted with their front surfaces flush with the face of the window casing. The narrow louvers require very little clearance space between the rear of the shutter and the window sash to open fully.

You'll get more light by choosing wide-louver shutters. They're handsome and distinctive, and widely available because they are very popular today. The louvers range from 1-1/2 inches to 4 inches wide. While they may be more expensive than traditional shutters, you can offset this higher cost by hanging the wide-louver shutters yourself.

The wider louvers require more clearance to open fully, so this kind of shutter is installed on hanging strips attached to the face of the window casing. The instructions here tell you how to do this in easy steps. The same procedures can be followed to mount narrow-louver shutters directly to the window casing.

MEASURE YOUR WINDOWS

To get shutters that fit properly, and to make installation as easy as possible, you must measure each window frame for three things: square, louver clearance, and shutter size.

Measure for square

Take inside diagonal measurements of the window frame from corner to corner—upper left to lower right, and upper right to lower left. If the measurements differ by more than 1/2 inch, the frame is out of square: The sides may not be parallel, the top of the frame or the interior sill may not be level, or there may be a combination of these problems. You can deal with an out-of-square frame when you mount the hanging strips and cut the shutters to size.

Measure for clearance

Many windows do not have enough clearance to allow wide louvers to be opened fully if shutters are mounted directly inside the window frame. However, if you mount hanging strips on the face of the frame and hang the shutters flush with the faces of the strips, you will increase the clearance by a distance equal to the thickness of the hanging strips.

To find out how much clearance your windows provide, measure from the window sash (the flat frame around the window glass) to the face of the window trim. That measurement should be equal to half the width of a louver, plus 1/2 inch. For example, 3-inch louvers need at least 2 inches clearance.

If you don't have quite enough clearance, you can either plan to use thicker hanging strips—which will move the back of the shutter farther out from the sash—or you can select shutters with narrower louvers.

Measure for size

To determine what size shutters you need, measure the width and the height of the window frame opening. Measure the width of the opening at the top, bottom, and center; use the smallest measurement. Measure the height at the left side and at the right side; use the larger of these two measurements.

If shutters are not available in the exact size you need, order a larger size and trim them down. But don't plan to trim more than 3/4 inch each off the top and bottom, or 1/2 inch off each side of a panel.

Measure window width at top, bottom, and middle of the frame opening. Measure height at both the left side and the right side. Use the narrowest width measurement and longest height measurement to choose shutter size.

Tools and Materials You Need

Tape measure

Carpenter's square

Level

Circular saw

Plane

Sanding block

Medium-grit sandpaper

Hammer

Nail set

6d finishing nails

Wood chisel

Wood or plastic mallet

Drill

Screwdriver

Paint sprayer and paintbrush

Alkyd primer and enamel

INSTALLING WIDE-LOUVER SHUTTERS

There are five steps to putting up the shutters:
- ▲ Mount the hanging strips.
- ▲ Cut the shutters to size.
- ▲ Mortise for hinges.
- ▲ Finish the pieces.
- ▲ Hang the shutters.

Here's how to do it.

Mount the hanging strips

You must attach the hanging strips to the window frame in order to measure for trimming the shutters, and to mark hinge locations.

▲ Cut strips from 1x2 stock, or thicker stock if you need a bit more clearance. Sand them smooth and attach them to the frame with 6d finishing nails. If the window frame is square, simply set their inside edges flush with the edges of the window trim.

▲ When the frame is not square, one or both sides may not be vertical. In that case, set the hanging strips flush with the sides of the frame at the narrowest point of the opening and use a level to get them plumb (vertical). Let them overlap the opening at the wider points.

▲ Measure between the hanging strips at the top and bottom and adjust as necessary to make sure that they are parallel to one another.

Cut the shutters to size

Trim the shutters equally on both sides to fit between the strips, with 1/8 inch between them—about the thickness of a nickel. If the top of the frame and the sill are level, trim equal amounts from the tops and the bottoms of the shutters to adjust their fit (Figures 1, 2).

▲ If the top of the window frame is not level, trim the tops of the shutters either to be level or to follow the line of the casing—whichever looks best. If the sill is not level, trim the shutter bottoms to follow the line of the sill.

Mortise for hinges

When the shutters have been trimmed to size, mark hinge mortises 2-1/2 inches from the top and bottom of each shutter.

▲ If the tops or bottoms have been trimmed at a slant to adjust for an unsquare frame, adjust the marks so that opposite hinges will align horizontally with one another.

▲ Set the shutters in place on top of nickels at each corner (Figure 3). The thickness of the coins will give just enough clearance for the shutters to swing freely when mounted.

▲ Transfer the marks from the shutters to the hanging strips. Then cut mortises in both the shutters and the hanging strips (Figure 4).

Finish the pieces

If you have varnished woodwork, you can finish the shutters and hanging strips to match, using a natural-color or clear varnish, or stain and varnish. However, if your woodwork is painted, paint the shutters to match or harmonize with the trim.

▲ Use an alkyd primer, followed by alkyd satin enamel topcoats (Figure 5). The glossier the enamel, the easier it will be to keep clean.

▲ Because the hanging strips are nailed to the frame, you will have to finish them in place. Set the nails and fill the holes, then carefully apply the finish with a brush.

▲ For best results with the shutter panels, use a spray gun to apply paint or other finish evenly to the louvers and frames. Finish-sand the bare shutters if needed before priming. When the primer is dry, sand with medium-grit paper and then apply two finish coats. Let the first coat dry completely and then sand it lightly before applying the second coat.

▲ An easy way to handle the shutters for painting is to drive a 3-inch finishing nail into each corner at the top and bottom edges, leaving about 2 inches protruding. Suspend each shutter by resting the nails on two sawhorses or other supports set an appropriate distance apart, with a drop cloth below. Lock the louvers in a fully opened position and spray on your paint or finish. Turn the shutter over and spray the other side.

Hang the shutters

Use screws to attach the hinges in the shutter mortises first, and then the mortises in the hanging strips (Figure 6).

▲ Check that the shutters swing freely and that the panels line up when they are closed.

▲ Finally, attach the hook and stud closure. The usual placement is midway between the top and bottom, but you may prefer to install the closure on the bottom rail for better appearance or convenience.

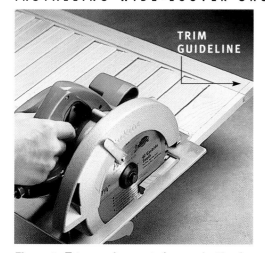

Figure 1. Trim equal amounts from each side of the panels and from the tops and bottoms. Use a circular saw to cut off more than 1/8 in.

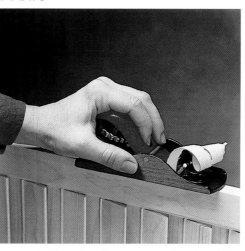

Figure 2. Plane the edges to remove less than 1/8 in. or to make minor adjustments in the fit. Plane the ends from the corners toward the center.

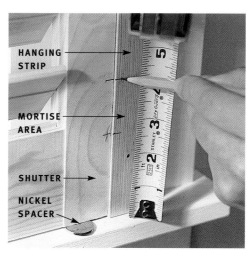

Figure 3. Mark hinge mortises on each shutter, then transfer the marks to the hanging strips. Set the panels on nickels for proper bottom spacing.

Mortising for Hinges

Be sure your chisel is sharp. If the handle has a metal cap, tap it with a hammer; if not, use a wood or plastic mallet.

OUTLINE THE MORTISE. Hold the chisel vertical to the surface with the bevel facing into the mortise area. Make the end cuts, across the grain, first. Then if the hinge leaf is not as wide as the wood edge, make a cut along the back of the mortise.

PARE OUT THE WASTE. Hold the chisel with the bevel facing downward and the blade at a low angle. For shallow mortises such as these, don't tap the chisel—use hand power.

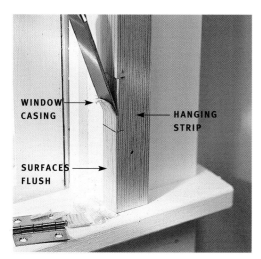

Figure 4. Cut mortises in the hanging strips and shutters with care so you don't gouge the window frame or split out the ends of the mortise.

Figure 5. Sand primed shutters with medium-grit sandpaper. Wipe with a tack cloth and spray on two coats of alkyd enamel paint.

Figure 6. Attach hinges to the shutters first, then to the hanging strips. Drill pilot holes and use the screws supplied with the hinges.

Install a Glass Block Window

For pleasant natural light, privacy, better security, and good energy performance, a glass block window may be just the thing.

With a preassembled panel and proper preparation, installation can take just a couple of hours.

A preassembled glass block panel can be installed with only basic tools, mortar, and grout. You'll be pleased with how easy it is to get professional-quality results.

CHOOSING A WINDOW

A glass block window is an excellent choice for a basement, a garage, or a wall next to a sidewalk, shared driveway, or other exposed location, for two major reasons. First, it would take a sledgehammer to break through a properly installed panel. Second, a glass block window admits light but prevents prying eyes from seeing the interior clearly.

Installing a glass block panel is much easier than you might expect. The secret lies in purchasing the panel preassembled, so you only have to slip it in place and secure it. This eliminates what would otherwise be the most difficult step: mixing up a batch of special mortar and laying up the blocks individually. Unless you are experienced in masonry work, building the panel one block at a time would take all day, because glass blocks are a good deal more difficult to lay than bricks.

A preassembled glass block panel is economical, too. It might cost 50 percent more than buying blocks, mortar, and other materials, but when you consider the savings in labor and time—and most homeowners' lack of experience—it makes sense to buy the panel.

MEASURING AND ORDERING

To order a preassembled glass block panel, make sure you measure the rough opening accurately, as shown below. Remove the old casing so you can measure the full width and height of the opening. Double-check the measurements and give them to a glass block fabricator when you choose the style and size of the blocks you want him to use for your window.

Perhaps the easiest way to find a glass block fabricator is to look in the Yellow Pages. Glass block masonry has become increasingly popular, so there are likely to be several dealers in your area. Visit some, examine the available panels, choose from the variety of sizes and styles offered, and compare prices. Ask questions, too. The dealers understand the problems of installation in various kinds of walls. They can give you some helpful advice, and they will build your panel to very close tolerances—usually within about 1/2 inch on the sides—to make the installation as easy as possible.

MEASURING FOR A GLASS BLOCK PANEL

Measure the window opening from inside the house. Remove any casings to expose the opening edges. For a basement window, like the one shown here, measure the masonry or concrete opening from side to side for width, and from the concrete sill to the structural member above for height. Measure the rough opening in a garage or other wall similarly.

JOIST

MUD SILL

SILL SEAL

WOOD JAMB

ROUGH OPENING HEIGHT

ROUGH OPENING WIDTH

WOOD SILL

CONCRETE SILL

MASONRY BASEMENT WALL

INSTALLATION TIPS

Installing a glass block panel is very straight-forward. Collect all the necessary tools and materials listed on the opposite page, and follow the step-by-step pictures. You'll be pleased at how quickly the project goes, and how good the finished results will look.

You can do all of the work yourself, but you will need a helper on the inside to support the panel when you lift it into place. A 2 foot x 3 foot panel weighs about 100 pounds and is awkward to handle.

When you remove the old wood, make sure you clean all dust and debris off the surface of the masonry sill and wall edges, so the mortar will bond securely to it. If the wall is brick, spray the exposed edges well with water before putting the panel in place. Dry bricks will draw water out of the mortar, making the mortar susceptible to crumbling and cracking with repeated changes in the weather.

Before starting to mortar the panel in place, check with a level to make sure that the joint lines are horizontal. Tap on the edges to make adjustments. Also use the level on the face of the panel to check that it is plumb. If not, make sure the top edge rests firmly against the temporary block and tap the base outward or inward as required (a helper is useful for this adjustment). Then recheck the horizontal alignment and adjust as necessary.

Step 1. Remove the old sash, then saw through the old sill and pry it out. Remove the side jambs and the header across the top of the window.

Step 2. Nail a 2x4 block to the upper wooden plate as a temporary stop for the panel. Position it to hold the face of the panel at the proper depth.

Step 3. Set two wedges on the sill and slip the panel into the opening. You'll need a second person on the inside to help guide and support the panel as you put it in place.

Step 4. Center the panel in the opening, and then level it by tapping on the wedges. Leave a 1/4-in. gap at the top. Check the face of the panel to make sure that it is plumb.

Step 5. Fill and pack the side and bottom gaps with mortar from outside and inside. Taper the mortar at the bottom away from the panel on the exterior for proper drainage.

Step 6. Caulk the gap at the top with exterior caulk on the outside; do the inside in the next step. Then insulate any gaps or open spaces in the adjacent framing from the inside.

Tools and Materials You Need

Measuring tape

Hammer

Saw

Prybar

2 wood wedges

Level

Preassembled glass block panel

Mortar mix

Mason's trowel

Caulking gun

Exterior caulk

Step 7. Remove the wedges at the bottom when the mortar sets, and then fill and smooth the holes. Remove the temporary block on the inside and finish caulking there.

The finished window becomes a permanent part of the wall. It transmits light while maintaining privacy, and is far more secure than a conventional window.

The flood of natural light from a skylight can dramatically change the character of almost any area of your home.

Install a Skylight

Once high-cost, complex architectural features, skylights are now both affordable and easy to install. Preassembled units make adding a skylight a practical do-it-yourself project.

A skylight is an excellent way to provide light and ventilation in a bathroom. Kitchens, family rooms, dens, and stairways are other popular places to install skylights.

REMODELING WITH SKYLIGHTS

Skylights offer a wide range of do-it-yourself remodeling options. A well-planned skylight will bring natural illumination into a room and brighten every corner. It can make a small room feel larger, brighten a shadowy stairway, balance lighting in kitchen work areas, and make any room more pleasant and inviting.

A skylight transmits more light than a window, and an operating or ventilating unit provides excellent air circulation. Modern skylights come preassembled, so all you have to do is set them into your roof. Easy-to-install flashing systems have almost completely eliminated leaks. And with the wide variety of sizes, styles, and features available, you can solve common problems like overheating, glare, heat loss, and condensation.

Installation options

If your room has a conventional horizontal ceiling, you can install a skylight with either a straight or flared shaft between the ceiling and the roof. You won't need any shaft at all if the ceiling follows the roof line.

Straight shaft. A straight shaft is the simplest to build, and may be your only choice, depending on the ceiling and roof framing.

Flared shaft. A shaft that flares from top to bottom opens a larger area of the ceiling than a straight shaft, giving the room a lighter, more spacious appearance.

Cathedral ceiling. If the room has a cathedral ceiling—one that slants with the roof line—installation is simple because you don't have to build a shaft at all.

Whatever kind of installation you plan to use, you can choose between a skylight constructed of conventional or thermal glass panels mounted in a metal frame, or a plastic dome mounted on a wood or metal curb. The dome may be single- or double-walled (for insulation), and either clear or tinted.

Skylights come in several standard sizes, and in fixed and ventilating models. You don't need a very large skylight to get a great deal of light. A unit with a 14-inch x 28-inch glass size is fine for a small room. For a bathroom, get a model that cranks open to exhaust moist air when someone uses the shower or tub.

Scope of the project

The instructions on the following pages show how to install a skylight with a flared shaft in a small bathroom. Even if you choose a different kind of installation, you can use the same general techniques in any room of the house.

Whatever the differences, your skylight installation project should proceed in the following stages:

▲ Plan the ceiling opening.
▲ Cut and frame the ceiling opening.
▲ Plan and cut the roof opening.
▲ Frame the roof opening.
▲ Set the skylight.
▲ Frame the shaft.
▲ Insulate and finish the shaft.

It will take you about a day each to frame the ceiling, frame the roof openings and set the skylight, and finish the shaft. Taping the drywall joints and painting will take a few additional hours, spaced over several days so you can allow various stages to dry.

You'll need a wide variety of materials for this project. Assemble them in advance, along with the skylight itself.

Tools You Need

Goggles or safety glasses

Dust mask

Tape measure

Carpenter's square

Bevel square

Chalk line

Plumb bob

Level

Circular saw with carbide-tip blade

Handsaw

Drywall saw

Pry bar

Hammer

Drill

Staple gun

SKYLIGHT SHAFTS

A straight shaft confines the light to a specific area and creates relatively dark corners. A flared shaft spreads the illumination, even from a small skylight, and softens shadows. An installation in a cathedral ceiling eliminates shadows and creates the most diffuse lighting.

Straight shaft

Flared shaft

Cathedral ceiling

Avoid Ceiling Damage

Do not nail into ceiling joists when framing the skylight opening and shaft. Instead, use screws. That way, you eliminate vibration from hammering which can cause cracks or nail pops to appear in the ceiling. You can use nails to fasten framing members to roof rafters, however.

PLAN THE CEILING OPENING

Plan to locate the shaft opening where the light can spread to the greatest area of the room. Sometimes the size and shape of the shaft will be limited by obstacles in the space above the ceiling—pipes, electrical wiring, or the roof design. Check your attic or crawl space and balance any problems against the cost and trouble of solving them. Moving wires is usually simple. Rerouting pipes is a good deal more work, and you may find that it is wiser to shift the skylight location instead.

Check the roof framing. If the roof is constructed with conventional rafters, you'll probably have no special problems. But if it is built with trusses, you'll have to work around them, because cutting any part of a truss weakens the entire structure. If you are in doubt, consult your local building inspector, an architect, or an engineer.

If there are no obstacles, you can make the ceiling opening almost any size you wish. Remember though, the wider you make it, the more ceiling joists you'll have to cut. If you need to cut more than two joists, consult your local building inspector, architect, or building engineer to be sure you won't compromise the roof's strength (the ceiling joists and roof rafters work together to support the roof).

Mark the opening on the ceiling. Construction will be made easier if you lay out one edge of the opening to run along a joist, so you won't have to add a trimmer on both sides of the opening when you frame it.

CUT AND FRAME THE CEILING OPENING

Before cutting through the ceiling, drive 16d nails up through the ceiling into the space above at the four corners of your proposed opening. Then go into the attic or ceiling crawl space, locate the nails, and look for any nearby electrical wires. If you find any, turn off the electrical power at the main circuit panel before you start sawing.

Removing part of the ceiling can be messy. Cover furniture, fixtures, and floor, and hang a covering over an arch or doorway. Wear goggles or safety glasses, a dust mask, and long sleeves.

Cut the opening

Cut along the marked lines with a drywall saw and remove the ceiling material in the opening (Figure 1). Work carefully so as not to damage the adjacent ceiling surface.

CUT THE CEILING OPENING

Figure 1. Cut the opening with a drywall saw and remove the section. Check first for obstructions above, and turn off the electrical power. Wear eye, nose, and mouth protection.

Strengthen the joists

Double the support on each side of the ceiling opening with additional joists screwed onto the original ones.

▲ Cut the new joists from the same size material as the old ones. Make them long enough to reach from the exterior wall plate to the inside bearing wall. Because the roof rafters are fastened to one side of the existing joists, you must place the new joists on the opposite side.

▲ Attach the new joists with 3-inch drywall screws spaced every 16 inches, one near the top and one near the bottom (Figure 2).

Install headers

The ceiling opening must have double headers across each end, both to frame the opening and to support the ends of the joists that originally crossed the opening.

▲ Cut off any joists that run through the middle of the opening (Figure 3). Mark the cut line 3 inches back from the edges of the opening, to allow for the added thickness of a double header at each end.

▲ If there is much weight on these joists from items stored in the attic, prop them up from below before cutting. Use 2x4's for braces, set between short 2x6 or 2x8 plates at the ceiling and floor to prevent gouges or scratches.

▲ Start the cuts with a power saw and finish them with a handsaw.

▲ Install a double header across each end of the opening. The headers are pieces of joist material cut to fit between the doubled side joists. Fasten the first header piece to the end of each cut-off joist using three 3-inch drywall screws (Figure 4).

▲ Fasten the second header over the first with two 3-inch screws top and bottom every 16 inches. Drive 3-1/2 inch screws at an angle (toe-screw them) from the face to fasten the header ends to the doubled joists.

Install trimmers

If either or both sides of the opening do not fall along the doubled joists, you must install a trimmer to support the ceiling drywall. Cut joist material to fit between the headers, tap the trimmer into place (Figure 5), and toe-screw it with 3-1/2 inch screws driven into the headers, three at each end.

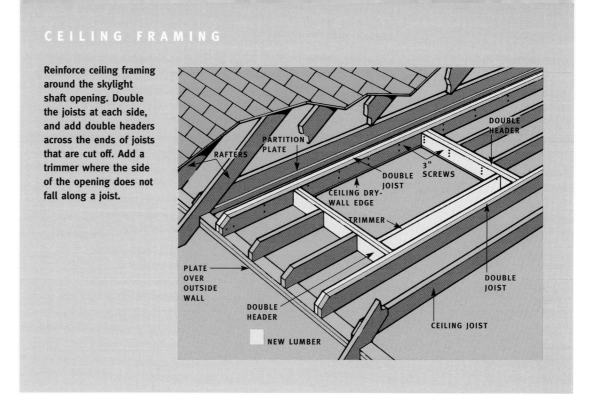

CEILING FRAMING

Reinforce ceiling framing around the skylight shaft opening. Double the joists at each side, and add double headers across the ends of joists that are cut off. Add a trimmer where the side of the opening does not fall along a joist.

RAFTERS

PARTITION PLATE

DOUBLE HEADER

3" SCREWS

DOUBLE JOIST

CEILING DRY-WALL EDGE

TRIMMER

PLATE OVER OUTSIDE WALL

DOUBLE JOIST

DOUBLE HEADER

CEILING JOIST

NEW LUMBER

FRAME THE CEILING OPENING

Figure 2. Double the joists on both sides of the opening, from the exterior wall to the interior load-bearing wall. Use 3-in. screws top and bottom, spaced every 16 in.

Figure 3. Cut off joists that run through the opening. Cut 3 in. back from the opening edges, to allow for double headers. Wear eye protection when using a power saw.

Figure 4. Fasten the first header with three 3-in. screws into each joist end. Use two screws every 16 in. for the second header and 3-1/2 in. toe screws at the ends.

Figure 5. Insert a trimmer between the headers to support an edge not located on a joist. Toe-screw each end. Fasten the ceiling to the trimmer with drywall screws.

Mark rafters for cutoff by first drawing along a straightedge laid from the ceiling opening to the marked edge of the roof opening. Measure 3 inches from that line along the bottom edge of the joist to locate the bottom of the double header. Mark the cut line at that point, at right angles to the joist edge, not parallel to the shaft edge.

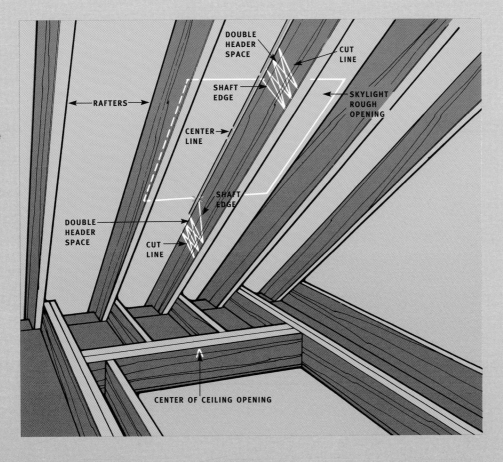

DOUBLE HEADER SPACE

CUT LINE

SHAFT EDGE

SKYLIGHT ROUGH OPENING

RAFTERS

CENTER LINE

SHAFT EDGE

DOUBLE HEADER SPACE

CUT LINE

CENTER OF CEILING OPENING

PLAN AND CUT THE ROOF OPENING

Before cutting into the roof, you must mark the opening on the underside of the roof sheeting.

Mark the opening location

The location of the roof opening will vary with the kind of shaft you plan to build.

Straight shaft. You must center the roof opening for a straight shaft directly over the ceiling opening; see the diagram at the left.

To lay out the roof opening, mark the center of the ceiling opening on the header at each end. Then hang a plumb bob from the roof sheathing and shift it until it is exactly aligned with the center mark at one end. Mark the roof at that point (Figure 6). Do the same at the other end. Then draw a line between the two marks; that is the centerline of the roof opening.

Flared shaft. If you center the roof opening for a flared shaft over the ceiling opening, the shaft will slant outward both at the sides and at the ends. If you align one side of both openings, and perhaps one end as well, you will save work cutting angled pieces to frame the shaft.

Whichever way you decide to build the flared shaft, mark the ceiling headers where the center of the roof opening will be located. Then use a plumb bob to transfer these marks up to the roof sheathing, and connect them to mark the centerline of the opening.

 Use a tape measure and carpenter's square to mark out the rough opening on the roof sheathing, working from the centerline (Figure 7). You can find the rough opening measurements in the skylight installation instructions, or simply measure the unit's outer dimensions and add an inch in each direction.

 Drive an 8d nail up through the roof sheathing and shingles at each corner of the marked opening (Figure 8). Then climb up on the roof and snap a chalk line between the nails.

Cut the opening

Start this phase of the project in the morning so you leave plenty of time to finish the roof work and set the skylight before nightfall.

Follow the chalk lines to cut through the shingles and roof sheathing from above (Figure 9). Use a power saw with a carbide-tip blade. Wear eye and hearing protection while cutting. Remove the roof material from the opening and lower it into the attic or over the side.

Be careful—climbing around on a slanted roof can be dangerous. Wear rubber-soled shoes. If your footing feels unsure, nail some 2x4 cleats to the roof with 16d nails. When you're all finished, pull them out and fill the nail holes with silicone caulk or roof cement.

Figure 6. Use a plumb bob to transfer the center of the skylight location from marks on the headers up to the roof sheathing. Do this at each end and then connect the marks.

Figure 7. Lay out the skylight opening on the roof sheathing, measuring from the marked centerline. Make sure that all your corners are square and that the sides are parallel.

Figure 8. Drive 8d nails up through the sheathing and roofing to mark the corners of the rough roof opening. Then go up onto the roof to mark and cut the opening from above.

Figure 9. Cut the opening with a power saw and a carbide-tip blade. Follow chalk lines snapped between the nails at the corners. Drive out the nails before cutting. Wear eye protection.

Reinforce roof framing around the rough opening. These are critical cuts, so measure twice before cutting anything. Add double rafters at the sides, cut off the intermediate rafters, and install double headers and trimmers. You can use either 16d nails or 3-1/2 inch drywall screws to fasten the framing.

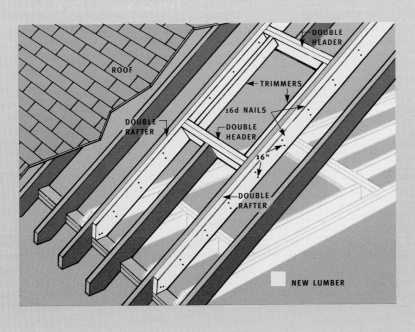

FRAME THE ROOF OPENING

Frame the roof opening as you did the ceiling opening: double the rafters (the roof equivalent of the ceiling joist), install headers, and install trimmers where needed.

Strengthen the rafters

Double the rafters on the sides of the opening the same way you doubled the ceiling joists. Make them identical to the existing rafters and fasten them with two 16d nails or 3-inch drywall screws every 16 inches (Figure 10). It may be easier to get the rafters into the attic by passing them in through the roof opening, rather than up through the ceiling opening.

Install headers

Now prepare to remove the rafter that runs through the middle of the roof opening and install double headers across the ends. The trick here is to make sure the headers won't obstruct the sides of the shaft. You can roughly determine the location of the shaft sides by running

FRAME THE ROOF OPENING

Figure 10. Double the rafters on both sides of the opening. Fasten the additional rafters with 16d nails or 3-in. drywall screws along the top and bottom edges, spaced every 16 in.

Figure 11. Cut off the rafters that run across the roof opening. The cut should be marked so the double headers will not interfere with the shaft sides. Then remove the roof and rafter section.

Figure 12. Frame the opening with double headers at the ends and trimmers at the sides. Fasten them like the ceiling headers and trimmers. See text about how to set trimmers for flared shafts.

a straightedge from the ceiling edge to the roof opening edge. Mark this line on the rafter. Mark the thickness of a double header behind the line and cut off the rafters (Figure 11). Install them the same way as the ceiling headers.

Install trimmers

The sides of the roof opening must be supported by trimmers. For a straight shaft or a slight flare, you can use lumber the same size as the rafters (2x6 or 2x8) for the trimmers. A shaft with greater flare may present a problem. Deep trimmers at the roof might extend downward far enough to interfere with the sides. To create enough space for the flared sides you may have to use 2x4's and perhaps move them back slightly from the edges of the roof opening (Figure 12).

To find out if this is necessary, run a straightedge up from a corner of the ceiling opening to the corresponding corner of the roof opening and try fitting pieces of scrap material where the trimmer must go. Use the deepest size that fits, but nothing less than a 2x4, and with a setback of no more than 1-1/2 inches from the edge. The mounting brackets on most skylights extend far enough to get proper support from trimmers offset this much. Install the roof trimmers in the same way as the ceiling trimmers.

SET THE SKYLIGHT

Once the openings are framed, it's easy to set and flash the skylight. Each manufacturer uses a slightly different system, so follow the directions for your unit. But all systems include these three basic steps:

▲ First, loosen the shingles within 6 to 12 inches of all sides of the opening by prying out the roofing nails with a flat bar (Figure 13). Do this carefully so you don't damage the shingles; you can reuse them when installing the flashing.

▲ Second, fasten the assembled skylight base, or curb, to the roof sheathing with screws through the mounting brackets (Figure 14). Check local regulations for curb height—it may be 6 inches or more in snow areas. Attach one point first, then level the skylight along the lower edge and check it for square with a framing square before fastening the other brackets. If it is out of square, the operating window won't close tightly enough to seal out water.

▲ Third, install the flashing made for your skylight (Figure 15). This is an important step because it deals with the most common complaint about skylights—leakage.

Step flashing is the best type. Place the bottom section of flashing across the bottom edge of the skylight. Then interweave the side pieces, alternating them with the shingles, working from bottom to top on each side. With this configuration, water running down the roof can't get underneath the shingles.

Do not nail through the flashing except at the top edge, into the skylight curb. These short nails will later be covered. If there is a short shingle you can't nail, glue it to the flashing with roof cement. Finally, slide the top flashing piece into place under the shingles above it.

You could now fit the glass panel or plastic dome in place. However, it will probably be easier to wait until you have installed the shaft framing, so you will have more working room.

SET THE SKYLIGHT

Figure 13. Pry out roofing nails along the edges of the opening with a flat pry bar. Remove shingles carefully where necessary; you can reuse them.

Figure 14. Secure the skylight curb with screws driven through the mounting brackets. Get the bottom edge level and the frame square before fastening.

Figure 15. Install flashing supplied with the unit. Begin at the bottom; work up the sides, interweaving the flashing with the shingles. Do the top edge last.

You can use 2x4 or 2x3 stock, because the framing only needs to support drywall; it has no other structural function. If any dimension between shaft corners is longer than 16 inches, add an intermediate framing piece. Be sure the faces are aligned, so the completed shaft will have the best possible appearance.

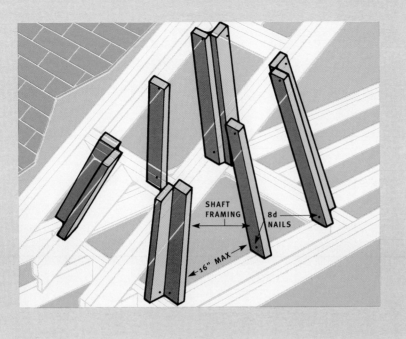

FRAME THE SHAFT

Because the roof and ceiling are self-supporting, the shaft framing needs to support only a drywall covering. Therefore, its alignment is more important than its strength. A flared shaft calls for a lot of angle cutting. You don't have to be precise on the cuts, but be sure to properly align the frame pieces when you nail them.

Use a sliding bevel square to measure the angles and transfer them to the shaft framing (Figure 16). Use a straightedge to establish the exact location of the shaft side—from the edge of the skylight to the edge of the ceiling—when measuring and nailing these pieces (Figures 17, 18). Be patient: you may have to cut the framing pieces several times before they fit. Begin with the corners and toenail the pieces with 8d nails. If any corner-to-corner span is greater than 16 inches long, add an intermediate framing piece.

FRAME THE SHAFT

Figure 16. Measure the angles for shaft framing with a straightedge and a sliding bevel square. Make trial cuts, and then recut them as necessary to get a good alignment.

Figure 17. Nail shaft framing in place with 8d nails. Use a straightedge to get the edges exactly in position. This is essential for proper installation of drywall on the sides of the shaft.

Figure 18. Use a straightedge to guide alignment. Place it between the bottom of the skylight and the ceiling edge at each point where the shaft framing will be installed.

INSULATE AND FINISH THE SHAFT

The shaft runs up through unheated space. It is important to insulate it well—especially in bathrooms—to avoid condensation. Staple insulation batts to the shaft framing all around, then staple plastic sheeting over the insulation as a vapor retarder (Figure 19).

Now hang drywall, using short drywall screws. Do the ends first; they will fit flat. However, you must gently bend the side pieces to get them into place (Figure 20).

Tape the joints and cover the screw heads with joint compound and smooth it carefully. Bright light pouring through the shaft will tend to show every finishing flaw, so taking care with the details is important. Finally, smooth a bead of caulk around the drywall–skylight joint and paint the shaft.

Figure 19. Insulate the sides of the shaft with batts stapled to the framing. Cover the insulation with a vapor-retarding barrier material, especially in a bathroom or kitchen.

Figure 20. Finish the shaft with drywall. Cut and fasten the ends with screws. Then carefully lay out and cut the sides. Flex them into place, fasten with screws, and tape all joints.

SKYLIGHT TIPS AND IDEAS

• Where protection from breakage is a concern—for example, next to a playground or a golf course—install a skylight glazed with tempered wire glass. Tempered glass is annealed for high impact resistance. Increased strength is provided by a wire mesh embedded in the glass. The hexagonal mesh pattern is similar to that of chicken wire.

• To admit sunlight but block much of the heat that accompanies it, choose a skylight constructed for low emissivity ("low-E"). Emissivity is the measure of heat radiated by a surface. Much of the infrared (IR) energy that accompanies the visible rays in sunlight is absorbed by ordinary glass, raising its temperature and causing the glass to radiate heat. Low-E windows have a transparent metallic coating on the glass or on a film placed between two layers of glass. This coating reflects the IR energy but lets the visible rays pass. It also reflects most of the ultraviolet (UV) energy that also is a component of sun light. UV radiation does not generate heat, but it can cause the colors in fabrics, paints, and wall and floor coverings to fade.

• For protection against cold, choose a skylight with double or triple glazing—that is, with two or three layers of glass. Air between the layers blocks the loss of interior heat when the exterior temperature is cold. To prevent condensation on the inner surfaces of the glass, the air between the layers must be completely dry when the space between the layers is sealed, and the seal must not be broken at any time. For this reason it is impractical to try double-glazing a skylight frame yourself. Triple-glazed units often have a middle layer with a low-E coating.

Doors

Add Security to Exterior Doors

Three simple, inexpensive improvements will make your entry doors far more resistant to break-ins. Here's what to do.

38

Replace a Hinged Door

Replacing a door is simple. Follow these instructions to get a proper fit and a professional-looking installation.

42

Install French Doors

French doors fit into many decorating styles far better than sliding patio doors—and they can open the doorway completely.

50

Home security begins with properly protected entry doors.

Add Security to Exterior Doors

Here are three ways you can make a door more resistant to break-in attempts. Each is inexpensive and easy to do, and each provides a measure of security and peace of mind far greater than the small amount of time and work involved.

THREE SECURITY MEASURES

Whatever kind of door you have at each entry to your home—wood, fiberglass, or metal-clad—you can improve the security it provides by installing any or all of three things: a strike box for the lockset bolt, extra-long jamb screws in the hinges, and a surface-mount deadbolt. These security devices are described here. Installation is shown on the next three pages.

Strike box

In most installations, the bolt of a lockset simply extends into an opening cut into the wood of the doorjamb. The opening is covered by a small metal strike plate, held with short screws. This arrangement can splinter out fairly easily if the door is given a few heavy blows in the area of the bolt, or a pry bar is used.

A strike box encases the bolt in metal, not wood. It is a plate with a metal box that extends into the pocket in the door jamb. The strike sits behind a cover plate that is longer and thicker than an ordinary strike plate. These components are mounted with 3-inch screws that extend through the jamb into the 2x4 framing around the door. There are screws at the bottom of the box as well as at the ends of the plates. Taken together, these features provide very high resistance to pounding, battering, and prying.

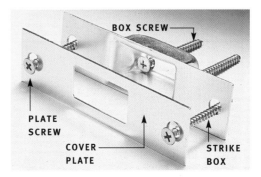

A strike box has two components: the box section with a front flange; and a cover plate. Both have mounting holes for extra-long screws.

Hinge screws

The hinge side of an exterior door is vulnerable to attack because hinges are usually installed with 3/4- or 1-inch screws. These are adequate for attaching the hinge to the door, but battering or prying can tear them out of the jamb. To correct this weakness, replace the jamb screws with 3-inch or longer wood screws that reach through the jamb into the framework studs.

Surface-mount deadbolt

A surface-mount deadbolt with a divided bolt that travels vertically to engage an L-shaped strike is judged by many to be the strongest door lock available. Because it requires only one relatively small hole for its lock cylinder, a surface-mount deadbolt does not weaken the doorframe as much as the type that is housed inside the door—called a cylindrical deadbolt—and it is easier to install.

The lock cylinder is operated by a key from the outside. On the interior side, some types have a thumb latch to operate the bolt; others have a matching key cylinder. The double-cylinder type is not a good choice for entry doors in residences, because when the bolt is thrown you must have the key to open the lock. That can be very dangerous or even fatal in case of fire or other emergency—especially where children are concerned—unless the key is kept in the lock, which undermines the security benefits of a double cylinder.

The lock unit can be mounted with long screws that reach almost to the front surface of the door. Or you can drill all the way through the door and put in bolts with round, smooth heads on the outside and nuts on the inside.

Most surface-mount deadbolts are supplied with a metal finish. To make them less obtrusive, you can spray paint the parts before mounting them, and touch up the heads of the mounting screws.

INSTALLING A STRIKE BOX

First, remove the old strike plate and use a 1-inch spade bit to enlarge and deepen the existing hole in the jamb to accommodate the box of the new strike (Figure 1).

▲ Next, hold the strike box in position and trace its outline onto the door jamb. Mark the outline with a utility knife, not a pencil, cutting clean lines into the wood.

▲ Use a chisel to create a recess about 1/8 inch deep for the combined thickness of the strike box plate and cover plate. Check the fit and adjust the depth so that the cover plate is flush with the surface of the jamb.

▲ Finally, put the strike box and cover plate in position and drill pilot holes for the screws in the plate and the back of the box. Then drive the long screws through the jamb into the studs of the doorway framing (Figure 2).

INSTALLING HINGE SCREWS

To maintain alignment, do one hinge at a time, and just two screws at a time.

▲ Remove the existing screws. Drill their holes deeper, and a bit larger if the new screws have a larger shank than the old ones. Keep the holes narrow and shallow enough so that the screw threads can bite into plenty of wood.

▲ Drive the new, long screws into these holes (Figure 3). Then remove the remaining original jamb screws from the hinge and replace them.

▲ Do the other hinges in the same way. Be careful: Don't drill or drive screws into adjacent sidelights or double doors.

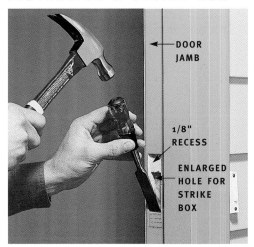

Figure 1. Enlarge the hole to accept the new strike box. Then carefully chisel a surface mortise for the larger, thicker flange and cover plate.

INSTALLING HINGE SCREWS

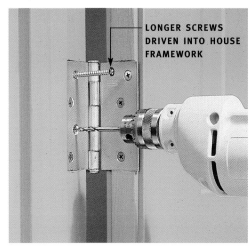

Figure 3. Replace standard hinge screws with 3-in. screws in the jamb leaf. Do two screws at a time; drill pilot holes for the new screws.

Figure 2. Mount the strike and cover plate with screws at least 3 in. long. Drive the outer screws first, then those in the bottom of the box.

Tools You Need

Utility knife

Hammer

Wood chisel

Screwdriver

Drill and twist bits

1" spade bit

Hole saw, sized to lock cylinder

Diagonal cutters or end-cut nippers

INSTALLING A SURFACE-MOUNT DEADBOLT

There are three steps to installing a surface-mount deadbolt:

- ▲ Mount the strike.
- ▲ Drill the mounting holes in the door.
- ▲ Mount the lock and the deadbolt case.

Mount the strike

Determine where the deadbolt will be located on the door. Hold the strike in its corresponding position on the frame and mark around it with a sharp utility knife (Figure 4).

▲ Chisel mortises into the side and edge of the jamb to receive the strike (Figure 5). You may have to temporarily remove or fold back the weatherstripping on the door jamb while you cut the mortise. Follow the lockset directions to cut the mortises to the proper depth. The strike shown in these photos had to be placed so that its front edge was flush with the door, and with a 1/8-inch gap between its flat side and the door edge.

▲ Drill pilot holes and install the screws through the strike (Figure 6). Use at least 3-inch screws from the side to reach through the jamb into the 2x4 framing stud behind. Use 2-1/2 or 3-inch screws from the front to reach well into the jamb from its edge.

Drill the mounting holes

The instructions supplied with the lockset include a template for locating the holes you must drill in the door—one hole for the lock cylinder and four holes for the mounting screws. Tape the template in place on the door and mark the center of each hole (Figure 7).

▲ Drill pilot holes for the mounting screws from the inside. Put a stop collar or a piece of tape on the drill bit so you won't break through the front surface of the door. If you plan to mount the housing with bolts, first drill all the way through with a small-diameter bit, then drill from each side with a bit having the same diameter as the bolt shaft.

▲ Use a hole saw to drill the cylinder hole (Figures 8, 9). Check the lockset directions for the required hole size. Brace or hold the door partway open so you can check the other side easily. Start on the inside with the saw perpendicular to the face of the door both vertically and horizontally. To prevent cracking or splitting the outer face, drill until the tip of the pilot bit breaks through the outside. Then drill back from the other side, with the pilot bit inserted into the hole and the hole saw squarely aligned to the door.

Mount the lock and case

First mount the lock cylinder and the backplate that secures it to the door (Figure 10). Slip the outside collar on the cylinder and make sure the cylinder connecting bar is in place as shown in the lockset directions.

▲ Insert the cylinder into the hole from the outside and turn the key slot to orient it the way you want it. Slip the backplate in place on the inside, insert the cylinder attaching screws, and tighten the cylinder and backplate in position. The screws have notches on the shafts so you can cut them off to accommodate a door of any thickness. Use diagonal cutting pliers or end-cut nippers, and wear safety glasses.

▲ Slide the lock into place, making sure that the connecting bar fits correctly into its slot in back of the latch. It is notched so you can cut it to length as necessary. Close the door and turn the latch so that the bolt enters the strike. If it binds against the strike, shift the case slightly to correct the alignment.

▲ When everything fits together and operates smoothly, drive the mounting screws into the door (Figure 11). Check the alignment and deadbolt operation before tightening the screws the last few turns. If you are mounting the case with round-head bolts, insert them with the heads outside and secure them with lock washers and nuts on the inside.

Figure 4. Mark the deadbolt strike position with a utility knife. Remove the strike and score the cuts deeper. Some strikes may mount on the surface without a mortise; check the directions.

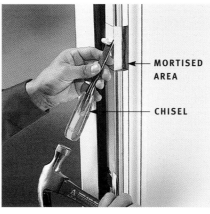

Figure 5. Cut the surface and edge mortises with a wood chisel. Work carefully to avoid splitting out the ends of the mortises. Place the strike in position so you can check for sufficient depth.

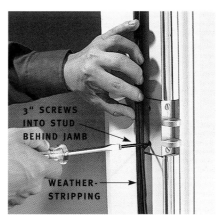

Figure 6. Drive strike screws into pilot holes. Use 3-in. or longer screws in the side, 2-1/2- to 3-in. screws in the edge. Be sure the pilot holes in the jamb edge are large enough to prevent splitting.

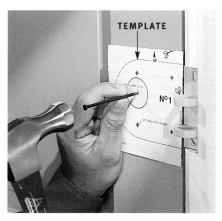

Figure 7. Position the mounting template for the deadbolt housing on the inside of the door, aligned with the installed strike. Tap a nail through the template to mark the centers of the screw and cylinder holes.

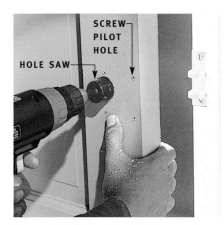

Figure 8. Drill pilot holes for the mounting screws. Use a stop collar or tape on the bit to drill to the proper depth. Then use a hole saw of the proper diameter to drill the hole for the key cylinder.

Figure 9. Drill the cylinder hole carefully, with the hole saw absolutely perpendicular to the door. Stop when the pilot bit breaks through, then move to the outside and drill back from the other direction.

Figure 10. Mount the cylinder and backplate in the hole. Make sure the key slot is positioned properly. Wear safety glasses when you cut the cylinder screws and connecting bar to length.

Figure 11. Check alignment and operation before installing the mounting screws. Tighten screws partway and check again. Move from screw to screw for the final tightening to equalize the pressure.

You can replace a worn or damaged door—or change to a different style—quickly and economically.

Replace a Hinged Door

To keep the project simple, use the existing door jambs and casing moldings—just replace the door itself.

For good-looking results you must fit the door precisely to the opening, and then hang it properly.

That's easy to do, and the project should take only a couple of hours.

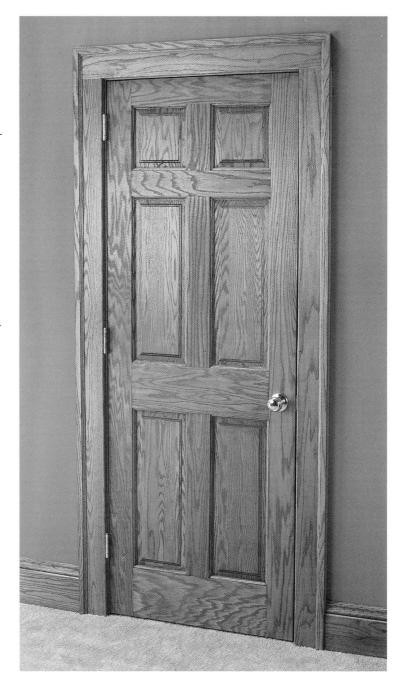

REPLACEMENT DOOR OPTIONS

There are several reasons for replacing an existing door. You may want to change the appearance of an entry, replace a damaged or worn door, or increase security or privacy by using a solid-core or paneled door in place of a hollow-core door. Whatever reason you might have, there are two replacement options: a prehung door or an unmounted door.

Prehung door

This is the more expensive choice, and necessary only when the existing door frame or casing moldings are unusable. A prehung door is an entire unit consisting of a preassembled door frame with casing moldings and the door hinged in place. Often the door has a mounted latchset and strike plate; if not, it is usually predrilled for this hardware. To install the unit you must remove the old casings and frame entirely. That's a messy job, and likely to damage the adjacent wall surfaces. It is more work than may be needed.

Unmounted door

An unmounted door is simply the door itself, without hinges or other hardware. If you can use the existing door jambs and casings, it is by far your best choice. An unmounted door is far less expensive than a prehung unit, it requires less work to install, and you have a wider range of styles to choose from.

The instructions on the following pages show you how to replace an existing hinged door with an unmounted door.

ORDERING AN UNMOUNTED DOOR

The primary concern in ordering an unmounted replacement door of any style is to get the proper size. That's a matter of measuring accurately. A second concern with some doors is to get the proper "hand." This means identifying the orientation of the hinged and latch edges of the door, as explained at right.

Measuring for a replacement

Residential interior doors are sold in a standard height of 80 inches, and standard widths of 30, 32, and 36 inches. Measure the height and width of the existing door and order the corresponding standard size. The existing door measurements will not be exactly the same as standard sizes, because most doors must be trimmed a bit to fit the door frame opening. Just be absolutely certain that the door you buy isn't smaller or it won't fill the opening.

Double-check the size when you order. The door industry uses foot-and-inch measurements, so the salesperson is likely to say "Two foot six by six foot eight," for instance, for a 30-inch x 80-inch door.

PREPARING FOR INSTALLATION

To install the new door, you must remove the old one. Use a hammer and small nail or an old punch to drive the hinge pins upward. Remove them and lift the door free. Do not unscrew the leaves attached to the jamb; you will reuse them. You will also reuse the leaves on the door. Remove them now, so they will not be bent or damaged as you move the door about. Label them clearly—top, middle, bottom—so you can match them properly with the jamb leaves when you hang the door. If you plan to reuse the latchset, also remove it at this time. Save all the mounting screws.

Left-handed Door   Right-handed Door

FIT THE DOOR TO THE OPENING

Mark and cut the new door to fit into the old jambs. Marking differs somewhat, depending on whether the door frame is square unsquare.

Square door frame

Use a carpenter's square to check if the top jamb is square with the hinge jamb (Figure 1). If it is, measure the height and width as follows.

Height. Measure the distance from the top jamb to the floor along the hinge side and along the latch side (Figure 2). Subtract the necessary clearances—1/16 inch on top, 1/2 inch at bottom (see box, below)—and mark the door for cutting across the bottom. If the two measurements are not equal, mark the bottom cutting line as described for an unsquare frame.

Width. Measure the width of the door frame at the top and bottom of the opening. If the measurements are equal, then the side jambs are parallel. Subtract 1/16 inch for hinge-side clearance and 1/8 inch for latch-side clearance, and mark one side edge for cutting. If you must remove more than 1/2 inch from the width of a paneled door, cut equal amounts from both sides if possible, in order to keep the panel pattern symmetrical.

Unsquare door frame

House walls settle over the years, often pulling a door frame out of square. This will affect how you trim the height or width of the door.

Height. If the top jamb is not square with the hinge jamb when you check it, use a level or straightedge to extend the arm of your carpenter's square across the opening and measure the difference at the opposite corner.

On the new door, lay your carpenter's square along the hinge edge and extend a square reference line across the width of the door. On the opposite side, measure up or down from the reference line the same amount you determined in the doorway and mark the door. Then draw the top cutting line.

To establish the bottom cutting line, measure the door frame height along both sides. Subtract the necessary clearances (1/16 inch and 1/2 inch), measure down from the top cutting line on the door, and mark the bottom line.

Width. Measure the width of the door opening at the top jamb and the floor. Subtract the side clearances (1/16 inch and 1/8 inch) and measure from the hinge edge to mark the latch side for trimming. If you must reduce the width of a paneled door more than 1/2 inch, mark it to cut equal amounts from both sides.

Cutting the door

Making clean, smooth cuts on a finished and sometimes quite expensive door requires care, patience, and a sharp saw blade.

▲ To avoid chipping, score the cutting lines with a utility knife and straightedge. Score the outside pieces or stiles deeply (1/16 inch), where the cut runs across the grain (Figure 3).

▲ To get a straight cut, clamp a straight board or other stiff straightedge to the door as a saw guide (Figure 4). Cut slightly outside the scored line with a circular saw to avoid chipping. If you must cut off the beveled edge of a door, make a square cut and restore the bevel when you plane the edges to fine-tune the fit.

▲ As soon as you have trimmed the door, use a wood file to put a 45-degree bevel on all the cut edges (Figure 5). This will prevent chipped edges when handling the door.

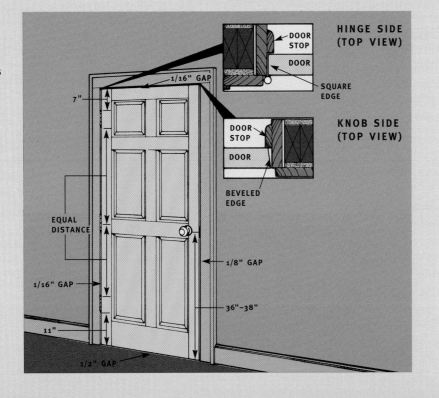

Figure 1. Check for square at the top corner of the hinge jamb. If not square, extend a line across the opening and measure gap at the latch side. Then measure height and mark the door as per text.

Figure 2. If the door frame is square, measure height from the top jamb to the floor along the hinge jamb and along the latch jamb. Use these measurements to mark the door.

Figure 3. Score the cut line on the face of the door with a utility knife to prevent the circular saw blade from chipping the surface as the teeth cut from below. Score cross-grain area deeply.

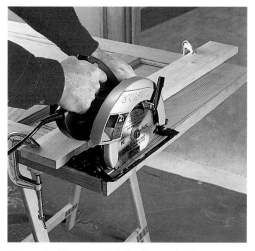

Figure 4. Clamp a straightedge to the door to act as a saw guide. Position it to cut just outside the scored cut line; plane or sand to the line when you are fine-tuning the fit.

Figure 5. File a 45-degree bevel along all of the cut edges. This bevel will prevent chipped edges when you handle the door in the succeeding stages of fitting and hanging it.

Tools You Need

Tape measure

Carpenter's square

Hammer

Punch

Utility knife

Circular saw

Wood chisel

Wood file

Drill and twist bits

Hole saw

Plane

Sander or sanding block

INSTALL THE DOOR

There are three basic steps to the actual installation of the door.

▲ Mark and cut mortises in the door for the hinges.

▲ Mount the hinges on the door.

▲ Hang the door.

When the door has been installed—and after you have adjusted the fit as shown in the box on page 48—you can install the latchset and finish or paint the door.

Mark and cut the mortises

Put the trimmed door into the door frame. Slip the hinged edge in position first. Be careful not to damage the door edge on the hinge barrels that are mounted on the jamb. Lightly drive wedges mounted along the latch edge to hold the door firmly against the hinge jamb.

▲ Place quarters on top of the door at each corner, to provide 1/16-inch clearance, and tap in wedges at the floor to shim the door and coins up to the top jamb (Figure 6).

▲ Use a sharp pencil to transfer the hinge positions from the leaves on the jamb to the door (Figure 7). This will show you exactly where to cut mortises for the hinge leaves that fasten to the door. Mark the top and bottom edge of each hinge accurately; stand on a stool if necessary to mark the top hinge. Precision is critical here; even a 1/32-inch deviation may keep the hinge leaves from fitting together easily.

▲ Remove the door from the frame and set it hinge-edge-up to mark the individual mortises. Measure the mortise width from the old door or from a hinge leaf on the door jamb (Figure 8). Measure from the surface of the door or the edge of the jamb (not the casing) to the back edge of the mortise or hinge leaf. Mark this width at each hinge location on the door edge.

▲ Now hold a hinge leaf at each position on the new door. Align it with the top, bottom, and width marks, and score its outline with a utility knife to mark the mortise (Figure 9).

▲ Deepen each mortise outline with a utility knife or chisel so the edges of the mortise will be crisp. Make cross-grain cuts at the ends of the mortise first, then score along the back edge of the mortise.

▲ Use a chisel to cut the mortise (Figure 10). Clearing out the waste wood in the mortise requires care. Make sure your chisel is sharp, and work slowly. Shave small chips, cutting with the grain of the wood toward either end. Keep the bevel of the chisel facing downward, and hold the angle of the blade low, less than 45 degrees above the edge of the door. In hardwood, tap the chisel with a mallet or hammer (if the chisel has a metal end cap). In softwood, you may find that you get better control by using both hands on the chisel to pare away the wood. Gradually deepen the mortise until the hinge leaf is flush with the surface of the wood when you check it.

Mount the hinges on the door

Lay each hinge leaf in its mortise and mark the positions of the screw holes. Use a punch, and mark each hole slightly off center toward the back of the mortise (Figure 11). That's an experienced carpenter's trick, so the screws will pull the hinge leaf tightly into the mortise.

▲ Drill pilot holes and attach the hinge leaves to the door. If you tighten all the hinge screws at this point, you probably won't be able to mount the door, since it's not likely that all the hinges will mesh perfectly. Leave two of the three hinges slightly loose and tighten the screws after the hinge pins have been inserted.

Hang the door

This step is easiest if you have a helper to insert the hinge pins as you maneuver the door into place. To do it alone, put a shim under the outer edge of the door to help support it while you slip the hinges together and drop in the pins. Then tighten all the hinge screws.

Figure 6. Put the door in place to mark hinge locations. Wedge it against the hinge jamb, and shim it upward to 1/16 in. from the top jamb.

Figure 7. Use a quarter as a spacer at each top corner to obtain a 1/16-in. gap. Mark the hinge locations on the door with a sharp pencil.

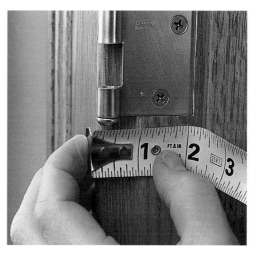

Figure 8. Measure mortise depth from the edge of the jamb to the rear of the hinge leaf, or measure the mortise on the old door.

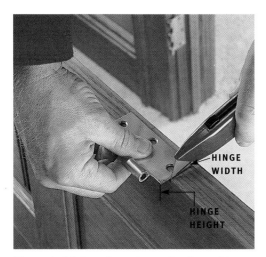

Figure 9. Mark each mortise outline from a hinge leaf held in position. Use a utility knife or sharp pencil. Then cut the outline deeper with a knife or a very sharp chisel.

Figure 10. Chisel out each mortise carefully. Use a sharp chisel, bevel side down. After cutting the outline, work from the center toward the ends to remove waste wood a little bit at a time.

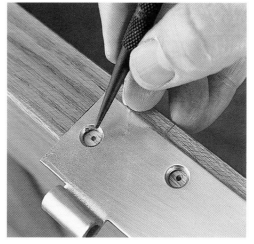

Figure 11. Punch guide holes for a pilot drill a bit off-center toward the back of the mortise. Drill pilot holes and insert screws. Drive them all partway in, then tighten alternately for even pull.

Figure 12. Cut narrow strips of cardboard as shims to adjust the hinge-side gap. Place them either behind the screws or in front as needed. See the diagrams below.

Figure 13. Plane or sand the edges to make an exact fit. Plane top and bottom from corners in toward center to avoid corner tearout. Bevel the latch edge about 3/32 in.

⚠ Begin by creating an even gap along the hinge jamb. It's very easy to make the gap wider or narrower by loosening the screws in the jamb leaves and inserting cardboard shims (Figure 12 and box below).

⚠ Next, swing the door partway open and let go. If the door starts to swing closed, loosen the hinges in the jamb and tap the top hinge with a hammer to move it outward slightly. If the opened door starts to swing open of its own accord, shift the bottom hinge outward in the same way. Another method is to remove the center hinge pin and tap it with a hammer to bend it slightly. When replaced, the tension will hold the door still.

⚠ Sand and plane the other edges for the final fit (Figure 13). Remove the hinge pins to take the door down to work on it. Plane a 3/32-inch bevel (3-1/2 degrees) on the latch edge to avoid rubbing when the door closes.

INSTALL THE LATCHSET

The trick in installing a new latchset is to position the latch so that it catches the old strike plate already in the jamb.

⚠ With the door in place, find the center of the strike plate and mark this point on the door. Put a strip of masking tape around the edge and over the face of the door so that your marks won't mar the finish and can be removed easily. Lay a square along the edge of the door and draw a reference line through the mark on the tape.

⚠ Mark the backset for the center of the knob along this line, measured from the edge of the door (Figure 14). The required backset may be stamped on the latch or given in the installation instructions. If you are using the old latchset, measure it directly from the old door. It is almost always 2-3/8 inches for interior doors.

⚠ Now cut the holes for the latchset. You'll need a hole saw for the knob assembly and a drill bit for the latch (Figure 15). Get the sizes from the holes in the old door or measure the knob and latch assemblies themselves.

Drilling a large hole with a hole saw can be a little tricky, so experiment on a scrap of wood if you haven't done this before. It helps to drill a pilot hole completely through the door first to guide the pilot bit in the hole saw. Keep the drill at right angles to the door. Work from one side until the pilot bit comes through, then drill back from the other direction.

⚠ Finally, drill the latch hole in the center of the door edge and chisel a mortise for the latch (Figure 16). Insert the latch, assemble the knobs, and tighten the mounting screws (Figure 17).

ADJUSTING A HINGE-SIDE GAP

To make the gap between the door edge and hinge jamb narrower, insert a shim at the rear of the mortise, between the hinge leaf and the jamb.

To make the gap wider, insert a shim at the front of the mortise.

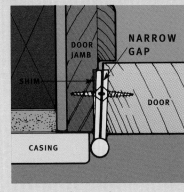

Narrow gap (top view)

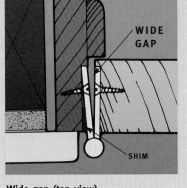

Wide gap (top view)

Figure 14. Mark the latch location on masking tape on the door, for easy removal. Center the latch on the existing strike plate. The backset locates the center of the knob hole.

Figure 15. Use a hole saw to make the knob hole. Drill a pilot hole first, then work from each side. Center the latch hole in the edge of the door.

FINISH THE DOOR

The finish performs double duty: It makes the door look attractive, and it slows moisture absorption by the wood. Moisture causes wood to swell. As the door expands, it will begin to stick or rub against the jamb.

▲ Remove the hinge pins and lay the door across padded sawhorses to work on it. If you prefinished the door, first restain all the places you've cut or planed (see Finishing Tip). Then seal the entire wood surface with a varnish or a polyurethane finish.

▲ If you are painting the door, remove the knob plates, finish-sand as necessary, and go over all surfaces and edges with a tack cloth. Then apply a primer, followed by a semigloss enamel finish coat. Your door should function without trouble for many years.

Finishing Tip

It is best to stain and seal the new door before hanging it. Otherwise it's difficult to sand off the oil and dirt the raw wood picks up from your hands. Don't worry about the slight marring that occurs from cutting, sanding, and planing the door edges. You can easily restain and seal these later. If you plan to paint the door, you can do all the finish work after cutting and hanging it.

Figure 16. Score the latch outline with the latch screwed in place. Then remove it and chisel a mortise so that the plate will sit flush with the surface of the door edge.

Figure 17. Assemble the latch and knobs as they were in the old door, or according to the instructions if you have a new latchset. Close the door and make adjustments as needed.

Install French Doors

Replacing an old patio door with new French doors can improve the appearance, energy efficiency, and value of your home.

This is a project with big impact, but one that's relatively simple to do—provided you select a new door unit that's close in size to your old one.

If you have do-it-yourself experience, you can complete the entire project in a day. If you're a novice, you should be able to get the basic installation done in one day, then finish up the remaining details in another afternoon.

SELECTING FRENCH DOORS

The key to making this an easy-to-do project is to select the right size replacement door unit. You must also choose a style that opens in an appropriate way for your room.

Size

A door that is too wide or too tall will call for major remodeling and structural work to change the size of the opening. Fortunately, several companies make replacement doors specifically designed to fit the 72-1/2 x 80-1/2 inch opening many old sliding patio doors fit into.

Try to locate a new door that's exactly the same dimensions as your old door (see Measuring and Ordering, page 52). If that's not possible, select one that's no more than 2 inches smaller in height and width; you can cover up these small gaps with wider trim. If necessary, you can get by with a door that's a little bit larger than your old door, but you must have at least a 3/8-inch gap between the door frame and the top and sides of the opening to provide room for adjusting the new unit.

Inward-swinging double French doors are the most typical installation.

Style

In addition to choosing doors that match the appearance of your home, consider the size and arrangement of the room, because that may determine how doors can swing. You have four basic options to choose from.

Inward-swinging double doors. By far the most commonly seen French doors are mounted in pairs, hinged at opposite sides and opening inward (photo, below left). Those with three- or five-point locking systems between the doors provide the best security. However, this style requires interior wall space on either side so the doors can be opened fully. Other available styles, described here, are shown in the box on the opposite page.

Inward-swinging single door. In some rooms the wall on one side of the doorway is blocked by shelves or furniture, or has a light switch or fixture that must not be covered. In that case, the solution may be a unit with one fixed and one swinging door. The swinging door is generally hinged at the center to the fixed door and it opens inward.

Outward-swinging double doors. Interior room space is no restriction if both French doors swing outward. This is especially useful for a doorway that leads to a porch or other enclosed, secure space. However, if you install this style in a doorway that leads directly outdoors, consider security carefully. The hinge barrels of outward-swinging doors are on the outside, which means the removable pins of ordinary hinges would be readily accessible. If you choose this kind of installation, be sure to buy doors with fixed-pin, hardened hinges.

Sliding doors. French door panels that operate like common patio doors are also available: one panel is fixed, and the other slides in a track. This offers the handsome appearance of traditional French doors without the need for any swinging space.

These styles make it possible to have French doors where space or other limitations prevent you from installing the standard inward-swinging double doors.

Inward-swinging single door requires minimum space to swing open, and does not cover any wall area. It is a good choice where you don't need to open the full width of the doorway.

Outward-swinging double doors require no interior space to operate and uncover the full opening. Tamperproof hinges are a must for security because the barrels are on the outside.

Sliding French doors require no swinging space inside or outside. With one fixed panel, half the doorway width can be opened. As with other styles, screens are available.

Checklist for Ordering French Doors

☐ SIZE. Are the rough opening dimensions and jamb depth correct?

☐ SWING. Which door opens, or opens first? Do the doors swing to the interior or exterior?

☐ SCREENS. Are they included in the price you've been quoted?

☐ DOOR HARDWARE. Is it included in the price? Is there a choice of finishes or styles?

☐ GRILLES. Are they included in the price? Do they mount inside or outside of the glass?

☐ GLASS. Do you want low-E or tinted glass? What about double- or triple-pane glass?

☐ COLOR. If the door is vinyl or metal clad, do you have a choice of colors?

☐ COST. Is there a discount if you're willing to wait longer for delivery? Is delivery included in the quoted price?

Other features to consider

As you look for French doors, compare the following features among the available units.

Security. Double, hinged French doors should have a three- or five-point locking system to secure the doors to each other as well as into the threshold and top jamb.

Energy efficiency. Many doors are available with double- or triple-pane glass for increased comfort and energy efficiency. Low-E and tinted glass are also available.

Screens. Most manufacturers offer some type of sliding or swinging screen door. Since screens partially obscure the view, many people remove and store them during the cooler, more bug-free months.

Finishes. Doors with a vinyl- or metal-clad exterior offer low maintenance, but are commonly available only in white, black, and perhaps bronze-colored trim. You must paint doors made of wood, but they can become whatever color you choose.

Ease of installation. To save work and get the best results, consider only preassembled units with the doors hung in the frame, weather-stripping and threshold in place, and much of the lock mechanism installed. You can save money buying individual or partially assembled doors, but you'll pay the price in extra time—and most likely wind up with a door that's less secure, less energy efficient, and (depending on your skill level) less attractive.

Appearance. True "divided light" doors contain rows of small individual panes of glass (called lights) set in a gridwork. These are quite handsome, but expensive. They're also more likely to allow air infiltration, and they require a thick grid or framework to support the panes. Most people now select doors with grilles that snap over the interior or exterior of a single large pane, creating the divided light look. Doors with double or triple glass or insulated glass panels use snap-in grilles.

Hardware. You may have many options when it comes to hardware; it depends on the door's locking system. Most manufacturers offer high-end brass hardware as well as many other, more affordable options.

MEASURING AND ORDERING FRENCH DOORS

You do not need to remove the existing door in order to measure for a replacement French door unit. Instead, use a pry bar to remove the moldings around the interior of the door. Be careful; you may be able to reuse them. And try not to mar the surrounding wall.

You'll need two sets of dimensions: the rough opening size, and the jamb depth.

Rough opening

Measure the distance between the 2x4 trimmer studs on each side of the door opening to determine the width of the rough opening (Figure 1). Then measure the distance from the bottom of the header—the wood beam over the door—to the floor under the door's threshold. This will give you the height of the rough opening.

Recheck the measurements; a mistake can be very costly. Make sure you're measuring the actual opening that will remain when the old door is removed. Usually there's a space of a half inch or more between the old door frame and the house framework. Drywall or plywood may jut into this opening and give you a false reading, so measure between the 2x4 trimmers, not between other materials.

Jamb depth

You must have this dimension when ordering a replacement unit so the moldings will lie flat and fit snugly. Measure or add together the combined thickness of the house framework, the interior drywall or plaster, and the exterior sheathing (but not the siding).

The wall shown in the diagram below (Figure 2) was built from 3-1/2 inch wide studs, 1/2-inch thick drywall, and 1/2-inch thick plywood sheathing, for a total wall thickness of 4-1/2 inches. Add to that 1/16 inch to account for gaps or a layer of roofing felt or other materials. The result is a jamb depth of 4-9/16 inches.

MEASURING AND ORDERING FRENCH DOORS

Figure 1. Measure the rough opening accurately. Remove interior moldings and measure width between the trimmer studs; measure height from header to floor. If necessary, probe with a wire to get the depth to the studs and add that to a measurement taken between drywall edges.

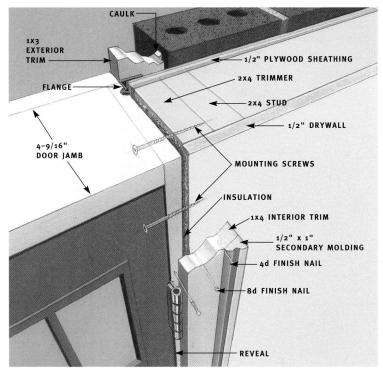

Figure 2. Jamb depth is the combined thickness of wall framing, exterior sheathing, and interior drywall, plus 1/16 in. This diagram also shows typical mounting and trim installation details. Instructions for your unit may call for a somewhat different installation.

Take the rough opening and jamb depth dimensions to your home center, lumberyard, or window and door dealer and place your order. Go over the order form yourself to see that all important details have been recorded correctly. Use the checklist on page 51.

REMOVING THE OLD DOOR

Don't begin dismantling your old door until the new door has arrived and you've verified that it's going to fit the rough opening.

▲ If you are replacing old hinged doors, simply drive the pins out of the hinges and take out the doors. If you can't remove the pins from the hinges, unscrew the hinges from the jambs. Then remove the fasteners securing the frame in the opening and pry out the old unit.

▲ If you are replacing a sliding door, it probably consists of two panels—one that moves and one that's fixed—set in a wood or aluminum frame. Begin by removing the screen, then slide the movable panel partway open and lift it to raise the bottom out of its track (Figure 3). Pull the bottom toward you until the top of the door drops free from the upper track. If the door is heavy, you'll need a helper who can support the top as you remove it.

▲ Next, remove any screws or brackets that hold the stationary panel in place. Slide it over a few inches to free it from the side jamb, then lift it up and out in the same way that you removed the sliding panel.

▲ Pry off any brick molding and wooden trim surrounding the exterior of the door (Figure 4). Remove the screws that secure the old jamb to the house framework. There will be several screws along the top and sides and perhaps a few through the bottom threshold. Use a small hacksaw to cut through stubborn fasteners (Figure 5). Lift the old frame out of the opening.

REMOVING THE OLD DOOR

Figure 3. Remove sliding door panels by lifting them upward and swinging bottom out. Sliding panel lifts out directly; stationary panel has brackets or screws that must be removed first.

Figure 4. Carefully remove brick molding and wooden trim with a pry bar. Position the tool so that you are prying against the door frame, not the siding, to avoid damage.

Figure 5. Remove screws on the sides and tops of the old door frame and the threshold; there will be several. Cut through difficult screws with a small hacksaw or drill them out if necessary.

INSTALLING THE NEW FRENCH DOORS

There's great variety in new doors and their suggested method of installation. Follow the manufacturer's directions for specific details; they generally are excellent. All installation directions cover the following steps. You'll probably need a helper to lift the door unit into place and hold it steady.

Level the sill

Rest a 4-foot level across the floor where the door's threshold will rest. If the floor slants more than 1/2 inch from one side of the doorway to the other, place varying thicknesses of wood shims every 6 inches, to create a level floor along the opening. If the floor slants less than 1/8 inch, you don't need to shim the threshold. If it slants some amount in between, level the threshold with shims after installing the unit but before permanently screwing it to the house framework.

Rough-fit the unit

Center the door unit in the opening, then secure it temporarily in place from the outside with a couple of 16d nails toenailed (angled) into the exterior sheathing. Stand back and examine it. If the gap between the door frame and the rough opening at the top or either side is wider than 3/4 inch, nail strips of wood or plywood to the house framework to reduce it to 1/2 inch or less.

For example, if there is a gap of 1-1/4 inches between the top of the door frame and the bottom of the header, nail a strip of 1x4 (which is actually 3/4 inch thick) to the bottom of the header, reducing the gap to 1/2 inch. This will give the mounting screws and molding nails something to bite into, while leaving enough room to level and plumb the door frame during final installation and truing-up.

Prepare the doors and opening

Carefully remove the door unit and lay it flat. If the door unit includes plastic flanges (which go behind the exterior finishing trim), use a block of wood and a hammer to tap them into the precut groove around the perimeter of the door frame (Figure 6).

▲ Remove any metal screw covers at this time too. Some doors have exterior screw covers for weather protection and a finished appearance.

▲ Place a strip of 15-pound roofing felt across the opening to serve as a moisture barrier under the threshold (Figure 7). Then apply a thick bead of silicone caulk on top of the felt strip, all along the outer edge, for a threshold seal.

Install and true-up the doors

Place the door unit so that the threshold is aligned with the strip of moisture barrier across the opening. Tip the door up into place (Figure 8), center it from side to side in the rough opening, and then again toenail it to the house with a couple of 16d nails to prevent the unit from falling out of its position.

▲ From the inside, place a 4-foot level along the side of one door. Install pairs of tapered wood shims between the door jamb and house framework, to hold the door unit perfectly plumb and straight (Figure 9). Small gaps may require only a single pair of shims, while wider gaps may require two or three stacked together. If your doors came with factory-installed spacers, leave them in place until all your shims are installed; they help maintain a consistent gap between the doors and frame.

▲ You must make the side jambs plumb from side to side and front to back, and the threshold and head jamb level. When you have this alignment, install four long screws—one high and one low on each side—to secure the door frame to the house framing (Figure 10).

▲ Test the doors by opening and shutting them several times; they should swing freely without dragging on the carpet or catching on the door frame. Open them halfway and let go; they should remain motionless, neither creeping open nor shutting on their own. If they do creep, remove the long mounting screws and recheck and adjust everything for level and plumb. Then replace the screws.

▲ When your doors pass the swing test, install the remaining screws. The unit shown in the photos required two long screws through each hinge plus several more along each side and the top. Screw covers conceal the screw heads in places that would be visible.

▲ Do not secure the door in place by nailing the plastic flanges to the house sheathing; this is a common mistake. Units mounted this way will loosen each time the door is opened or shut, resulting in shaky, leaky, sagging doors. The flanges are designed to be gap fillers and air blockers, not mounting devices.

Figure 6. Lay the door flat to prepare it after rough fitting. Tap weather-blocking flanges, if any, into the precut groove with a hammer and block of wood; don't hammer the flanges directly.

Figure 7. Lay a strip of roofing felt across the opening as a moisture and draft barrier. This is essential if the threshold will rest on concrete. Apply a bead of caulk on the felt, along the outside edge.

Figure 8. Raise the French door unit into place after aligning the bottom across the opening. You'll need a helper. Center it side-to-side in the opening, then hold it temporarily with angled 16d nails.

Using Tapered Shims

Use shims in pairs, with the thin end of one beside the thick end of the other. To adjust the shim thickness, tap on the thick ends to drive them further together. Because of the tapers, the outer sides will remain parallel, so whatever the shim is bracing will twist out of alignment.

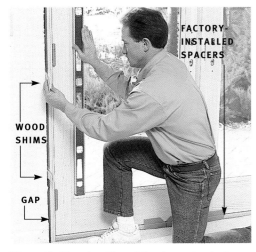

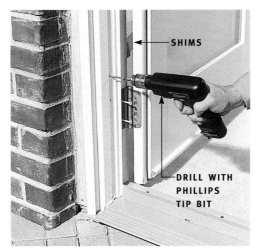

Figure 9. Use a level to get the doors plumb at both ends. Insert doubled shims to hold the unit in position. Leave the factory-installed spacers in place until all mounting screws have been driven.

Figure 10. Install long screws through the hinges and the door frame at all points indicated in the mounting instructions for the unit. Test the doors for proper operation as described in the text.

TRIMMING AND FINISHING

To enhance the appearance of your new doors, take care to do a neat, precise job in adding exterior and interior trim and in painting or staining the doors and trim.

Install exterior trim

In rare cases, you can simply reapply the old interior and exterior moldings and be done. But chances are you'll have wider, narrower, or uneven spaces to cover so your new door blends gracefully with its surroundings.

Use a circular saw and rip guide to cut 1x4's (1x6's for wider spaces) to the correct width to fill in the space between the exterior door frame and the existing brick or siding (Figure 11). The widths of the pieces may be identical or quite different from one another and from the old standard brick molding, depending on how close a match in size the old and new doors are. Position these pieces, then nail them in place using 8d galvanized casing nails (Figure 12). Apply a bead of caulk where the exterior molding meets the brick or siding.

Install interior trim

To avoid having to touch up the wall paint around the door—or having to locate and patch in skinny strips of wallpaper—select an interior trim molding wide enough to slightly overlap onto the existing paint or wallcovering. Position one edge of the molding on the door frame and use the other edge as a guide to mark the baseboard (Figure 13). Pry the end of the baseboard a few inches away from the wall, then trim it to length using a fine-tooth handsaw. Before nailing the trim in place, lightly pack strips of fiberglass insulation in the gap between the door frame and the framework of the house.

Figure 11. Cut new exterior trim to fill the gaps between the door frame and the brick or other siding material. Use 1x4 clear pine or other defect-free wood and rip it to width as required.

Figure 12. Position and nail the exterior trim in place. The trim covers the plastic weather flanges, if any. Install the top board first, then the side pieces. Caulk between the trim and masonry siding.

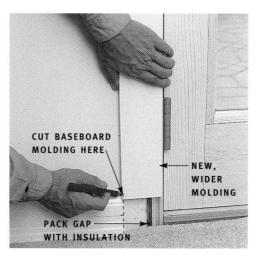

Figure 13. Mark baseboard molding for cutting by holding a piece of new interior trim in position as shown. Pry baseboard carefully away from wall and cut it to length with a fine-tooth saw.

Figure 14. Dress up the new, plain interior trim by adding a secondary molding, such as a small doorstop molding, to its face. Miter the corners. Set and fill the nailheads before finishing.

If the new, wider and plainer trim looks out of place next to the existing baseboard or other molding in the room, you have two options. You can install all new moldings in the room so everything matches, which would be a major undertaking. Or you can keep the project simple and add a secondary molding atop the plain trim so that it blends better with the existing moldings (Figure 14).

Finishing touches

To prevent warping, paint or stain and finish all bare wood surfaces on the doors and frame immediately after installation. Don't forget the top and bottom door edges; they're the first to be affected by moisture.

Install the locking and operating hardware. If hardware is supplied with your doors, it probably will require no drilling and can be installed in a few minutes without difficulty.

You may need to apply a thin wood or metal transition strip to cover gaps or jagged edges where the threshold meets the existing carpet, hardwood, or other interior flooring. With that done, your French doors are complete.

The finished installation will give you pleasure, comfort, and security. Most modern French doors have excellent weather seals and multiple-point locking hardware.

Walls

Hanging Wallcoverings

Transform a room in one day with new wallcoverings. Here's everything you need to know about hanging them.

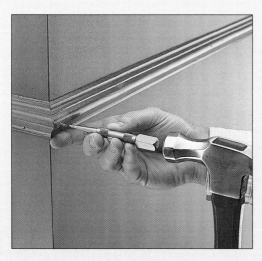

A new wallcovering can change the look, feel, and texture of a room literally overnight.

Hanging Wallcoverings

Hanging wallcoverings is one of the easiest and most popular do-it-yourself projects. The tools and materials needed are widely available and all are quite reasonably priced.

You can learn the necessary skills quickly, and with practice and patience do professional-looking work.

What's more, you'll enjoy the results for many years to come.

Modern materials provide wallcoverings suitable for any room in the house. A new wallcovering goes up rapidly and easily. Eighty percent of the wallcoverings DIYers buy, they hang themselves. That's because prepasted papers and easy-to-use tools make paper hanging nearly goof-proof.

CHOOSING A WALLCOVERING

Although many people still say "wallpaper," a great number of modern wallcoverings are made of other materials such as vinyl, grass cloth, fabric, and foil. Paper coverings are still available, but have advantages over the wallpaper of old. Most have a plastic coating for durability and ease of cleaning. The major considerations in choosing a wallcovering are suitability both to your decorating tastes and to the location, the quantity you need, and whether the covering is prepasted or unpasted.

Suitability

When you consider various wallcoverings, bring home some samples and tape them in place to see if the color and pattern are compatible with the carpeting, lighting, furnishings, and character of the room. In general, small prints or light colors will make a room seem larger; big bold patterns and dark colors will make the same room feel smaller.

Also consider the suitability of the material for the location. A smooth, washable surface is essential in kitchens, bathrooms, children's rooms. Textured surfaces are good for living and dining rooms and bedrooms. Foil and other specialty materials work well in entrance halls, informal family rooms, and similar locations.

Quantity

Wallcoverings are sold in rolls 15 to 54 inches wide. A single-length roll contains about 35 square feet of material; a double-length roll, or "bolt," twice as much. You'll actually get 15 to 20 percent less coverage—say 25 to 30 square feet with a single roll—because of waste and trimming. Check the average coverage figures on the labels when you shop for wallcoverings.

To determine how much you need to cover a wall, proceed as follows.

▲ Measure the height from the top of the baseboard to the ceiling in feet, and add one-half foot for trimming waste at top and bottom. Multiply that amount by the length of the wall in feet. The result of this equation is the area to be covered in square feet.

▲ If there is a large patio door, picture window, or bay window, figure its area in square feet and subtract that from the wall area. Do not subtract the area of normal-width doors or windows, because you will hang full-width strips there and cut out the necessary portions.

▲ Figure the area of each wall to be covered, add the individual wall areas to get the total room area, and divide by the average coverage figure for the paper (or by 25 if none is specified). The result is the minimum number of rolls of wallcovering you need.

▲ If the covering has a repeated pattern, you must allow for some waste in matching the repeat. Add 10 percent to your final figure, or—for a pattern where the repeat spacing is 12 inches or more—a half-roll. Round off the total to the next full roll.

Prepasted or unpasted?

Many wallcoverings come prepasted. You simply moisten the back to activate the paste just before hanging each strip. This is the easiest kind of covering to work with and is the kind used in the project illustrated here. It should be the choice for your first wallcovering job.

Unpasted materials require that you apply wet adhesive to the back of the covering with a wide wallpapering brush or a roller. You must be sure to use the kind of adhesive specified for the wallcovering—vinyl, for instance, requires a special vinyl adhesive—and there may be activators or other additives required.

Working with an unpasted wallcovering is a bit messier, and handling the strips is sometimes trickier than with a prepasted covering. However, the techniques of hanging, fitting, and trimming shown on the following pages are the same for both types of wallcovering.

WALL PREPARATION

Your finest efforts will be wasted unless you prepare the walls properly before hanging any covering. The surfaces must be smooth: Even a small, detailed pattern in the covering cannot hide underlying irregularities when light strikes a wall at an angle. The surfaces must also be sealed for the adhesive to bond securely. Here's what to do in the three situations you're most likely to encounter.

Unpainted drywall. Prime with an oil-base primer, and then follow with an acrylic wall-covering undercoat.

Painted drywall or plaster. Prime with an acrylic wallcovering undercoat.

Wallpapered walls. Strip the old paper off by peeling and scraping. To soften the paste in difficult spots, apply hot water or wallpaper remover, or rent a steamer. Prime the stripped wall before hanging new wallcovering.

In all situations, fill gouges, cracks, and dents with patching or drywall taping compound. Fill alligatored paint or similar irregular surfaces with a feather coating of compound. Sand all filled and patched areas with medium-grit paper and seal with primer.

Make certain there are straight, well-defined edges along all moldings, so you can get crisp, straight lines when you trim the new covering.

Finally, *turn off electrical power* to any outlets and switches in the walls you will be covering and remove all wall plates. Electricity, metal tools, and wet wallcovering do not mix safely. If you need power for a worklight, run an extension cord from an adjacent room.

Drawing the First Line

It is essential to get the starting reference line absolutely plumb. It is equally essential to precisely align the edge of the first drop with that line. Each succeeding drop is butted against the edge of the one before it, so if anything is at all crooked, the problem will be carried across the entire wall to the first corner.

For the same reason, it is essential to get the reference line you draw after turning a corner plumb, and to get the drop edge there precisely aligned with it.

HANGING THE WALLCOVERING

If you have never hung wallcovering before, choose a closet or a small room for your first project to get the feel of working with the tools and materials. The techniques for hanging wall-covering are not difficult to learn. They include:

- ▲ Marking the layout
- ▲ Cutting, pasting, and booking a strip— called a "drop"
- ▲ Hanging drops
- ▲ Seaming and trimming
- ▲ Turning corners
- ▲ Hanging drops around windows, doors and similar features
- ▲ Dealing with common problems

MARKING THE LAYOUT

There are two stages to marking a layout for hanging wallcovering: planning seam locations and establishing a starting line.

Seam locations

Begin by laying out full-width intervals around the room, to see how seams will fall near corners and at the very end. The end is important because you probably will need to cut a partial-width strip for the last drop, which means the pattern will not match exactly. So it makes sense to have the final seam fall in an unobtrusive place: behind a door that usually stands open, for instance, or in the darkest corner of the room.

▲ Choose an appropriate starting point and mark with a pencil where each seam will fall. Do not draw lines, just make tick marks, because you may want to shift the starting point to get the best layout, and you will be marking a fresh starting reference line every time you turn a corner.

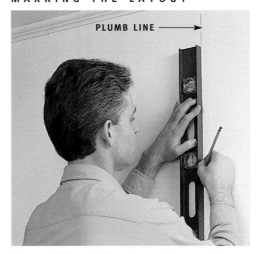
PLUMB LINE

Figure 1. Plan strip locations so they extend past corners by 4 in. or more. Then mark a plumb reference line for positioning the edge of the first section of wallcovering (the first drop).

There are two major points to watch out for in marking the layout:

▲ A full-width measurement should run at least 4 inches around any inside or outside corner. This will ensure having enough of the strip extending onto the second wall to make an overlap joint (see Turning Corners, page 65).

▲ Seams should not fall close to the edge of a door or window frame, a fireplace, or a similar built-in feature. The aim is to avoid having to cut very narrow strips, which stretch or tear easily during handling and which would put two seams very close together, making them more clearly visible.

Starting line

Once you have a layout that puts projected seams at convenient places, you can mark the starting reference line. Measure one full width from the point where the last seam is to be located, going in the direction you plan to work—left to right is easiest for most people, but not absolutely necessary. At that point, use a level to draw a plumb (vertical) line from the ceiling or bottom edge of the ceiling molding to the top of the baseboard (Figure 1).

CUTTING, PASTING, AND BOOKING A DROP

You'll need a worktable big enough to unroll strips of wallcovering for cutting and pasting. Plywood or an old door laid across sawhorses is suitable. It should be at least as wide as the full width of your wallcovering. Since you'll be working with water, protect the floor from drips.

Cutting and pasting

Unroll a strip of wallcovering face down on the table and cut off a drop—a length equal to the baseboard-to-ceiling dimension of the wall plus 4 inches; this allows for 2 inches of trimming waste at the top and the bottom.

With a prepasted covering, "pasting" is simply a matter of wetting the adhesive on the back until it forms a milky paste. Moisten a short-nap paint roller in a tray of lukewarm water and roll it across the drop (Figure 2). Wet thoroughly, especially the edges and ends.

If you are using an unpasted wallcovering, mix the required adhesive according to the manufacturer's directions and spread it thoroughly over the back of the drop with a wallpapering brush or a paint roller.

Booking

Lightly fold the drop in half, end to end, pasted surfaces together; then fold it in half again. This is called booking the drop (Figure 3). Do not press on the folded drop; you do not want creases, and you do not want the surfaces to stick together. Before lifting the drop from the table, peel back the upper right corner so you can apply it to the wall easily.

HANGING DROPS

Carry the booked drop up your stepladder and position the top end with about 2 inches of overlap at the ceiling (Figure 4).

▲ Smooth the drop lightly against the wall as you align the edge with the reference line. Then go over with a vinyl smoother, pressing the covering firmly into place along the line (Figure 5).

▲ Next, smooth across the width of the drop to work large bubbles toward the outer edges. Unbook the drop carefully as you move down the wall and continue to align it with the reference line. It will overlap the baseboard 2 to 4 inches at the bottom.

▲ Prepare the next drop, carry it to the wall, and hang it beside the first one, butting the edges together (Figure 6). Continue to hang drops for the next 15 minutes or so, then return to the start to roll the seams and trim the top and bottom edges (page 64).

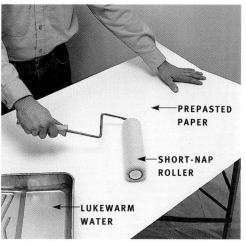

Figure 2. Wet the back of a prepasted drop with lukewarm water until a milky paste forms. Be sure to wet all the edges and ends. If you use paste, mix and apply according to instructions.

Figure 3. Book a drop by folding the pasted faces loosely together and folding the drop in half again. Take care not to crease the paper. Peel back one corner before lifting the drop.

Tools You Need

Tape measure

Level

Short-nap paint roller

Paint roller tray

Vinyl smoother

10" broad knife

Razor knife and blades

Metal straightedge

Seam roller

Stepladder

Worktable

Figure 4. Position the edge of the first drop exactly along the plumb line, starting at the top. Smooth the edge along the line with your hand. The drop ends should overlap floor and ceiling moldings.

Figure 5. Flatten the drop against the wall with a wallcovering smoother. Be careful not to stretch the covering. Work large bubbles out toward the edges. Tiny bubbles will disappear with drying.

Figure 6. Hang the second drop with its edge butted against the first one. Match the pattern. Be careful not to open the seam as you smooth the drop. Continue to hang subsequent drops in the same way.

SEAMING AND TRIMMING

There are two important finishing steps in hanging wallcovering drops: seaming and trimming. Both require care for a first-rate job.

Seaming

Seaming actually means rolling the butt seams to make sure the edges lie flat and are securely adhered to the wall. About 15 to 20 minutes after hanging two drops, go over the seam between them with a seam roller (Figure 7). Use light pressure and roll the seam just once; overworking a seam can squeeze out all the adhesive at various points, which can lead to separation and peeling later. A little bit of adhesive will squeeze out in any case. Wipe the roller clean frequently, and wipe the surface of the wall covering clean with a damp (not wet) sponge or cloth immediately after rolling the seam.

Trimming

Trim the overlap at the ceiling and baseboard using a 10-inch broad knife as a straightedge and a razor knife to do the cutting (Figure 8). A razor knife is a handle with a head that clamps a razor blade in place with one edge exposed for cutting. Do not use the pointed edge of scissors, or a utility knife. Their thicker blades are likely to produce ragged or torn edges.

Press the broad knife firmly into the joint at the ceiling, ceiling molding, or baseboard and draw the razor blade along it to cut off the excess wallcovering. Have plenty of razor blades on hand—they're inexpensive—and change blades often to get a clean, crisp cut every time.

SEAMING AND TRIMMING

Figure 7. Roll seams to make sure they adhere well, using light pressure. Give them a single rolling when the adhesive becomes tacky, about 15 to 20 minutes after hanging. Wipe each seam clean.

Figure 8. Trim the excess wallcovering at the top and bottom. Press a broad knife firmly against the molding or ceiling corner, then draw a sharp razor knife along the edge.

TURNING CORNERS

Whether your house is new or old, it is almost certain that you will not find any corners that meet at exactly 90 degrees, or that are perfectly plumb. The differences can make it impossible to hang wallcovering around a corner—without using a special technique.

Fortunately, the trick is easy to do, and it is the same whether you are dealing with an inside or an outside corner: You make an overlap seam instead of a butt seam, with the overlapping piece hung to a reference line on the new wall. That way, any discrepancy is concealed and vertical alignment is maintained on each wall. Here's how to do it.

▲ When you reach the point where the next drop will go around a corner, measure from the edge of the drop that is already in place to the corner at the top, bottom, and two places in between (Figure 9). Add 1/2 inch (or 1/4 inch; see Corner Tip) to the largest measurement and cut the next drop to that width (Figure 10). Save the remaining piece.

▲ Paste and hang the width you have just cut, folding the extra 1/2 inch around an outside corner or pressing it all the way into an inside corner (Figure 11). Smooth the narrow strip firmly onto the adjacent wall. Cut a slit in the overlap at the ceiling and baseboard so the covering will lie flat when it turns the corner.

▲ Measure the width of the remaining cutoff section of the drop. On the new wall, measure out that distance from the corner—not from the edge of the drop you have just hung, but from the corner. Draw a plumb reference line on the wall at that point.

▲ Now paste the cutoff section of the drop and hang it with its outside edge exactly on the reference line (Figure 12). Smooth it back into the corner, overlapping the strip of covering that is there. If the wallcovering has a pattern, there may be a slight mismatch, but because it falls in a corner it will be virtually unnoticeable.

Figure 9. Measure from the corner to the edge of the preceding drop in three or four places. Add 1/2 in. (or 1/4 in.; see sidebar) to the largest measurement to get the trim width of the corner drop.

Figure 10. Cut the corner drop to the required width using a razor knife and a straightedge. Cut a clean edge and save the leftover piece. You will use it to complete the corner with an overlap seam.

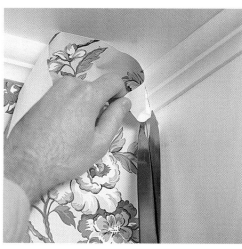

Figure 11. Hang the first strip of the corner drop, then snip the corners and trim the edges at the moldings. Crease and smooth the excess into and around the corner. Press the drop firmly onto both walls.

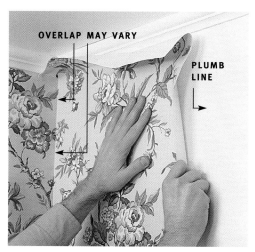

Figure 12. Complete the corner by hanging the cutoff piece to a plumb line drawn on the second wall. Smooth the drop back toward the corner. The amount of overlap will vary with corner irregularities.

Corner Tip

If you think a 1/2-in. overlap seam will create too noticeable a break in the pattern, you can trim the first drop for only a 1/4-in. overlap onto the second wall. This is feasible if the corner is almost plumb, but not if it is badly out of line or is irregular.

Before cutting an entire drop, trim a scrap of covering to width for a 1/4-in. seam and try it at several points between floor and ceiling to make sure there is adequate overlap onto the second wall.

If you do use a 1/4-in. corner seam, be very careful in hanging the first drop. It is difficult to get the very narrow strip around the corner and firmly into place without tearing or stretching it.

Finishing Tip: Borders

If your room does not have a ceiling molding, you can add a finishing touch by applying a paste-on border over the new wallcovering. Many patterned coverings have optional matching or harmonizing borders, and there is a wide range of borders available for unpatterned and specialty papers.

Hanging a border is simple and straightforward. Cut the lengths required, wet or paste them, and hang them with the top edge against the ceiling. Be very sure that the border adhesive is compatible with the wallcovering, otherwise the border may pop or peel loose. Make 1/4-in. overlap seams in the corners rather than in the middle of a run, if possible.

Figure 13. Hang full drops at a window or door. Draw a plumb line on the far side as a guide. Drape the wallcovering over the opening, taking care not to crease it before making corner cuts.

Figure 14. Make a diagonal cut from the outside corner of a window or door casing to the edge of the waste portion. Then you can press the covering to the wall around the molding corner.

Figure 15. Trim the excess around odd profiles by making many small cuts with a razor knife. Make long cuts by pressing the covering against the molding and drawing the knife along the crease.

HANGING DROPS AROUND WINDOWS AND DOORS

When you come to a window or door, hang a full-width drop overlapping the opening and make diagonal cuts from the waste area to the corners of the frame so you can press the covering flat to the wall all around it (Figures 13, 14). Then trim around the molding, using a broad knife as a straightedge along the straight sections. Trim around profiles and detail edges freehand, making several small cuts as necessary (Figure 15).

The short edge of the drop above a doorway or above and below a window does not provide enough length to guide you in hanging the next drop vertically. So measure from that edge a full width and draw a plumb line on the wall on the far side of the door or window frame. Hang the next drop to that line, and smooth it back to butt against the previous edge. Cut out the waste and trim the edges as before.

DEALING WITH COMMON PROBLEMS

You're bound to encounter some obstacles and difficult details. Here's what to do.

Outlets and switches. You should have turned off the power at the electrical panel and removed the wall plates before starting. Let the drop cover the outlet or switch. Cut an X from corner to corner of the opening with a razor knife, then trim and remove the flaps along the edges of the electrical box. Paste pieces of the covering to wall plates, positioned so the pattern will match on the wall when the plates are mounted. Slit the covering at the corners so you can fold it around onto the back of the plate, concealing all the edges.

Air bubbles. Slit the covering over the bubble and glue the edges down with seam adhesive. **Loose or curling edges.** Apply seam adhesive to the edges, then flatten with a roller. You may need to temporarily secure really stubborn edges with pushpins or thumbtacks. **Working procedures.** Many problems are caused by overworking the paper—pulling the paper off the wall and repositioning it too many times. Rolling the seams more than once or stretching the paper with the smoother can cause problems, too.

Moldings are a wonderful way to dress up a room at very modest cost.

Install Chair Rail Molding

Horizontal molding at about hip height —called a chair rail—protects the wall from being banged by furniture. It also provides a decorative break that allows you to combine different wallpaper patterns, borders, or paint colors. Installing a chair rail is an excellent first project. Once you have experience with the techniques explained here, you can tackle other molding jobs with confidence.

SELECTING MOLDING

There are four matters to consider when selecting molding for use as decorative trim:

▲ Profile: the molding's contour or shape
▲ Quantity required
▲ Cost
▲ Kind of wood

Profile

There are profiles specifically called "chair rail" in molding charts that you can consult at your local lumberyard or home center. But you don't have to limit your choice to those types, or even to just one molding (see Moldings for Chair Rails, page 68). If you find a molding design or shape that you like, use it. Just about any style will work as a chair rail.

In the project explained here, two moldings frame a decorative border, top and bottom. The lower molding is a true chair rail; the upper one is a profile called a "panel cap."

Quantity

To determine how much molding you'll need, measure the length of each wall and round up to the next full foot. For example, a wall 9 feet 3 inches long requires a 10-foot length of molding. Moldings are generally available up to 16 feet long, so unless your room is unusually large you shouldn't have to splice two pieces together. Add the individual wall requirements together to get the final amount.

If this is your first molding project, buy an additional 8 to 10 feet to use for practice cuts and to test paints and finishes. The slight additional expense will be well worth it.

Cost

Moldings are usually priced by the running foot, although some outlets often have "per piece" specials in a standard length, commonly 8 feet. The cost per foot may seem high compared to flat lumber, but keep in mind that moldings must be specially milled and the profile had to be cut out of stock that was free of flaws. A good part of the molding price is the cost of the wood that was cut away.

Kind of wood

Most of the moldings you're likely to use will be fairly close in price, regardless of the species of wood. However, pine is generally cheaper than oak and other hardwoods. Specialty woods are very beautiful, but also very expensive; they are generally used in moldings for cabinetwork rather than for room trim.

Each type of wood has its own advantages. Pine is easier to work with when it comes to fitting inside corner pieces. Oak, birch, and other hardwoods are more resistant to bumps and nicks. Oak also shows more grain and is more attractive than pine when stained.

If you are going to paint your molding, grain won't be a concern, so choose the less expensive pine. Also, pine molding is often made up of relatively short sections of stock glued end-to-end with finger joints. These joints, while invisible under paint, would look terrible with a stained or natural finish.

PREPARATION

Make a rough sketch of the room and write down the dimensions from corner to corner, or to window and door frames, built-in shelves, and other features along the path of the molding. You will remeasure just before cutting, to ensure accuracy, but these notes will help you allocate your molding stock for the project.

▲ Also mark the kind of cuts you must make at each joint: inside corner, outside corner, flush cut, or return.

▲ Next, mark a level horizontal line on the walls at the height of the molding. That dimension is determined by the height of the furniture in the room as well as by whether you're planning to use one or two rows of molding.

For example, in the nursery shown on the opposite page, the lower chair rail molding was installed with its bottom edge 28 inches from the floor. The top panel cap molding was installed 9 inches above the lower piece, measured between the top edge of the chair rail and the bottom edge of the panel cap. Nine inches was the width of the border paper that was to be pasted between them.

In your room, position the chair rail at whatever height looks the best and is the most functional in protecting the wall.

▲ As the final step in preparation, paint or stain the molding before you begin. This prevents the oils and dirt on your hands from being absorbed by the wood as you handle the molding. It also is a real timesaver that makes finishing the trim a lot easier. Once the molding is installed, you'll only need to fill the nail holes with wood putty and apply a final finish coat. If your molding is stained, give it the first coat of varnish or polyurethane before you install it.

CUTS, CORNERS, AND JOINTS

Just a few basic cuts will allow molding to fit together in a variety of ways. The cuts are for:

▲ Inside corners
▲ Outside corners
▲ Flush-cut (butt) joints
▲ End returns
▲ Scarf joints

The techniques for making these cuts and joints are explained on the following pages. Precise cutting is easiest with a power miter saw; you'll often be fine tuning the length and angle at the ends of the molding. A handsaw and miter box are much slower and often less accurate. They won't work as well unless you have some experience using them.

If you don't own or can't borrow a power miter saw, rent one. They're available at most rental equipment stores, usually for less than $25 a day. (This project probably won't take longer than one day.) Make sure the saw has a good, sharp finish-cut blade.

If you are a beginner, don't expect your first cuts and joints to look very satisfying. In fact, they can be discouraging. But after a few practice cuts, your corners will start fitting nicely.

For more information about miter boxes and cutting molding for various joints, see Making Crown Molding Fit, pages 133–143.

Moldings with several different profiles are milled specifically for use as chair rails. These moldings range from 2-1/4 to 3 inches wide and from 5/8 to 1-1/8 inches thick.

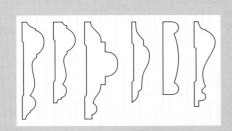

Other kinds of moldings can also be used as chair rails. These panel moldings range from 1 to 1-1/2 inches wide and from 3/8 to 11/16 inches thick.

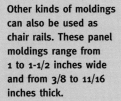

Tools You Need

Tape measure

Chalk line

Miter box and saw

Coping saw

Rasp

Drill and twist bits

Hammer

Nail set

Painted moldings are an easy way to add decorative trim to a room.
The horizontal border in this nursery is made from chair rail and panel cap
moldings that frame a decorative strip of wallcovering.

INSIDE CORNERS: COPED JOINTS

A professional-looking inside corner is made with a "coped" joint. It consists of one piece of molding cut to butt against one wall, and another piece of molding on the adjacent wall that is cut out (coped) so its end contour fits over the profile of the first piece. This produces a tight inside joint even in an unsquare corner, and it will not reveal a visible gap even when the wood dries and shrinks.

A mitered inside corner, with the ends of both pieces cut at 45 degrees, is almost impossible to make invisible because wall corners are never truly square and because shrinkage will always produce a visible gap.

Although a coped inside corner is the toughest joint to master, it's the best one to start with, because after you learn how to make it the others will seem like child's play.

Flush cut

To make a flush or butt cut at the end of the first piece of molding, set the miter saw for a 90-degree angle, insert the molding, and make the cut. This end will butt against the adjacent wall.

Coped cut

To make the coped cut for an inside corner, first cut the end of the molding at an angle, then cope out the profile.

▲ Begin by setting the miter saw to cut the molding at a 45-degree angle so the unfinished profile is exposed (Figure 1). As you look at the cut from the front of the molding, the back edge is longest, the front edge is shortest, and the angled cut exposes the face of the wood between the two edges.

▲ To make sure the miter saw is positioned properly for this cut, follow these rules: If the coped cut will be at the left end of the molding, swing the saw 45 degrees to the right and feed the molding from the right to make the cut. If the coped cut will be on the right, swing the saw to the left and feed from the left.

▲ Next, use a coping saw with a sharp new blade to cut out the profile. Follow the edge between the finished and unfinished surfaces, and keep the saw blade angled at 35 to 40 degrees so that it undercuts the edge of the molding (Figures 2, 3).

This is tricky, so take your time. Slow, deliberate strokes will do the job right. If you hurry, you'll end up with a rough edge and a bad-looking joint. Keeping the coping saw blade angled backward under the molding edge removes enough wood so you can make the joint fit tightly even if the corner of the wall is not 90 degrees.

▲ Test-fit the coped end against the flush-cut piece (Figure 4). Check the fit of the contour. If it's not snug, remove some of the wood from the underside of the coped area with a rasp (Figure 5). You may have to do this several times to arrive at a tight fit (Figure 6).

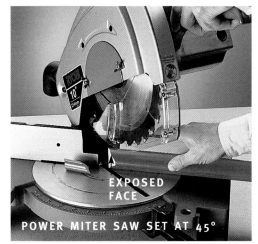

Figure 1. Cut the end to be coped at a 45-degree angle so the unfinished face is exposed. Work from the right as shown for a coped left end. Shift saw and molding to the left for a coped right end.

Figure 2. Cope the end by angling the coping saw 35 to 40 degrees to the side, almost perpendicular to the angled face of the molding. Maintain that angle as you cut away the exposed wood.

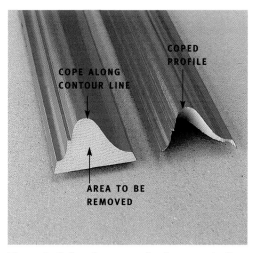

Figure 3. Follow the contour line between the finished and unfinished areas. Use deliberate strokes for a clean edge. The coped cut removes wood from the back of the molding.

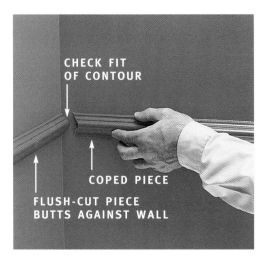

Figure 4. Test the fit of the coped end against the contour of the flush-cut piece that is already installed on the adjacent wall of the inside corner. It should fit tightly at all points.

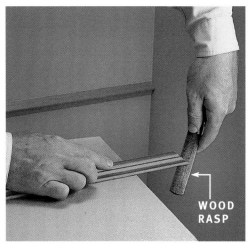

Figure 5. Shave any high spots with a rasp to adjust the fit of the coped end. You may need to do this several times to get a tight fit. Be careful not to damage the edge or corners of the coped piece.

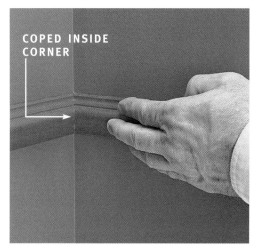

Figure 6. A tight-fitting coped joint at an inside corner is a professional detail that yields the best appearance now and tomorrow. It will not reveal an unsightly gap if the wood shrinks.

OUTSIDE CORNERS: MITERED JOINTS

Outside corners don't require coping, but they're tricky, too, because almost no corner is a perfect 90 degrees. To check the squareness of an outside corner, cut a perfect 90-degree outside corner from two pieces of scrap molding, each 8 to 10 inches long (Figure 7).

Cut these outside corner pieces as follows: For the right side piece (as you face the corner), swing the saw 45 degrees to the left and insert the molding from the right side of the saw. For the left side piece, swing the saw 45 degrees to the right and insert the molding from the left. Put the two pieces together around the outside corner (Figure 8) to see if the corner is over-square or undersquare.

Oversquare corner

If the corner angle is oversquare—greater than 90 degrees—the back edges of the two pieces won't meet (Figure 9). To correct this, you need to adjust the angle of the cut on the molding. Recut one of the corners at one or two degrees less than 45 degrees and recheck the fit. If the fit is still not right, cut the other piece slightly under 45 degrees and check again. Repeat these steps until the corner fits. Then use the test pieces to set the blade at the exact angles for the cuts in the actual molding.

Undersquare corner

If a corner is less than 90 degrees, the test moldings will have a gap in the front (Figure 10). To correct this, recut one of the pieces at slightly more than 45 degrees. A power miter saw will let you do this. Recheck the fit and, if necessary, cut the other piece of molding slightly more than 45 degrees. Repeat this process until the joint fits properly. Then use the test pieces to align the angle of the saw for the actual cuts.

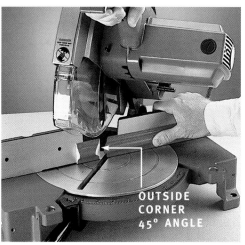

Figure 7. Cut test pieces for an outside corner by making opposite 45-degree cuts to form a 90-degree angle. Cut the right side piece from the left, as shown; cut the left side piece from the right.

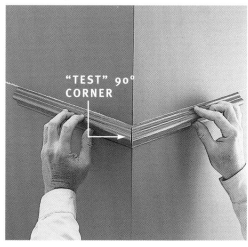

Figure 8. Check the squareness of each outside corner with the test molding pieces. Almost every corner will be either oversquare or undersquare.

Figure 9. An oversquare corner spreads test pieces so a gap is formed at the rear of the joint.

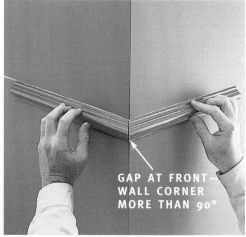

Figure 10. An undersquare corner is indicated by a gap at the front of the joint between the test pieces.

FLUSH CUTS

A flush or butt cut is most often used when the molding end fits against door or window trim (Figure 11). It's the easiest joint to make: Cut the molding at a 90-degree angle and butt it against the edge of the trim.

If you have a piece with a mitered joint at one end and a flush cut at the other end, make the mitered cut first. Then cut the flush end a bit long so you can trim it to adjust the fit of the mitered joint if necessary.

END RETURNS

An end return is used when the chair rail neither finishes in a corner nor butts flat against something, but is left with an end exposed.

You could simply flush-cut the end and let it go, but that would reveal end grain that's hard to cover with paint or stain.

An end return provides a finished end (Figure 12). It actually is an outside corner with one very short length.

▲ To make an end return, first cut the end of the long piece of molding as for an outside corner—with a cut angled 45 degrees to the rear.

▲ Next cut the end of another piece at the opposite 45 degrees, as for an outside corner.

Then cut off the angled end with a 90-degree cut exactly aligned with the back of the 45-degree cut (Figure 13). This little end is the return piece. Match its 45-degree face with the angled end of the long piece.

▲ The best way to secure the return is to glue it to the longer piece with wood glue—either hold it in place for about 30 seconds or secure it with masking tape—before you install the longer piece (Figure 14).

FLUSH CUTS

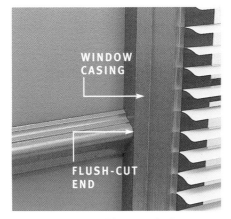

Figure 11. Make a 90-degree flush cut wherever a molding end butts against a window or door casing or other feature with a flat edge. This is the easiest cut to make and fit.

END RETURNS

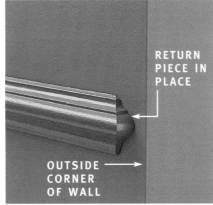

Figure 12. An end return gives an exposed end a finished, professional look. The return can be made either directly at the wall corner, or set back a bit as shown here. A set-back return generally looks better.

Figure 13. Make an end return by first cutting an outside corner at a 45-degree angle. Then cut off the return piece with a 90-degree cut aligned with the back corner of the angled end.

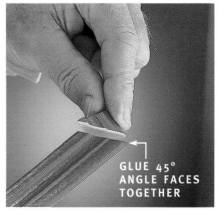

Figure 14. Secure the short return piece to an outside angle cut in the end of the longer piece of molding; use wood glue. An end return is actually just an outside corner with one very short piece.

SCARF JOINTS

With molding available in lengths of up to 16 feet, it is unlikely that you will need to extend a straight run. However, if it is necessary do not cut the ends square and butt two pieces together. They will invariably separate, leaving a visible gap as the molding dries and shrinks. Instead, make an overlapping, angle-cut splice called a scarf joint. Position this splice over a wall stud for secure nailing.

▲ To cut the pieces for a scarf joint, set the miter saw at a 22-1/2-degree angle cut either left or right (it does not matter which). Place one piece of molding in the saw from the left and cut the end. Then, with the blade in the same position, insert the other piece of molding from the right and cut the end.

▲ To assemble the scarf joint, lap one piece over the other for a continuous finished surface. Even if the pieces do shrink a bit after installation, there will be no visible separation, because the angle-cut face of the rear piece will cover over any gap.

INSTALLING MOLDINGS

Install moldings to a level line. The best way to mark the line is to snap a chalk line at the desired height. You'll need a helper to install the longer lengths of molding. You can't do a precise job by trying to hold a long piece in position and fasten it at the same time.

▲ Secure the molding to the wall studs. You'll need a stud finder to locate them. The electronic type, available at hardware stores and home centers, works best and is not expensive.

▲ Install molding with finish nails; 6d nails are long enough (2 inches) to reach through most moldings and into the studs. Drill pilot holes in the molding to avoid splitting the wood.

▲ When driving the nails, don't try to drive them completely flush with a hammer; you'll dent the molding face. Instead drive the nail until about 1/8 inch of the head remains exposed. Then use a nail set and hammer to recess the head into the molding.

▲ When making an outside corner joint, first position the pieces square and snug, and secure them to the wall. Then, to keep the outside corner from separating, drive a 3d finish nail through the face of one piece into the end of the other (Figure 15). Drill a pilot hole in the thickest part of the molding so that driving this nail will not split the angled ends.

▲ In a scarf joint, drill a pilot hole exactly centered in the overlap, left to right and top to bottom, and drive a 3d nail through the front piece into the angled face of the rear piece.

▲ Use a nail set to recess all nailheads. Then fill the recessed areas with wood putty and apply the finish coat of paint or varnish.

INSTALLING MOLDINGS

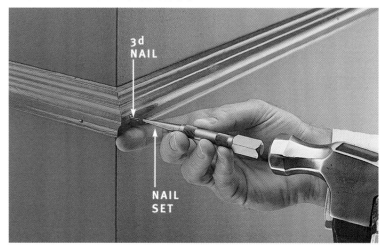

3d NAIL

NAIL SET

Figure 15. Fasten moldings in place with finish nails. Secure an outside corner joint with a 3d finish nail driven squarely through the face of one piece into the end of the other. Drill a pilot hole first to avoid splitting either piece of molding.

Wood paneling will make a striking change in the character and style of a room.

Formal Oak Paneling

Oak paneling is rich in color and texture, and is quite practical, too.

A formal installation will look like the work of a professional cabinetmaker, but ambitious DIYers can do it in just a couple of weekends, with no special joinery or millwork.

The oak paneling puts a powerful decorative stamp on this dining room. The formal appearance of the vertical grain patterns and tall narrow panel shapes is balanced by the light-colored stain and simple, clean lines of the early 1900's Craftsman style.

PANELING THE SIMPLE WAY

Floor-to-ceiling oak paneling always looks like it calls for special woodworking experience and skills. But this project is an exception. The paneling is actually 4x8 sheets of 1/4-inch oak veneer plywood nailed and glued to the wall. The vertical battens and horizontal trim are a framework of 1/2-inch x 3-inch oak strips nailed over the panel background.

Although no special skills are required for this simplified method of construction, installing this paneling is not a beginner's project. There's a lot of exact measuring, cutting, and fitting, so you will need plenty of patience for all the detail work. But taking care with the cutting, the fitting, and the installation will produce spectacular results.

SCOPE OF THE PROJECT

Paneling a room may seem like a great deal of work. But if you divide it into stages, it's not overwhelming or difficult. You should be able to complete the entire project in two weekends.

As far as cost is concerned, this is a major renovation. Make a rough estimate of materials and price them at your local lumberyard before you commit to the full job. When you're ready to start, here are the steps to take.

▲ Draw a plan of each wall to determine how much material you will need, and to establish the spacing of the battens.
▲ Prepare the wood for the project.
▲ Install nailers for attaching the paneling.
▲ Install the paneling.
▲ Finish the job.

DRAWING A PLAN

This project requires careful planning. The diagram in the box below shows the information a layout plan must include. You don't need to make a finished drawing like this, but you must draw each wall on a sheet of graph paper, showing its dimensions and the locations of windows, doors, and other details.

▲ On each wall, lay out the widths of the plywood sheets, with a full-width sheet at each corner. Place any sheets that must be cut to partial width next to windows and doorways.
▲ Next, sketch in the panel widths—the spacing between the vertical battens—at the size you want them. Allow for the width of the battens, and adjust the sizes slightly so whole panels fit at the corners.

Remember that a batten must be placed over the seam between two sheets of plywood. If you need a bit more or less width, divide the difference between the panels on either side of a doorway or window. However, if that produces two panels that are very much wider or narrower than the others, refigure the basic panel width.

▲ On a wall without a window or door, you may have to trim two or more plywood sheets in order to get the seams to fall under the panel battens. However, the panel size on one wall can differ somewhat from the size on another wall. Even an inch of difference won't be readily noticed. And that may make it unnecessary to cut the plywood.

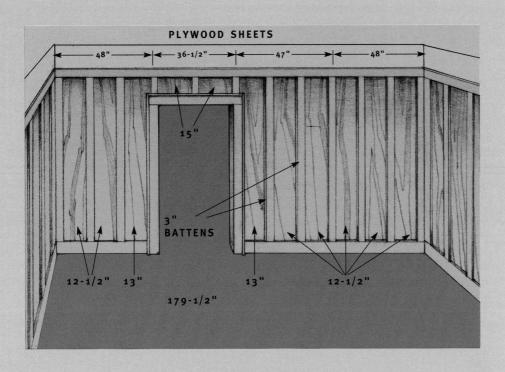

PLANNING PANEL SIZES

Draw a plan for each wall of the room, to set all the details of layout and spacing, and to determine how much material you need. These dimensions are for one wall shown in the photos.

WHAT YOU NEED

First, figure out how much material of each kind and size you need. Then you can select the actual materials and get them ready for use.

Figure your needs

Use your plans to make a shopping list of the lumber needed.

Nailers. As a supporting structure, install nailers running the length of each wall spaced 16 (sometimes 12) inches apart from floor to ceiling. Use construction grade pine 1x4's.

Panels. Count the number of 4x8 plywood sheets you need to cover the walls. Figure carefully to use the cut-offs where possible; hardwood veneer plywood is expensive.

Battens and trim. This is all hardwood lumber to match the plywood veneer. The vertical battens are 1x4's. The trim includes:

- ▲ 1x4's for a top rail
- ▲ 1x4's and 1x8's at the ceiling
- ▲ 1x8's for a baseboard
- ▲ 1x6's or 1x8's for door jambs
- ▲ Corner molding to trim around the door and window casings
- ▲ Shoe molding to finish the baseboard where it meets the floor

Usually, 1x4, 1x6, and 1x8 boards are standard stock. In the installation shown, the 3-inch wide pieces used for the battens and top rail were ripped to that width from 1x4's and milled to 1/2-inch thickness. If you have a table saw and planer, you can do this yourself. If not, most lumberyards will do the work for a reasonable charge. Many millwork shops will plane your wood to exact dimensions also, although they'll probably charge a bit more.

You'll also need 1-1/2 inch drywall screws; 4d, 6d, and 8d finish nails; stain; colored wood putty; and a clear finish.

Select the wood

For stained formal paneling, you'll want to use knot-free wood, which can be quite expensive. Holding down the cost is one of the reasons for using veneered plywood rather than solid planks for the panels. The battens and trim should be solid wood, however.

Investigate the kinds of wood readily available from a hardwood lumber dealer. Red oak is usually plentiful, the least expensive, and shows nice grain when stained, but you may like other species equally well. When choosing boards for the trim pieces and battens, consider the grain pattern as well as the final color. Oak exhibits different grain patterns depending upon how it's milled. Quarter-sawn boards have an even vertical grain pattern but may cost up to 15 percent more than plain-sawn boards. Oak plywood is also available in several veneer grain patterns. Choose one that matches the trim. The panels shown in the photographs have a moderately vertical grain pattern called plain sliced. Since appearance is of great importance in this project, check all the wood carefully to avoid highly irregular coloration or pattern.

PREPARE THE WOOD

Sand and stain the oak plywood, battens, and trim before installing them (Figure 1). This can be a big job, and is an important step, so allow time to do it well.

▲ Use a power finish sander to save a lot of work, although a hand sanding block will work fine, too. Use 100- or 120-grit paper, and sand with the grain of the wood, not across it. The plywood veneer will already be smooth, but a light sanding will help it receive the stain more evenly. The trim boards may have marks left from planing, which will require additional sanding to remove. When finished, wipe the material clean with a tack cloth (or a cloth dampened with paint thinner) to remove sawdust before applying an oil-base stain.

▲ Make some tests before staining to get the degree of lightness or darkness you want. Also, the oak veneer plywood may stain somewhat differently than the solid oak boards. For example, in the room shown in the photos a colonial maple stain was used on the plywood. The solid boards, however, required a mixture of mahogany and colonial maple stains to get a close color match.

Once you have determined what to use, stain the veneer side of the plywood sheets, and the good face and both edges of the solid oak boards.

Tape measure

Level

Saber saw

Circular saw

Hammer

Chisel

Router or table saw

Miter box and saw

Nail set

1-1/2 " drywall screws

4d, 6d, and 8d finish nails

Wood putty

Stain

Clear finish

PREPARING THE WOOD

Figure 1. Stain the wood with an oil-base stain before beginning installation. You can precut the plywood before staining, but the solid boards must be cut to fit later, so stain them full-length.

INSTALLING NAILERS

Begin by removing the old casings, baseboard, and ceiling molding if any. If the existing door jambs will harmonize with the paneling, or can be refinished in place, leave them; otherwise remove them. Then install horizontal 1x4 boards as nailers.

The nailers provide solid support for attaching both the 1/4-inch plywood and the battens in place. There are two ways to install them. One is to cut away the drywall or plaster at each nailer position. The other is to remove the entire wall covering, which is at least as much work and much messier. In either case, the exposed wall studs must be notched so that the face of each nailer will lie in the same plane as the original wall surface. The first method is the one shown in the photographs and explained here.

Mark nailer positions

Snap chalk lines on the wall to mark the top and bottom edge of each nailer (Figures 2, 3).

▲ Start with the bottom nailer and mark its position so that the center of the board is 7-1/4 inches above the floor, which will put it behind the top edge of the baseboard.

▲ Work up the wall, marking the other positions so that the nailers are spaced 16 inches on center. (If you have removed all the drywall, more support will be required. Mark the positions on the studs, 12 inches on center.)

Cut the wall

Cut along each marked line so you can remove the drywall or plaster between them (Figure 4). If you don't mind a huge cloud of plaster dust and a great mess, use a circular saw with an old blade. Set the blade for a cut 3/4 inch deep. That setting will score the studs the proper depth for the nailer to lie flush with the wall surface when you have chiseled out notches in the studs.

▲ To create much less mess, use a saber saw with a very short blade to cut the drywall. The short blade will also help avoid nicking any electrical wires. If the insulation is damaged, that entire run of wire must be replaced, which can be a big job. The only sure way to avoid this is to locate all wires in advance by breaking through the wallboard in each stud space and looking for them. Then turn off those circuits at the main panel when sawing near them to avoid potential shocks.

▲ Once the drywall is removed, use a circular saw to cut four or five 1/4-inch deep kerfs in the studs (Figure 5). This will speed the job of chiseling notches to the required depth in the studs. Use a saber saw to cut kerfs in corner studs, where the circular saw cannot be used.

▲ While the studs are exposed, lightly mark their positions on the ceiling, so you can nail the ceiling trim into them.

Attach the nailers

Use 1-1/2 inch drywall screws to fasten the nailers to the studs (Figure 6).

▲ Make sure a nailer lies flush with the surface of the wall at each stud position before driving any screws. Shave the stud notch deeper or insert a thin shim if needed.

▲ When all the nailers are in place, replace the door jambs and casing and the window casings, or cut and install new ones if the old wood will not look good with the paneling.

Figure 2. Snap chalk lines to mark positions for the nailers. Remove door and window casings first. Center the bottom nailer at the top edge of the baseboard; space the others 16 in. on center.

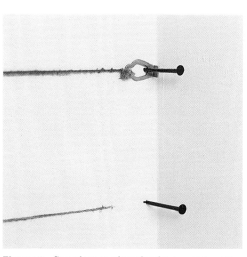

Figure 3. Speed up marking by driving nails at the proper intervals at one end of the wall, for hooking the end of the chalk line. Make pencil marks at the other end and stretch the chalk line to them.

Figure 4. Cut along the chalk lines with a saber saw and remove the drywall between the cuts. Shut off the circuit electricity at the main panel and use a short saw blade to avoid nicking wires.

Figure 5. Cut kerfs in the studs with a circular saw. Use a saber saw for corner studs. Then chisel out smooth notches deep enough so the nailers will lie flush with the surface of the wall.

Figure 6. Fasten the 1x4 nailers to every stud with 1-1/2 in. drywall screws. When they are all in place, replace the door and window casings, or install new ones as required.

Refer to this diagram when installing the veneer plywood, and later for details of the ceiling trim, baseboard, top rail, and battens.

1X4

1x6

3"X3"X1"
DENTILS

1/2"
DRYWALL

1/2"x3"
BATTENS
AND TOP
RAIL

1/4"
PLYWOOD

1X4
PINE
NAILER

1/4"
PLYWOOD

1/2"x3"
BATTEN

1x8

1/4"x
1/2"
NOTCH

BASE SHOE

Install corner molding before the baseboard or battens. It conceals the joint between the plywood and the door and window casings, and adds dimension and a finished appearance.

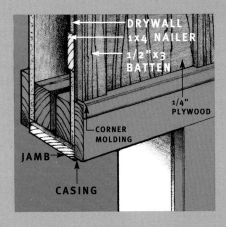

DRYWALL
1X4 NAILER
1/2"x3"
BATTEN

1/4"
PLYWOOD

CORNER
MOLDING

JAMB

CASING

INSTALLING THE PANELING

There are five steps to installing the paneling:
1. Put up the plywood.
2. Add ceiling trim.
3. Add the corner moldings and baseboard.
4. Install the top rail.
5. Install the battens.

Construction details are shown in the box at the left. Specific procedures follow.

Put up the plywood

Cut and install the pieces of plywood one at a time to ensure a good fit (Figure 7). Follow your plan, but recheck the measurements from the wall before making a cut.

▲ Cut the length to extend 1/2 inch below the top of the baseboard for a clean joint there. At windows and doors, run the plywood up to the casing, but leave a 1/16- to 1/8-inch gap to allow for expansion; this gap will be covered by new corner molding.

▲ To mount the plywood, turn the sheet face down and spread continuous beads of construction adhesive over the back (Figure 8). Lift the first sheet into place and push its top edge against the ceiling. You may need a helper to hold it while you check with a level to get the edge plumb. Tap over the face of the plywood with the heel of your hand or with a piece of smooth 1x6 and a hammer to press the adhesive securely against the wall surface.

▲ Drive 4d finish nails through the face of the plywood into the nailers. Position all the nails so they will be covered by the battens and drive them flush (Figure 9).

Add ceiling trim

The ceiling trim is made up of a 1x4 flat against the ceiling and a 1x6 just below it, against the plywood.

▲ At corners, cut the top boards at an angle so their ends will meet in a mitered joint. Make

trial joints with scrap wood to find the exact angles of the cuts, because the wall corner may not be square.

▲ Make a square (flush cut) butt joint at the corners where the boards that lie flat on the walls come together.

▲ Preassemble each run of ceiling trim: Nail the 1x4 into the top edge of its 1x6, then lift the assembly into position to install it; you'll need a helper here. Drive two 8d finish nails through the 1x6 and plywood into each stud; refer to the marks that you made earlier to locate the studs.

▲ Do not add the dentils at this time. Wait until the battens have been installed so you can align each dentil directly above a batten.

Add the corner moldings and baseboard

The L-shaped corner moldings around the door and window trim conceal the joint between the plywood and the casings.

▲ Install the corner moldings before installing the baseboard and battens that butt to doors and windows. Miter the corner joints and use 4d finish nails to fasten them in place.

▲ Use 1x8 stock for the baseboard. With a router, cut a rabbet (notch) 1/2 inch deep and 1/4 inch wide in the top edge of the baseboard to cover the bottom of the plywood on the walls. Nail the baseboard in place with 8d finish nails driven near the top, into the nailer (Figure 10). Do not add the baseboard shoe molding at this time.

Install the top rail

Cut the top rail for each wall from the 1/2 x 3 inch boards (Figure 11). Nail it into position, tight under the ceiling trim on the plywood; drive 8d nails into the studs. Because the ceiling trim is a full-thickness board, it will overhang the top rail by 1/4 inch, providing a nice visual accent.

Install the battens

Work on just one wall at a time.

▲ Mark out the positions of the battens on the plywood and then measure the height of each one individually. Because the ceiling and floor are probably not absolutely parallel, the battens may well differ in height.

▲ Cut each batten for a snug fit between the top rail and the baseboard (Figure 12). Start with the longest one and work down to the shortest. That way, if you make a mistake you can recut the piece for use where a shorter batten is required. The battens will lie flush with the 1/2-inch thick top rail and the exposed 1/2-inch edge of the baseboard.

▲ Use a level to make sure each batten is plumb before nailing it. Then drive two 6d finish nails into each nailer. Look at the nail positions in the plywood to locate the nailers.

FINISHING THE JOB

Cut 3x3-inch dentils from 1x4 stock and install them on the ceiling trim, above the top rail. Use 6d nails to secure them, and be sure each dentil is directly above a batten.

▲ If you have a wood or tile floor, cut shoe molding and install it along the bottom of the baseboard. Miter the inside corners and use 6d nails to fasten it in position.

▲ Examine each wall, setting all nailheads and filling the recesses with colored wood putty. Check for any nicks or scratches; touch them up with stain and a fine brush as necessary.

▲ Finally, wipe the walls clean with a tack cloth or thinner-dampened cloth. Then brush on two coats of a clear finish. Follow the instructions that come with the finish, and be sure to let the first coat dry completely before applying the second.

Figure 7. Cut the plywood to match your sketched plan. Lay out each piece on the wall to measure it precisely. Turn the plywood veneer-side down and use a straightedge to guide the saw.

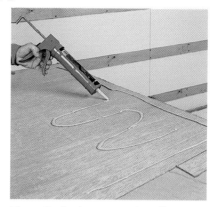

Figure 8. Apply construction adhesive to the back of each panel with a caulking gun. Make continuous beads over the entire surface, spaced as suggested in the cartridge instructions.

Figure 9. Position the first sheet of plywood and get its edge plumb. Use pressure to bond the adhesive, then drive 4d finish nails into the nailers where the heads will be covered by the battens.

Figure 10. Fasten the baseboard to the nailers with 8d finish nails; predrill holes for the nails. A 1/4-in. notch routed in the top edge covers the lower edge of the plywood on the wall.

Figure 11. Install the top rail against the upper trim boards, and fasten it with two 8d finish nails into each stud. The nail positions in the trim above will show where the studs are.

Figure 12. Nail the battens between the top rail and the baseboard with 6d finish nails, two nails at each nailer. Mark the spacing from your plan before starting to nail the battens in place.

Because painting is so simple and so common, it's easy to think there's not much to it.

Paint a Room

However, there are several steps you can take to make your painting faster and easier, with better results.

Here's a basic guide to painting a room, with working tips that will help you even if you've painted a dozen rooms before.

New paint can totally transform a room in just a few hours. The keys to making the job quick, easy, and fun are proper preparation, the right tools and techniques, and the professional tips included here.

THE PROFESSIONAL APPROACH

Watch a professional painter at work and you'll see that there's more to painting a room than most do-it-yourselfers realize. The room is ready and everything required is at hand before the job begins, so the work can progress without interruption. Tools and materials are of good quality—no makeshifts or bargain counter specials that can produce only mediocre results at best. The work follows the most efficient pattern, so there's no backtracking to work on areas or details more than once. Mess is minimized, and cleanup is rapid and easy. And the finished appearance is excellent.

A professional doesn't have secrets; he or she has working experience. Here are tips from experienced professionals to help you with one of the most common home-improvement projects: painting an average room and achieving considerably above-average results.

TOOLS FOR PAINTING

Everything you need is readily available at good paint stores and home centers, and most large hardware stores. Here are some things to consider in buying tools; how to use them is explained on the following pages.

Basic equipment

The basic tools for painting are pretty commonplace. They include:

Rollers and tray. Rollers 8 to 12 inches long make fast and easy work of covering large areas. Get a tray wide enough for your longest roller. For easy cleanup, line the tray with kitchen foil.

Brushes. You can buy short rollers and rollers with angled faces for corners and painting trim, but for the best results you need brushes. Get a 3- to 4-inch wide brush with a square end for corner work, and a "sash" brush 1 to 1-1/2 inches wide with an angled end for trim.

If you want professional-looking results, don't buy cheap brushes or roller covers. Money spent on good-quality brushes and rollers buys you a better-looking paint job.

Stepladder. You'll need a sturdy stepladder, one that is easy for you to handle and that has a fold-down shelf below the top step to hold a paint can or roller tray.

Drop cloths. Get plastic drop cloths to protect furniture and floors, and fabric drop cloths for safety, as explained later.

Goggles and painter's cap. Get goggles to protect your eyes from roller spatters, especially when you look up when painting the ceiling. Wearing a painter's cap is optional, but it makes personal cleanup easier.

Preparation tools. You probably already have the basic tools for preparing surfaces for painting: a bucket, sponges, putty knife, caulking gun, scraper, and sanding block.

Additional equipment

Two additional items in particular will make painting a room much easier, and the final results much better.

▲ The first item is an extension handle for your paint roller. This tool is not just for high places; leave it on your roller all the time for less stooping, craning, reaching, and ladder climbing. It's worth every penny of its cost, especially if you have any back problems. A handle that has two or three screw-together sections is most useful. You can use a single section to work on walls from floor to normal ceiling height, and two or three sections for higher areas and ceilings.

▲ The second item is a bright work light. Soft lighting is great for romantic dining, but if you try to prepare walls or to paint in dim light, you'll miss spots and make mistakes. A simple clamp-on light is fine. Get one with a dishlike reflector, so you can position it within your range of vision without having to look at the glare of a bare bulb.

Tools You Need

3" or 4" square-end brush

1" or 1-1/2" angled sash brush

8" to 12" roller

Roller with extension handle

Paint tray

Work light

Stepladder

Drop cloths

Goggles

Putty knife

Caulking gun

Sanding block and sandpaper

Bucket

Sponges

Scraper

Masking tape

SAFETY AND HEALTH

Painting is pretty safe if you pay attention to three very basic things:

▲ Use your ladder properly and safely. Never stand on the top or next-to-top step, and never lean so far to one side that your hips are beyond the foot of the ladder. Get down and move the ladder; it takes only a moment.

▲ Wear goggles when you paint the ceiling.

▲ Beware of toxic fumes.

The problem is, which fumes are toxic? Some latex paints have a noticeable odor, others do not, but that is not a reliable indicator. In general, latex paints are much safer than some brands of "stain-killers" used for sealing wall stains, and so-called deglossers—weak paint strippers sometimes used on trim before repainting. To cut down on fumes, use a latex- or shellac-base stain-killer, and stick to sandpaper for taking the gloss off of trim. At all stages of the job, regardless of the kind of paint you are using, be sure to have plenty of cross-ventilation through the rooms.

If you are sensitive to the odors of latex paints, you can wear an inexpensive disposable respirator. However, this kind of mask is not adequate protection from toxic fumes or paint spray, and a simple dust mask—useful when cleaning and sanding—does not stop odors.

ORGANIZING THE JOB

Paint is messy stuff, and there are few things as frustrating as dripping on a surface you want to keep clean. Keep the work and the mess to a minimum by doing your room-painting project in logical order.

▲ Get the room ready. Clear it out, mask items not to be painted, and repair cracks and holes.

▲ Seal and prime all surfaces as necessary to ensure good-looking results with the finish coats.

▲ Paint the ceiling and walls.

▲ Paint the trim, windows, and doors.

▲ Clean up and restore the room to order. A general rule of painting is "work from the top down." Paint the ceiling first, masking any trim that you don't want to spatter. Paint the walls next, then the trim. The baseboards will usually be the last item you paint.

GETTING THE ROOM READY

Clear the room, protect the floor and items you can't remove, and clean the surfaces before doing repairs or painting.

Clean and clear the room

Move the furniture out of the room or into the center. Put padding on finished surfaces that could be damaged. Cover chandeliers or ceiling fans with plastic bags (Figure 1). If you have any wallpaper on the walls, remove it now—don't paint over it.

▲ Remove door and window hardware, and duct vents, but not switch plates and outlet covers. Remove those only after you have washed the surfaces to be painted.

▲ Drop cloths are absolutely essential. Plastic drop cloths are cheap; put them everywhere. However, plastic is slippery underfoot, so it's wise to put old sheets or canvas drop cloths on top. The fabric will also absorb the paint and keep you from tracking it all around.

▲ Once the room is prepared as above, wash the walls, ceiling, and trim before you paint (Figure 2). To save work, use a cleanser that doesn't require rinsing.

When the walls have been washed and repaired, remove the switch and outlet wallplates, and cover the switch handles and outlet faces with masking tape.

Repair cracks and holes

Paint cannot hide even little nicks and holes in a wall. The walls, ceiling, and trim must be flat and smooth for repainting. Shine your work light across the surface to throw any imperfections into relief. Don't be satisfied with surfaces that look smooth; run your hand over them—they should feel smooth, too.

▲ Scrape and sand any loose, peeling, or chipping paint. Wear a dust mask and wash your hands after sanding to avoid ingesting potentially toxic paint dust.

▲ Sand trim thoroughly to smooth it out and remove the gloss. Vacuum off the dust. If your trim is in really bad shape, you may need to strip the finish. If so, get a stripper recommended for the kind of finish on your trim, and be sure to follow the directions exactly.

▲ Use latex spackling compound to fill dents, nail holes, and damaged spots up to about 1/8 inch wide (Figure 3). Sand the spackling compound after it's dry and vacuum off the dust.

▲ Caulk any cracks at the top of the baseboard, around the window and door trim, and along any ceiling moldings (Figure 4).

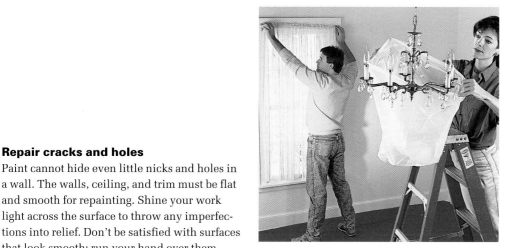

Figure 1. Protect everything from paint spatters. Remove as much as you can and cover everything else with plastic. Leave only the switch and outlet covers in place. Put down drop cloths.

Figure 2. Wash all surfaces to be painted—ceiling, walls, and trim—with water and detergent. Use a brand that requires no rinsing. Remove switch and outlet covers when that is done.

Figure 3. Fill cracks, holes, and dents in walls, and trim with latex spackling compound. Sand until smooth, vacuum the surface, then apply primer over the compound to seal it.

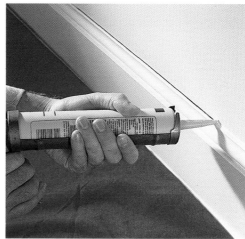

Figure 4. Caulk gaps, especially along the top of the baseboards and around window and door trim. Use paintable latex caulk and cut just a small hole in the tip of the caulking tube.

Preparation Tip

When you remove outlet covers and switch plates, immediately screw their tiny mounting screws back in place. Otherwise, they will disappear as soon as you turn your back.

SEALING AND PRIMING

Most homeowners are confused about sealers and primers, and as a result don't use them. Sealers (stain-killers) are essential when you use latex paints to keep stains on the wall from bleeding through to the surface of the new paint. Primers help paint adhere and keep the sheen and color uniform.

▲ Coat all stains and smoke marks with sealer (Figure 5). If there are heavy smoke or cooking stains, paint the entire ceiling or wall with sealer. Be sure to prime after you apply the sealer, because sealer has a higher sheen than wall and ceiling paints and would show through the final paint coat.

▲ If you are repainting the room in the same color, you don't need to prime the walls or ceiling. Just spot-prime any spackling compound or other patched or sealed areas.

If you are changing colors and must apply two coats of paint, or if you have many repairs, it's easier to paint the whole room with primer as the first coat. Have the primer tinted at the paint store to match the final coat.

▲ For trim, use a primer especially designed for enamel (often called an "enamel under-coater"). Trim will need two coats—a primer as a first coat, and an enamel as a second coat. Have the primer tinted to match the enamel.

Wherever you apply primer, sand it lightly when dry and vacuum the dust before applying the final coat of paint.

Sealing Tip

Use a disposable brush with plastic foam in place of bristles to apply a shellac-base or lacquer-base sealer or sealer-primer. Those materials are very difficult to clean out of bristle brushes completely, and foam brushes are very cheap.

DISPOSABLE FOAM BRUSH GOOD FOR SHELLAC-BASE SEALERS

Figure 5. Seal stains to keep them from bleeding through the paint. Use a latex- or shellac-base stain-killer, as recommended for your paint. Prime the sealed areas before painting.

PAINTING THE CEILING AND WALLS

There are two basic painting techniques, cutting in and rolling on. The best way to work is to have one person cut in the ceiling and wall edges while another person paints the open areas with a roller (Figure 6). If you're doing the job by yourself, cut in just a few feet at a time, then roll paint on the adjacent section of the wall or ceiling.

Cutting in

Start along a narrow side of the room. Brush a strip of paint 2 to 3 inches wide on the ceiling, adjacent to the wall. This is "cutting in."

When you do the walls, cut in the top edges next to the ceiling in the same way. Also cut in at the corners, and along all trim. If you try to roll paint into those areas, the end of the roller will leave scrape marks on the adjacent surface.

Rolling-on paint

Applying paint with a roller is a three-part process as follows:

1. Roll the paint onto a section of the wall in a zigzag pattern (Figure 7).
2. Work the roller in the opposite direction to even out the paint (Figure 8).
3. Roll lightly in long, even strokes to minimize roller marks (Figure 9).

Don't roll the paint too thinly: 6 to 9 square feet is the most to cover with a single roller-full of paint. On walls, work from the top down, and finish with long, light roller strokes from the ceiling down to the floor.

When working on a new section, roll back into the adjacent section you have just finished painting, so that the wet edge of the painted area never has a chance to dry.

Figure 6. Paint the ceiling first, then the walls. Two people make the job efficient and pleasant: one cutting in the edges with a brush and the other rolling paint onto the broad areas.

Figure 7. Rolling-on, Step 1: Apply the paint in a zigzag pattern. Don't try to cover too much area. A roller-full of paint will cover 6 to 9 square feet without spreading the paint too thin.

Figure 8. Rolling-on, Step 2: Work the roller in the opposite direction to even the paint out. On walls, work from ceiling to floor, and work back into the wet edge of paint to prevent lap marks.

Figure 9. Rolling-on, Step 3: Make light strokes from top to bottom to create a texture and eliminate roller marks. An extension handle helps when making long vertical strokes.

Wall and Ceiling Tip

If you can't paint a room in a single session, never stop in the middle of a wall or ceiling—a lap mark will show; always work to a cut-in edge. Keep an eye on the amount of paint left so you don't run out in the middle of a wall.

PAINTING TRIM, WINDOWS, AND DOORS

Paint the trim in the room from the top down: ceiling moldings first, then windows and doors, and finally baseboards. Give all the trim a coat of enamel undercoater and an enamel top coat (Figure 10). Brushing on each coat of paint is a three-step process:

1. Apply plenty of paint along the length of the trim, working in one direction.
2. Brush across the first strokes to spread the paint evenly.
3. Give a final light brushing in the long direction to even out the brush strokes. Check after 10 minutes for drips and sags and brush them out.

Painting windows

Paint each window as shown below (Figures 11, 12, and 13). Adapt the general pattern to fit the style of your window.

The most difficult step is the first one: painting the wood where it meets glass. There are three good approaches to this step, listed below. Whichever method you use, there is one thing you must be sure to do: Leave 1/32 to 1/16 inch of paint on the glass. This forms a seal so that condensation can't get under the paint film and cause it to start peeling.

▲ Put masking tape over the glass, with just a sliver of glass exposed next to the wood. This is time-consuming but gives you very straight paint lines and is best if you don't trust your hand to be steady.

▲ If you do have a steady hand, just paint the trim, using an angled-tip sash brush. This is fast and—with practice—gives a straight paint line that just laps onto the glass. If you get too much paint on the glass, wipe it off with a paper towel wrapped around a putty knife.

▲ Paint the wood and allow the paint to get onto the glass without worrying about getting a straight, finished line. When the paint is partially dry, scrape it off the glass with a razor blade in a holder (available at paint and hardware stores). Make a scoring cut on the glass first, parallel to the wood, then scrape the paint to that line.

▲ Paint the window casings and interior sill using the three-step process described under Painting Trim, at left.

Window Tips

Tape window glass with a special blue masking tape, made by 3M. It is more expensive than ordinary masking tape, but can remain in place for days—even in direct sun—without becoming glued-on or leaving a residue that is difficult to remove.

When the sashes have been painted, open and close a window every hour or two until the paint dries, to keep it from sticking.

PAINTING TRIM, WINDOWS, AND DOORS

Figure 10. Enamel is the best top coat for trim; apply it over an enamel undercoater. Work carefully next to the newly painted walls and ceiling. Use an angled sash brush and a generous load of paint.

Figure 11. Paint windows in the numbered order, regardless of type. See text for techniques of painting around the glass. Do the sash frames next, then the casing, and finally the sill and apron.

Figure 12. Whichever method you use to paint around the glass, you must leave a fine line of paint on the glass to seal it. Wipe away the excess as you work, or scrape it away later.

Painting doors

Since doors are large, you must work quickly to prevent lap marks. It's helpful to use a roller to apply the paint, then brush it out smooth. Follow the sequence shown below (Figure 14). You can paint a door in place, in which case you should be very watchful of sags and drips. Or you can drive out the hinge pins and remove the door to paint it on sawhorses. If you do that, be very careful putting it back on the hinges to avoid marring the new surface.

Paint the door casings and jambs in the same way as window casings.

Painting baseboards

Baseboards are like window and door casings, except that they are horizontal. Paint them in the same way as the casings. Protect the floor with a strip of masking tape or a piece of thin plastic or metal that you move along as a shield (cardboard gets soggy and gummy). If you buy a plastic or metal paint shield, wipe it clean as you work. You can reuse it for years.

Figure 15. Paint is toxic—don't just wash it down the drain. Strip excess paint from rollers and wipe out the tray before washing. Let rags, cans, and papers dry before disposing of them.

CLEANING UP

Paint isn't garbage, it's toxic waste. So don't just pour it down the drain. Remove the excess from rollers (Figure 15), and wipe out roller trays and brushes with newspaper before washing them. Be sure to let the newspaper dry before you throw it away.

If you use oil-base paints, clean brushes with mineral spirits. Save the cleaner; you can let the sediment settle and pour off the clear liquid to use in other cleaning sessions.

Paint can leach into the ground water from landfill sites, so let paint cans and used rollers dry hard before you throw them out. Some communities have specific disposal regulations or special pick-ups for paints and similar waste. Be sure to check for any special requirements in your area.

Door Tip

If a door between rooms is painted in different colors, paint the edges of the door so that as you open the door, the edge you see is the same color as the room you are in. In one room, the edge you see will be the hinge edge; in the other room, it will be the latch edge.

Figure 13. Paint the meeting rail where the two sashes of a double-hung window overlap, if you can reach it. If not, paint the top side thinly, to avoid runs and drips on the visible front side.

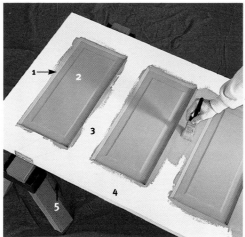

Figure 14. Paint doors quickly, so the paint doesn't dry before you're done, creating lap marks. Paint in the order shown. You can also paint doors in place, following the same sequence.

Floors

Lay Sheet Vinyl Flooring
No flooring goes down faster than sheet vinyl, and none is easier to install, especially with the techniques given here.

92

Vinyl Floor Tile

Tiles let you design your own patterns, borders, and accents. You can fit them into any room in your home.

99

Glue-down Wood Floor

Hardwood flooring is unmatched for rich, warm beauty. Glue-down flooring strips take almost all the work out of installation.

106

Ceramic Tile Entryway

An entryway floor gets hard, dirty wear. Use ceramic tiles for appearance, maximum durability, and ease of cleaning.

112

If your once-beautiful floors now leave something to be desired, sheet vinyl flooring may be just the answer.

Lay Sheet Vinyl Flooring

Vinyl flooring comes in a wide range of patterns and colors to meet all tastes. It is perhaps the least costly but most highly durable covering you can choose, and it's not hard to install.

Here's how to get it down right—without having to remove the old flooring.

Laying sheet flooring isn't especially difficult. With the proper tools and materials on hand, you can probably do the job in one weekend. Take care with preparation and details, and you'll get first-rate results.

CHOOSING VINYL FLOORING

Since its introduction in the 1960's, sheet vinyl flooring has been the choice of homeowners and apartment dwellers who don't want to sweat over their floors—either caring for them or paying for them. Always a great value, today's materials and designs make vinyl flooring tougher and more eye-pleasing than ever.

Cost

A sheet vinyl floor will cost between $5 and $40 a square yard. And, as with most things in life, you get what you pay for.

▲ More expensive, higher quality vinyl generally has a thick wear layer on the surface, which makes it tough and long lasting. It also has thicker backing than low-cost materials, which makes it more sound absorbent and easier on the feet. The simplest way to judge the quality of flooring is to inspect it and compare samples. If you want precise information, ask a salesperson at a flooring store to look up exact measurements for the wear layer and the backing.

▲ The warranty a floor carries is another measure of quality. Any flooring you buy should be warrantied against defects. A long-term warranty—5 to 10 years—tells you the manufacturer has confidence in the product.

▲ Of course, color and pattern will weigh heavily in your choice. The range and character of these qualities also vary with cost. Look carefully, and consider all the possibilities. If you are covering a floor in a small room, you may be able to get a high-quality floor at a low price by picking up a remnant, but your choice of patterns is likely to be quite limited.

Types of flooring

There are two basic types of sheet vinyl: rotovinyl, made only from sheets of vinyl; and inlaid, which contains vinyl chips. Laying inlaid vinyl is a job only for an experienced installer; you should consider only rotovinyl.

▲ Rotovinyl comes with either felt or flexible backing. Both kinds can be installed by a do-it-yourselfer. Felt-backed rotovinyl is slightly more difficult to handle only because you have to be careful not to accidentally tear the felt off the facing in spots as you work, but this is not a serious drawback. Felt-backed rotovinyl is the type shown in the photographs.

▲ Flexible-backed rotovinyl was designed with the idea that it could be installed by nonprofessionals with excellent results. Brand names for this kind of product commonly end in "-flex." It's generally more expensive than felt-backed vinyl, but you won't have to rent a floor roller or buy as much adhesive.

INSTALLATION METHODS

Most felt-backed vinyl flooring must be glued down all over. Flexible-backed vinyl should be glued or stapled around the edges and at seams only. Different brands—and even different pattern designs—can require different adhesives. Seemingly small mistakes can lead to big headaches, so always follow the manufacturer's instructions, right down to the size of notches in the trowel you use to spread the adhesive. Most manufacturers offer specific directions to follow when installing their products. A flooring retailer can provide them.

▲ Many home centers and flooring stores sell installation kits for under $20 that include a large paper template you tape together, lay in the room, and cut to fit. You then place the template on the flooring, cut around it, and have a perfectly tailored sheet of vinyl.

▲ The professional techniques shown here are usually faster than the template method. But if the room has a complex shape or if your cutting and fitting skills are shaky, a template may be the way to go. You can make your own template out of large sheets of wrapping paper or other thick paper. In any case, be careful about marking the face of vinyl flooring. Ink may damage some types of flooring, so check the manufacturer's instructions.

Whichever way you choose to install the flooring, the instructions and photos on these pages will help you do it right.

WHAT YOU'LL NEED

The tools and materials for installing vinyl flooring are itemized in the accompanying lists. Here's some information about a few of the various special items.

▲ For best results you should cover old flooring with underlayment. The most widely used underlayment is 4x8 sheets of 1/4-inch lauan plywood, but other types are available. They include underlayment-grade plywood, hardboard, particleboard, chipboard, and even cement panels. The flooring manufacturer or dealer can tell you which types of underlayment may be used with it.

▲ To put down the underlayment, rent an underlayment stapler and mallet. The rental dealer will also sell the staples you need.

▲ If your flooring is to be glued down just around the edges and seams, you'll need only a hand-held roller. You can buy the kind used for wallpaper quite inexpensively. If your flooring needs to be glued over the entire area, rent a 75- to 100-lb. floor roller. (You won't need a floor roller until late in the job, probably the second day. To save on rental fees, pick one up when you drop off the stapler.)

Tools You Need

Utility knife and extra blades

Tape measure

Straightedge

Pen or pencil

Hammer

Pry bar

Handsaw

Circular saw or saber saw

Notched trowel for adhesive

Wide putty knife for floor patch

100-grit sandpaper

Drill

Nail set

Underlayment stapler and mallet

Floor roller

PUTTING DOWN UNDERLAYMENT

It's best to cover your old floor with 1/4-inch underlayment instead of pulling it up. Older flooring may contain asbestos, which becomes dangerous when disturbed. In any case, tearing out old flooring is likely to create more problems than it solves.

Clear the area

You'll have to move out all the furniture and any appliances that aren't built in. Be sure to turn off appliances and gas lines before disconnecting them. You may want to rent moving rollers or dollies to move appliances in and out. When moving them back in, put down strips of hardboard or plywood to roll on. Many a magnificent flooring job has been ruined while putting the refrigerator back.

Prepare the floor

First, carefully remove all baseboards with a pry bar. When the flooring is laid and you replace the baseboards, you'll cover the edges of the sheet and hide any small mistakes you made while trimming the vinyl.

▲ Next, undercut door casings by laying the blade of a handsaw on a scrap of underlayment and horizontally cutting off the bottom of the casing. This will allow you to slide both the underlayment and the vinyl under the casing, instead of trying to trim around it.

▲ If you have a squeaky floor, deal with it now. If you can work from below, add braces along joists or insert shims or inject glue between joists and the subfloor where it is loose. If you can't get at the floor from below, drive screws through the floor from above, into the joists below. Drive them flush or a bit below the surface; they will be covered by the underlayment.

▲ Cut out any loose areas along the seams of the old flooring and fill the holes with floor patch compound (Figures 1, 2). Most floor patch powders can be mixed with water, but use liquid latex instead of water, because it won't promote mold and mildew growth. Don't mix up more floor patch than you can use in about 15 minutes; it hardens fast.

Install the underlayment

Measure the room and draw a rough floor plan. Sketch a layout that will use as many full sheets of underlayment as possible. This will leave you with less cutting and fewer seams to staple and fill. Stagger the seam pattern so that four corners never meet.

▲ One side of the underlayment will be smooth and should face upward; the other side may be full of holes and wide cracks. If you mistakenly put the rough side up, fill any holes or cracks with floor-patching compound.

▲ Cut underlayment with a plywood blade in a circular saw, or with a saber saw. Support the thin panels well when sawing so the edges will not tear or splinter.

▲ Fasten the underlayment in place with 7/8-inch chisel-point staples, which bend over to "fish hook" as they're driven in, to grip permanently (Figure 3). Space staples in a 4-inch square pattern over the field of each panel, and 2 inches apart along all edges. You'll need about 360 staples for each 4x8 sheet of underlayment. They are commonly supplied in clips of 60. Don't be gentle when you drive the staples with the stapler; they have to sink well below the surface.

▲ Flatten any protruding staples with a hammer and fill the hammer marks with floor-patching compound. Also fill the underlayment seams (Figure 4). When the patching compound is dry, after about 30 minutes, sand everything smooth.

▲ Finally, sweep and vacuum the floor thoroughly. Be obsessive about getting every last bit picked up. Because vinyl flooring is shiny and flexible, it will telegraph any bumps or ruts beneath the surface.

Figure 1. Prepare the old floor to receive underlayment. Cut out any loose spots and trim away any curled edges along seams of the old flooring with a utility knife. A sharp blade will make the job easier.

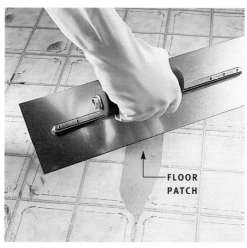

Figure 2. Fill the cut-out areas and any other holes or depressions with floor-patching compound. Use a small trowel or a broad putty knife; feather out the edges of the patch all around.

Figure 3. Staple underlayment every 4 in. in the field, and every 2 in. around the edges. Flatten any staples that might protrude above the surface using a hammer.

Figure 4. Fill underlayment seams with floor-patching compound. Sand all patching after it dries to get a perfectly smooth surface. Then sweep and vacuum the floor thoroughly.

Materials You Need

Vinyl sheet flooring

Underlayment

Floor-patching compound

Flooring adhesive

Seam sealer

Liquid latex

Shoe molding

Threshold cap

INSTALLING THE VINYL FLOORING

You must first cut the vinyl so it fits neatly around cabinets and corners and up against the walls. Then you can glue it permanently in place with flooring adhesive.

Cut and fit the vinyl

If there's space, unroll the flooring in the room where you want to install it (Figure 5). If there is not sufficient space in your room, you'll have to do some rough cutting in a bigger area. But don't try to cut the sheet to the exact size of the room—leave as much excess as you can. Work on a clean floor so you don't drag unwanted grit into the room.

If the room has a wall with an outside corner, or base cabinets that form one, cut a rectangular section out of the flooring so that the sheet will fit around the corner and up against adjoining walls. Unroll it from there.

If the room doesn't have an outside corner, start against the longest straight wall or a long row of base cabinets.

▲ Be sure the flooring is positioned so that the pattern will lay out properly. If your flooring has a pattern of lines, for example, and you want them to run parallel to a wall, adjust the sheet before you begin to cut inside corners and trim along walls. Once you've started slicing, it's too late to reposition the flooring.

▲ First cut out the excess at an inside corner (Figures 6, 7). Then make the straight cuts along the adjoining baseboard or cabinet base (Figure 8). A common error when laying felt-backed vinyl is to tear the backing off when forcing it into corners. If that happens, just glue the backing to the face with flooring adhesive.

▲ Work along one wall to the next corner and make the corner cut there. Then go back to the starting corner and work along the adjoining wall. When you reach a corner, cut it and work along the next wall. Finally, do the last wall. When you are finished, all the edges will have been cut and the flooring will lie flat in place.

▲ If the vinyl isn't wide enough to cover the entire area between two walls, you'll have to make a seam (see box, Making No-Show Seams).

Glue down the flooring

There are two stages in gluing the vinyl in place. First, spread adhesive evenly over the underlayment and then put the vinyl in position. Second, apply pressure with a floor roller for proper adhesion in all areas.

▲ Make sure you have the kind of adhesive specified for your sheet flooring, and use a trowel with the specified size and shape of notches, either square or triangular. Spreading adhesive with the notched edge leaves small ridges that flatten out into a uniform layer when the flooring is put into place and rolled.

Sheet vinyl and adhesives often contain VOC's (volatile organic compounds), which

are unpleasant to breathe in concentration and may be injurious to health. So open the windows and run a fan or two while laying the flooring, and keep the room well ventilated for a couple of days after the job is done.

▲ To begin, roll back the flooring from one long side of the room to about the middle. Be careful: Rolling up a sheet of vinyl face-in can damage the wear layer. When you roll back the sheet to spread the adhesive, roll it loosely and unroll it as soon as you can.

▲ With half the underlayment exposed, kneel on the flat part of the vinyl and reach across the roll to spread adhesive on the floor all along the length of the roll and as far out as you can reach (Figure 9). Use sweeping strokes and get a uniform coating of ridges. When you have covered the area that you can reach, unroll the flooring onto it and move forward to do the next section. Continue until you reach the wall.

▲ Now roll back the flooring from the opposite wall to the center of the room and glue down the second half just as you did the first.

▲ Once everything is glued down, go over the surface with a floor roller to eliminate bubbles and bulges (Figure 10). Work from the center out to the edges in all directions, and overlap each path of the roller.

Bubbles sometimes form under the vinyl after it's been rolled. If the adhesive hasn't begun to set, you should be able to work them out with a roller. If it has set, puncture the bubbles with a needle and roll them down to squeeze the air out. Then put a drop of seam sealer—a liquid that bonds vinyl and seals the surface—over each hole. Use the type of sealer specified by the flooring manufacturer.

There may be some places where your knife slipped or you made a cut longer than you intended. After the floor is glued down, treat those spots with seam sealer too.

Figure 5. Lay the flooring along base cabinets or a straight wall, then unroll and position it. Let excess flooring lap up on the walls. Use a piece of duct tape to keep outside corners from tearing.

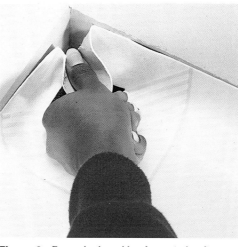

Figure 6. Press the knuckle of your index finger into inside corners from the face, and reach behind and grasp the flooring to mark the point of the corner with your thumb.

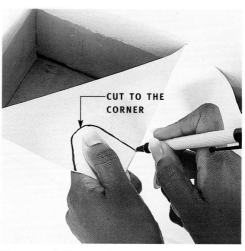

Figure 7. Pull up the flooring at the corner, draw a U shape, and cut it out with a utility knife. When in doubt, start with a small cut; it's better to repeat the cut than to remove too much at first.

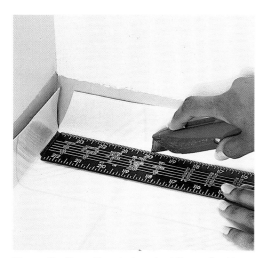

Figure 8. Force the vinyl against the wall with a metal straightedge and trim the excess along the first wall. Then do the adjoining wall. Change knife blades frequently.

Figure 9. Roll back the sheet about halfway across the room, sweep the area, and spread adhesive. Roll back the other half and repeat. Once laid on the adhesive, the vinyl can't be moved.

Figure 10. Roll out bubbles and bulges with a floor roller. Start in the middle and work outward in an overlapping pattern. Use a hand roller wherever the floor roller won't fit.

FINISHING THE EDGES

When the flooring has been laid and rolled, replace the baseboards along the walls to cover the edges. If there are mistakes or edges that the baseboards do not cover completely, add a shoe molding at the floor line (Figure 11). You can also add molding along the bases of cabinets to conceal the flooring edges.

▲ Adding underlayment and a sheet of vinyl will have raised the floor by a bit more than a quarter-inch above the floors in adjoining rooms. Cover the uneven thresholds with a metal or wooden cap designed to bridge uneven floor levels (Figure 12).

▲ Set all nails in the molding and threshold caps and fill the holes.

▲ You can walk on the floor and move the appliances back as soon as it's laid. But keep furniture and heavy foot traffic off until the adhesive completely sets, usually in about 24 hours. In the case of a room like the kitchen, this may be a nuisance. On the other hand, it's a good excuse to go out to dinner to celebrate a job well done.

FINISHING THE EDGES

Figure 11. Cover edges around base cabinets with shoe molding. You may want to paint or finish the molding before you attach it. Reinstall baseboards along the walls.

Figure 12. Place a cap of wood or metal over the threshold to bridge between different floor levels. Cut the cap to fit a door or archway precisely. Use a hacksaw on metal caps.

Vinyl tile is so easy to install that it's an excellent home-improvement project, even if you think your do-it-yourself skills are quite modest.

Vinyl Floor Tile

Tiles are available in a wide array of beautiful colors and patterns. Because they are made in standard square sizes, it's easy to design your own pattern using inexpensive solid-color tiles. That will give you a beautiful as well as unique floor.

Design your own floor with easy-to-install vinyl tiles. This floor uses solid-color tiles: black and red for the border, and the same red tiles for accents in the large field of white tiles. Only simple straight-line cuts were required.

Tools You Need

4' level

25' measuring tape

Chalk line

Utility knife and plenty of replacement blades

Carpenter's square

Pry bar

Hammer

Nail set

60- and 100-grit sandpaper

Sanding block

Fine-tooth file

Smooth-edged trowel

Notched trowel

100-lb. floor roller (rental)

CHOOSING VINYL TILE

There are generally two kinds of vinyl tile available for do-it-yourself installation:

1. A thin tile, about 1/16 inch thick, with adhesive on the back. You simply peel off the backing paper and stick the tile to the floor.

2. A thicker tile, 1/8 inch, that you install by applying a separate adhesive to the floor and setting the tile in place.

Although the second type is somewhat more expensive than peel-and-stick tiles, and requires a bit more work to install, it is far superior. According to the manufacturers, these tiles resist damage and stains and are very durable. They are generally designed for both commercial and residential use.

Vinyl tiles are manufactured in standard square sizes: 9, 10, and 12 inches. Your best choice is 12-inch tiles. They make it easy to figure layouts and trim measurements, and they cover the floor area faster than the smaller sizes.

Your choice of colors and the number of tiles you need will depend on the character of the room and your intended layout.

PLANNING A LAYOUT

Whether you choose peel-and-stick or adhesive-laid tiles, you need to plan a layout on paper. This will help you check the design and figure how many tiles you will need.

▲ Use graph paper, letting each square represent one tile. Measure the length and width of the room, and draw it to scale on the graph paper. The scale will depend on whether the squares represent 9-, 10-, or 12-inch tiles. Then measure cabinets, appliances, and other features that the tile must be laid around and draw them to scale on the plan. Make some photocopies of this basic outline so you can sketch a variety of layouts.

▲ Draw possible layouts on the plan copies. You can lay tiles so that the seams run at right angles to the walls of the room or diagonally. You can use full tiles or cut them in half (both straight and on the diagonal), nip off triangle-shaped corners, or inset small squares. If you intend to use tiles of different colors, you can color in a section of squares with appropriately colored pencils or markers, to get an idea of how a particular arrangement will look.

▲ Include a border in your layout. A border offers two advantages. It provides a finished, unifying appearance, and it makes it easy to lay out even quite complex field patterns without difficult measurements or trimming.

The length and width of a room are seldom equal to a full number of tiles. A border will let you use full- and partial-size tiles freely in the field; any adjustments for the room dimensions can be made in the width of the border. If you are laying the field tiles diagonally, that will save a lot of work, because border tiles are commonly laid square to the walls. It is much easier to make a series of straight cuts to trim the width of an outer border row than to trim an equal number of diagonally laid tiles.

In the vinyl installation shown in the photograph on page 99, the border consists of one full black tile and a red accent tile, cut to size. The field tiles are white, with red triangular insets at every third tile in every other row. The insets and the spaces for them were made simply by trimming the corners off tiles. Two other border and field designs are shown below, but there are many other possibilities.

ALTERNATE BORDER AND FIELD DESIGNS

This vivid border is made by alternating black and red tiles that have been cut in half from corner to corner. Using white field tile with triangular insets on the corners provides contrast and interest.

The border at the right uses full-size red tiles; the field tiles are a toast color. Spaces for the 2-inch black accent squares were created by trimming the corners where four full tiles meet.

PREPARING THE FLOOR

For a permanent, long-lasting installation, your new tile cannot be laid directly on top of old tile, sheet flooring, or wood-strip flooring.

If the old floor is resilient tile, linoleum, or a similar material, removing it could pose a health threat. Both the flooring and the adhesive used to secure it may contain asbestos, even if manufactured until the late 1970's. Left in place, asbestos doesn't pose a real threat. However, breaking it up and removing it does. That's why it's usually best to put down a 1/4-inch subfloor over the old flooring and lay your new tile on top of that.

There are a few situations where vinyl tile is not recommended (see the tip, Don't Do It). However, assuming that you can install vinyl tile, proceed to prepare the floor as follows.

Fix the old floor

Inspect the old tiles or sheet flooring for low spots. Lay a 4-foot level at successive points across the floor, in at least two directions.

▲ If you find any low spots 3/8 inch deep or more, level them out with latex underlayment patching compound. You may have to apply multiple coats of patching on deep depressions to get the surface as smooth and level as possible. Also fill any holes or broken corners with the patching compound.

▲ Sand the repairs. The underlayment patch dries almost rock hard, but you can sand it with 60-grit paper over a sanding block.

▲ If you have a wood-strip floor, check it for low spots, breaks and splinters, and irregularities. Fill with underlayment patch where necessary. If edges are warped up or sections of the floor are uneven (common in old kitchen wood floors), drive all nailheads below the surface with a nail set and level off the area with a power sander. Rent a floor sander if a large area requires work.

Install underlayment

Once you have made sure that the original floor surface is level, cover it with underlayment (Figure 1). Use only 1/4-inch-thick APA-stamped (American Plywood Association) plywood underlayment with a fully sanded face. It is sold in 4x8-foot sheets.

▲ Carefully remove the baseboard with a pry bar before putting down underlayment. (Replace the baseboard or molding after the tile is laid. Alternatively, leave the baseboard in place and add shoe molding over the edge of the tile at the end of the job.)

▲ Lay the underlayment with the sanded face up and position the sheets with butt joints staggered in successive rows (as in laying bricks) so that four corners do not meet at the same point.

Secure the plywood with ring-shank underlayment nails every 6 inches (Figure 2). To speed up nailing in a uniform pattern, snap a grid of chalk lines spaced 6 inches apart over the face of the underlayment. Nail spacing is very important. An improperly nailed subfloor will void most tile warranties, should a problem occur later. Place nails opposite one another across the seams. Countersink all nailheads.

▲ When nailing is finished, use a smooth-edged trowel to fill all the nail heads with underlayment patch (Figure 3). Also fill any gaps where the underlayment sheets butt together. Taper or feather the edge of the patching compound as much as possible to reduce sanding time. Sand any rough or high spots with 60-grit sandpaper and a sanding block.

▲ Seal the underlayment. Most manufacturers recommend applying a coat of shellac or other wood sealer to the plywood to prevent the tile adhesive from being absorbed into the plywood. The sealer must be dry before you begin applying the tile adhesive.

Don't Do It

■ Do not apply vinyl tile directly onto particleboard or lauan plywood, or over cork or rubber floor coverings. These must be removed.

■ Do not apply vinyl tile on a wood subfloor that rests on a concrete slab directly in contact with the earth.

■ Do not install vinyl tile on a wood subfloor that "gives" or springs when you walk on it. In this situation, you may want to contact your building inspector to make sure there isn't a structural problem with your floor.

PREPARING THE FLOOR: UNDERLAYMENT

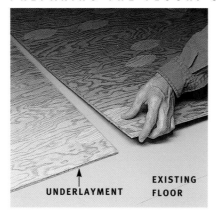

Figure 1. Install 1/4-in. thick plywood underlayment directly over the existing flooring. Fill low spots in the old flooring with latex underlayment patch before installing the new plywood.

Figure 2. Nail the plywood every 6 in. along the edges and over the entire surface with 1-1/4-in. long ring-shank nails. A grid pattern marked on the plywood ensures proper nail spacing.

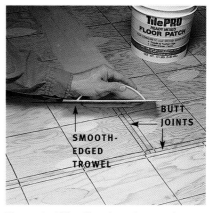

Figure 3. Fill nailheads and gaps where the underlayment sheets butt together with the latex underlayment patch. Feather the edges of the patches; sand smooth with 60-grit sandpaper.

MAKING A TRIAL LAYOUT

Your graph paper plan is useful for figuring tile quantities and for guiding you in putting down the tiles in the proper pattern. However, the plan is somewhat idealized because it assumes that everything in the room is square.

In real life, few rooms have walls or floor cabinets that run at perfect right angles to one another. For that reason you need to mark some guidelines on the floor in order to make the tile layout centered and square in the space.

You also need to dry-lay some tiles in a trial pattern to make sure the borders and field fill the space without gaps. You're almost sure to find that a guideline must be adjusted before you start installing the tiles permanently.

Mark guidelines

Refer to the box below and to Figure 4 to see how to apply the following steps.

1. Measure the longest dimension of the floor along one wall of the room. Locate and mark the middle (half the length) of that measurement on the floor.
2. Measure the same distance along the opposite wall and mark that point.
3. Snap a chalk line between the two points to mark the center of the floor length.
4. Following the same procedure on the two remaining walls, snap a chalk line between them, crossing the first.
5. Use a carpenter's square to make sure the angles of the intersecting lines are square.

The spot where the two perpendicular center lines intersect is the center point of the floor. If you're laying tiles on the diagonal from the center of the room or oriented on a corner, you must now mark diagonal lines. Follow the procedure explained in the tip Marking a 45° Angle.

Marking a 45° Angle

To mark a 45° angle between two lines that form a right (90°) angle, you need only a tape measure and a pencil.

Measure out the same distance along both lines, say 24 in., and mark those points. Draw a line connecting the two points and find its middle. Draw a line from the midpoint of the connecting line back to the square corner. It bisects the right angle into two 45° angles.

Use the same method to divide any angle into equal halves—for example, to run a layout line from the corner of a room where the walls do not form a right angle, or to subdivide angles for cutting decorative patterns from flooring materials.

MARKING GUIDELINES

Locate the center of the floor by snapping chalk lines between the midpoints of opposite walls. Check with a carpenter's square: If they do not form an exact 90° angle, adjust the shorter line.

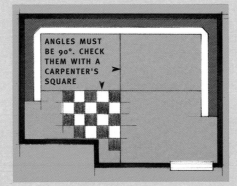

ANGLES MUST BE 90°. CHECK THEM WITH A CARPENTER'S SQUARE

Mark 45° diagonals by bisecting the right angles of the first set of lines (see sidebar). For both square- and diagonally laid tiles, precisely equal angles are required for symmetrical results.

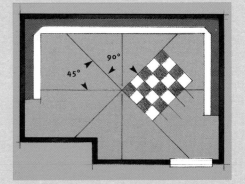

90°

45°

Dry-lay a trial placement

It may be necessary to adjust the position of one or both guidelines in order to have a symmetrical layout, without slivers of tiles along one edge, and to get borders of equal or nearly equal width. To check, make a trial layout of dry-laid tiles.

In the trial run (Figure 5), the black and red border tiles were put in place along two adjacent walls. Then, starting at the center point, enough field tiles were laid along the diagonal guidelines to check tile placement against the borders in two directions.

The trial layout showed a gap when the first field tile was positioned at the center and the last tile was butted against the border (Figure 5). Moving the tiles together toward the border eliminated the gap. A new diagonal line was marked from the adjustment (Figure 6).

Two lines of tiles were then laid out from the new lines to the opposite walls to check the spacing and to see if any border-trimming was necessary there.

If you discover that a border must be adjusted, you have two options. If the border runs up to a row of appliances or cupboards, you can trim up to about 1-1/2 inches there without it being particularly noticeable. If the border runs to a wall, or a greater amount must be trimmed away, divide the amount equally between opposite borders and shift the field tiles accordingly.

MAKING A TRIAL LAYOUT

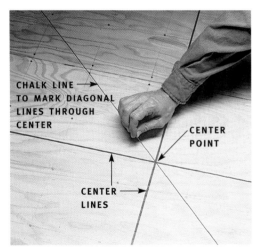

Figure 4. Chalk lines are the best way to mark guidelines on the underlayment. It takes only a second to snap a line, and it can be quickly erased if a line must be moved.

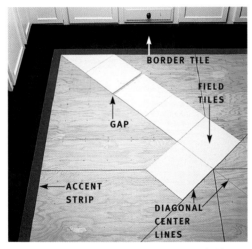

Figure 5. Dry-lay the border, accent, and field tiles, using your guidelines to determine tile placement. If a gap occurs, move the starting lines or plan to adjust the borders to eliminate it.

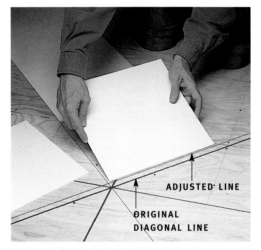

Figure 6. Recheck the layout after moving a starting line. Also dry-lay tiles in the other direction to make sure the adjustment hasn't created a new problem somewhere else.

INSTALLING THE TILES

Vinyl tiles are easy and safe to work with because they don't contain asbestos, as older tiles almost certainly do. Installation with adhesive—the procedure explained below—is straightforward, too.

To lay tiles, the temperature of the room and tiles should be kept at least 70°F for 48 hours before and after installation. Place them in the room for a day or two before starting. Work when the humidity is relatively low, less than 50 percent. If necessary, delay the project until the conditions are favorable.

There are three steps in installing tiles:
1. Cut the tiles.
2. Spread the adhesive.
3. Set the tiles.

Cut the tiles

To make the job of laying tiles go faster, precut as many tiles as possible and sort them into piles of matching shapes and color.

▲ Cut tiles from the back, not the face. Lightly mark the cut lines with a sharp pencil and a straightedge. Score along the cutting line using a utility knife with a sharp blade; change blades often. Draw the blade along a metal straightedge two or three times to score the tile (Figure 7); you don't need to cut completely through to the face.

▲ Grasp the tile firmly and snap along the scored line (Figure 8). Place the tile face down with the scored line on the edge of a smooth work surface for easier snapping.

▲ Check the snapped edge and smooth any rough spots with a fine file or 100-grit paper on a sanding block. Take your time. Move the sanding block or file along the entire length of the tile so that you get a straight, square edge. Sanding in just one spot, or holding the sandpaper in your fingers will only make the trimmed edge more uneven.

Spread the adhesive

Make sure the room is well ventilated when you apply adhesive. This will keep fumes from the adhesive to a minimum and help control the humidity. Sweep or vacuum the underlayment just before beginning to work.

With a notched trowel, start spreading the adhesive at one wall and work toward the center of the room (Figure 9). Check the label on the adhesive can for the appropriate trowel notch size and any special instructions, precautions, or helpful suggestions.

The label will also tell you how much adhesive to put down and its "open" time—how much time you have to lay down the tile before

INSTALLING THE TILES

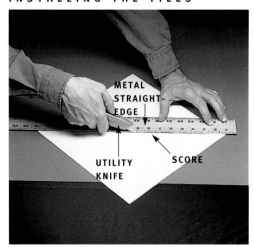

Figure 7. Score the back of a tile for cutting, using a utility knife and metal straightedge held firmly in position. Score the tile two or three times, but don't cut through to the face.

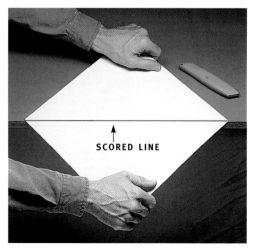

Figure 8. Snap the tile along the scored line. To make a clean break, place the scored line on the edge of a table or work surface. Smooth rough edges with a fine file or sandpaper.

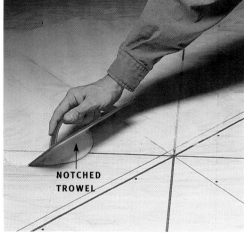

Figure 9. Sweep the floor thoroughly, then spread tile adhesive over no more than one-half of the floor area, using a notched trowel. Start spreading at a wall and work back to the center lines.

the adhesive will no longer bond properly to the tile. Don't try to cover more than half the floor at a time; less is better if this is your first vinyl tile project. Most vinyl tile adhesives have an open time of 40 to 50 minutes.

Set the tiles

To lay the tile in the area you have covered with adhesive, start at the center of the room and work toward the walls.

▲ Hold the first tile by its outer edge and align the inner edge with the guideline, which will be visible between ridges of adhesive. Lower the inner edge directly onto the guideline with the tile almost flat, then lower the rest of the tile into place.

▲ Butt the next tile against the first. Be sure to lower each tile into place; do not slide it.

Sliding scrapes adhesive from the floor and builds it up along the edge. This buildup will squeeze out onto the surface, creating a mess as the tiles are butted together. When this happens, wipe off any excess adhesive that rises between the tiles with a damp cloth.

▲ When your pattern calls for an inset piece, set the large tiles first, then position the inset against it (Figure 11). Do the insets as you go; you may find it necessary to trim or file some of them to make them fit. The same is true of the border tiles set along the edge of a wall or at the base of a cabinet.

▲ Once all the tiles have been set in place, use a 100-pound, three-section roller to firmly set them into the adhesive. This is probably the only tool you will have to rent. As you use the roller, be careful not to scratch or shift the tiles.

FINISHING UP

Allow 24 hours' drying time before moving furniture or appliances onto the floor and avoid foot traffic as much as possible. If you are careful, and lay down a sheet of hardboard to kneel on, you can replace the baseboards or install shoe molding after only two or three hours. When you do move any appliances back into place, be careful. Lay a sheet of plywood or hardboard over a large open area to take the pressure of rollers or casters.

Finally, apply the manufacturer's recommended finish to keep the floor looking great during the drying period.

Figure 10. Start at the center lines and work toward the wall. Set each tile cleanly in place. Don't slide tiles into position, because that creates a buildup of adhesive on the tile edge.

TRIANGULAR INSET

Figure 11. Place inset or accent pieces into the pattern as you go, in the same way as the other tiles. When all the tiles have been laid, roll the entire surface with a 100-lb., three-section roller.

A handsome hardwood floor in your dining room, living room, or bedroom can stop being a dream and become a reality.

Glue-Down Wood Floor

With modern glue-down wood flooring, you can do the job yourself and get beautiful results for 20 to 25 percent less than the cost of a professionally installed floor.

A finished floor can be installed in just a day when you use prefinished, glue-down hardwood strips. You don't need any special tools or woodworking skills to get fine-looking results like this.

PREFINISHED GLUE-DOWN FLOORING

Glue-down hardwood flooring is easy to install and, best of all, it is prefinished. You need little woodworking experience to lay this kind of floor. Simply set the precise tongue-and-groove wood strips in adhesive spread over a properly prepared subfloor, and that's all there is to it. It's much like installing a ceramic or vinyl tile floor. In contrast, traditional 3/4-inch-thick wood-strip flooring requires the skill of an expert to install, and must be carefully sanded, stained, and finished after installation, which adds at least two days' work to the job.

Glue-down floors are versatile. You can install them directly over a wood, concrete, or vinyl floor. Because they're only 3/8 inch to 1/2 inch thick, they blend well with floor coverings in adjoining rooms.

The flooring can be so thin without sacrificing durability because the strips are laminated —layers of wood glued together like plywood. Laminating makes a prefinished floor more stable in regions with wide humidity and temperature swings during the year.

There are some limitations. The top hardwood layer is only 1/16 inch to 1/8 inch thick, so you'll have to keep dirt and grit off to reduce wear. And even a laminated floor won't survive long in a bathroom with a shower or tub, or in a damp basement. In fact, the manufacturers don't recommend installing a glue-down floor below ground level.

BUYING PREFINISHED FLOORING

It's always a good idea to visit a flooring dealer to examine samples of prefinished flooring firsthand before you buy. Don't rely on photographs. Compare the stains, finishes, and thicknesses of the top layer of hardwood.

Edge styles and joints

Also compare and evaluate the edge styles. The strips fit together with tongue-and-groove joints. Some types have beveled edges on the top surface that form a V-shaped groove at the joint. Other types have square top edges to fit flush at the joint. However, sometimes the flush fit is slightly off, leaving sharp edges that could pinch bare feet on a bedroom floor. Perhaps most widely usable is a third type that has slightly rounded edges at the joint—no sharp edges, but no noticeable V-groove either.

Quantity

Determine the amount of material you need by multiplying the length and width of your room to find its area in square feet. Add about 5 percent for waste. Dealers sell prefinished flooring strips in boxes containing from 20 to 30 square feet, costing from $100 to $150 a box. If your figures show that you're likely to have most of a box left over, ask if you can purchase a partial box, so you won't have money tied up in a significant amount of unused material.

Discuss with the dealer the types of transitions you must make where the wood will meet other types of floors, like carpeting, vinyl, or stair treads. Then buy the special transition strips that you need, or make them yourself. Also purchase the glue recommended by the flooring manufacturer and the notched trowel you need to spread it.

Materials You Need

Flooring

Glue (mastic)

Sandpaper

Packing tape

Concrete or wood patching compound

Mineral spirits

3d finish nails

Tools You Need

- Measuring tape
- Carpenter's square
- Chalk line
- Pry bar
- Handsaw
- Hammer
- Nail set
- Trowel with smooth and notched edges
- Paint scraper
- Mask with organic vapor filters
- Saber saw
- Miter box and saw

PREPARING A SUBFLOOR

The most difficult, but important, step in the project is preparing the old floor to receive the new one. If you are redoing a finished room, remove the baseboards and undercut the door-frame (Figures 1, 2). Then turn your attention to the existing floor. All manufacturers insist that the old surface be dry, solid, flat, and clean.

Dry floor

You can easily glue down wood flooring on a concrete floor that does not rest on soil. But always test a ground-based concrete floor for moisture; for an easy method, see the box Concrete Floor Moisture Test, opposite.

A wood or vinyl underfloor won't usually pose moisture problems unless the wood is new, damp plywood. Let new plywood cure for at least a week in dry weather before gluing down the hardwood strips.

Solid floor

In a concrete floor, chip out any loose material and fill the holes with concrete-patching material, mixed with a latex additive, not water (Figure 3). You can buy both at home centers.

If you're working with a wood subfloor, fasten down any loose boards with ring-shank nails or drywall screws.

Flat floor

Lay a straight 10-foot board on edge across the floor and look for any high and low spots that cause 3/16-inch or larger gaps.

▲ If the floor is concrete, fill and smooth the low areas with the concrete-patching material. To remove high spots, rent a surface grinder. Wear a good particle mask and eye protection when using the surface grinder.

▲ With a wood subfloor, the task is easier. In rough or high spots, set all nailheads below the surface and sand the spots down with a belt sander (consider renting a floor sander if most

of the floor needs work). Fill low areas with wood-patching compound.

▲ If the old wood floor is extremely rough and uneven or if it has a layer of old glue, put down a layer of 3/8-inch grade C/D plywood as a subfloor. Use screws or ring-shank nails, and fill any voids in the plywood with patching compound. The extra plywood layer will raise the overall floor height, so you will have to undercut door frames and trim to accommodate the new thickness of the flooring.

Clean floor

Glue won't adhere to dust, grit, paint, varnish, wax, or oil. Scrape, strip, or sand a floor clean, then sweep and vacuum it thoroughly. You can work by hand on a concrete floor (Figure 4), but to scour the surface with the least amount of work, rent a floor buffer and put a steel wool pad or sandpaper on it. Be obsessive about getting the surface clean, especially concrete that has been sealed or painted.

PREPARING A SUBFLOOR

Figure 1. Remove the baseboards carefully so they can be reused. Place a wood block against the wall to protect the surface as you pry the baseboard free.

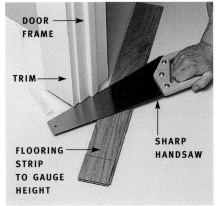

Figure 2. Undercut door frame and trim with a handsaw so that the flooring will fit underneath. Use a flooring strip as a spacer for the cut.

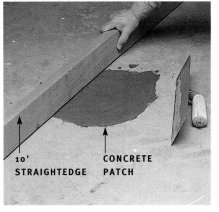

Figure 3. Lay a long straightedge on the floor and fill low spots where the gap exceeds 3/16 in. with a special concrete-patching material.

Figure 4. Scrape and scrub paint, dirt, and oil off the concrete. Flooring glue will not bond to foreign materials. Sweep and vacuum the surface clean.

MARKING A STARTING LINE

To keep the flooring perfectly straight, snap a starting line with a chalk line. Orient this line with the most prominent feature of the room—a fireplace hearth, a wall, or a doorway—so you can run the wood flooring strips parallel or at right angles to it. The diagram in the box below shows the procedure. The strips were laid to run at 90 degrees to the doorway. Because there is no guarantee that two adjoining walls form an exact right angle, the layout guide line—line B—was established as follows.

Line A runs parallel to the doorway wall. It was marked by measuring out an equal distance at each end of the wall and snapping a chalk line between those points. Next, an origin point was chosen on line A directly opposite the edge of the doorway. Then layout line B was marked, with a chalk line, using the 3-4-5 method (explained at right) to get it exactly perpendicular to line A. Locating line B next to the doorway made it possible to spread glue throughout most of the room and still get in and out easily.

The 3–4–5 Method

The sides of a triangle with a right angle have a length ratio of 3:4:5. You can use this fact to quickly and easily lay out a right angle.

Draw a base line and mark an origin point on it. Attach a string that is 4 feet long at this point. Measure along the base line 3 feet from the origin point. Then attach a string that is 5 feet long at that spot. Now hold the ends of both strings together and move them back and forth until both are taut. The 4-foot string is now perpendicular to the base line. Mark its path.

MARKING A STARTING LINE

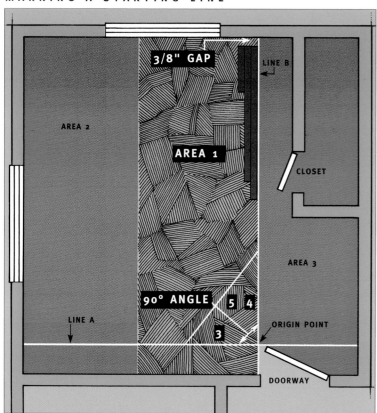

Use a chalk line to mark a starting line to keep the wood strips straight. The 3-4-5 method is used here to get line B at right angles to the doorway. Divide the work into sections of about 60 sq. ft. each. Leave the entry area for last.

CONCRETE FLOOR MOISTURE TEST

Moisture rising from damp concrete will cause flooring glue to fail and wood flooring strips to buckle. Because moisture penetration can be caused by damp ground, a high water table, or periodic heavy rains, most manufacturers won't guarantee their hardwood floors in basements or below ground level. New concrete or a concrete floor at ground level could also contain too much moisture. Here's how to test your floor.

Tape 2 foot x 2 foot squares of 6-mil plastic tightly to the concrete floor in three or four places. Stretch the tape along all four sides to completely seal the plastic. After 24 hours, lift the plastic. If the concrete surface is damp or has darkened, it is too damp for a glued floor.

If you're uncertain about the results of this test, hire a flooring contractor to check your concrete with an electronic moisture meter.

INSTALLING THE FLOORING

Once the subfloor is ready and you've marked a starting line, you can lay a new floor in a modest-sized room in one day. If you have not already done so, remove all doors and floor-mounted duct covers in the room. You'll cut the new flooring to go around the ducts and reinstall the covers later. If there are radiators, prop them up so you can fit the flooring under their legs. You can work in a series of areas, spreading glue and laying the strips in one area before proceeding to the next.

Spread the glue

The glue for your flooring is a specially formulated adhesive often called mastic. Read the label on the container and be sure to follow the directions printed there exactly.

Most mastics, once spread, take about an hour to "flash," that is, stiffen enough so the wood strips stick down. Then you have about two hours to lay the wood strips in the glue.

After that, any glue you haven't covered will harden, and you'll have to scrape it up—a tough job—before putting down more.

▲ If this is your first floor project, spread less than 60 square feet of glue at a time. Divide the room into areas of that size, and work so that you will end up laying flooring around the entrance door last.

▲ Your trowel should be smooth along one long and one short edge, and notched on the other edges. Starting from the guideline marked on the floor, spread the glue with the smooth side of the trowel. Then rake it with the notched side, holding the trowel at a 45-degree angle so that ridges form (Figure 5). The glue is sticky, so put some muscle into spreading it.

Lay the flooring

To install the strips of flooring, simply lay them into the mastic. Set each strip cleanly in place; do not slide it, because that will build up mastic on the tongue or in the groove along the edge,

which will prevent a tight joint when the adjacent piece is put into place. Keep mineral spirits and a cloth nearby so you can clean glue smears off the finished surface of the wood and off your hands as you work.

▲ Align the tongue edge of the first row of strips even with the guideline, pressing each strip into the glue (Figure 6). Leave a 3/8-inch gap at all of the walls to allow for floor expansion. When you reinstall the baseboard it will overhang this gap, hiding it from view.

▲ To lay the second row, insert the tongue of each piece into the groove of the first row, then lower it into the mastic.

The first row is likely to slide out of place when you interlock the second row of wood strips. If you're working over a wood floor, drive 3d finish nails into the tongues to hold the first row in place. Use a nail set for the last taps on the nail to avoid crushing the edge of the wood and to countersink the head so it won't interfere with the adjacent strip.

INSTALLING THE FLOORING

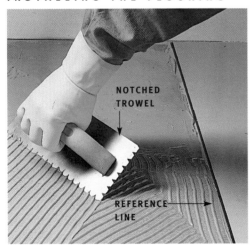

Figure 5. Hold the trowel at a 45-degree angle. Sweep on an even layer of glue with the smooth edge, then use the notched edge to make ridges. Keep the angle consistent for equal-size ridges.

Figure 6. Press the first row of strips into the glue with their tongues aligned with the guideline. Wear a mask for vapor protection both when spreading glue and when laying the flooring.

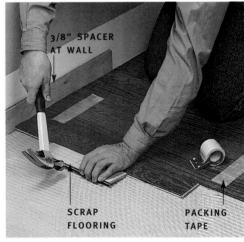

Figure 7. Fit tongues and grooves together tightly. Tap as shown if necessary; use packing tape to hold stubborn joints tight until the glue dries. Leave a 3/8-in. expansion gap at all walls.

If you're working over a concrete floor, you can't drive nails to stabilize the first row. Instead, hold it with your knees until two or three more rows have been added.

▲ Make sure the joints close tightly as you lay each row. If necessary, lay a scrap piece of flooring against the edge of a strip and tap it into place with a hammer (Figure 7). Hold difficult joints closed by driving 3d nails into the grooves of one piece, or use packing tape over the surface of the strips. Discard the occasional strip that isn't straight. It isn't worth the trouble of trying to force it into place. Some strips may bow upward. Don't worry if they won't stay down initially. After you complete the first glued area, press the strips firmly into the glue by stepping on each one. If they don't stay down, weight them with heavy books or other objects.

▲ Cut strips with a saber saw to fit around corners, into closets, and the like (Figure 8). Slide the strips under door frames and trim.

Work section by section, ending up at the entryway. Trim the transition piece to fit across the doorway and glue it in place; nail it also, if possible (Figure 9). Borrow or rent a power miter box with a sharp carbide-tipped blade to cut the strips square and make clean, tight joints with the transition strip. The diagrams at the right show the three most common kinds of transitions between different flooring.

When all the flooring has been laid, let the glue set for 24 hours, then reinstall the baseboard to cover the exposed edges of the floor.

Figure 8. Trim strips as necessary to fit around corners and built-in features; use a saber saw. Make long straight cuts with a circular saw. Slide strips beneath undercut door frames and trim.

Figure 9. Glue and nail a transition strip in place before laying flooring up to a doorway or archway. Butt the flooring into the transition strip. Use a power miter box for clean, accurate cuts.

TRANSITIONS TO OTHER TYPES OF FLOORS

Transition strips conceal the edge of the wood flooring and help it blend smoothly with other types of floor coverings. You can buy transition strips or make your own.

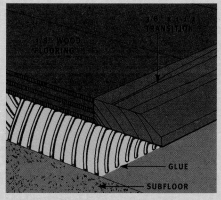

Full transition to lower level

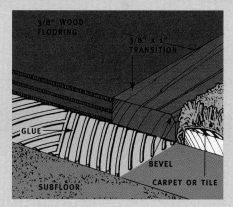

Transition to carpet or tile

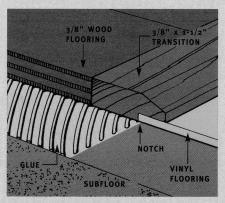

Transition to vinyl flooring

The entryway inside the front door is the first thing a visitor sees in your home. It also must bear the heaviest traffic.

Ceramic Tile Entryway

To lend your entryway a distinctive appearance and the highest possible durability, replace the existing floor with ceramic tile.

A tile floor is colorful and virtually maintenance-free.

Best of all, it's not difficult to install.

A ceramic tile entryway is visually striking, long lasting, and easy to clean. You can choose from a wide range of tile colors and shapes, and create a pattern that complements the style of your entry.

SELECTING AND BUYING ENTRYWAY TILE

When you choose tile for an entryway, there are two major considerations: physical characteristics and appearance.

Physical characteristics

The physical characteristics of tile are durability, size, surface, and material.

▲ Many tiles made for bathroom walls and floors won't stand up to the foot traffic and wear that entryway tiles receive. Tiles often have a wear rating listed either on the back or in the manufacturer's specification sheet; a tile rated "3" or greater is acceptable for entry floors.

▲ In general, square or hexagonal tiles 6 inches or 8 inches across will look better in an entryway than the 4-inch and smaller sizes often used in bathrooms and kitchens. They are also easier to lay and cover a given area faster.

▲ Tiles are available with unglazed or glazed surfaces. Unglazed tiles, often called quarry tiles, are not the best choice for an entryway. They must be sealed after installation to prevent them from absorbing moisture and dirt. To maintain this protection, the surface must be thoroughly cleaned and new sealant applied at least once and preferably twice a year.

By comparison, glazed tiles are virtually maintenance-free. However, a glossy surface can be slippery, and it will show every little scratch. It's better to select tiles with a matte or textured glaze surface.

▲ Tiles are also broadly classified as earthenware or porcelain, according to the kind of clay used and the temperature at which it was fired (baked). For an entryway, choose a true porcelain tile. It is colored all the way through, which makes scratches essentially invisible, and it is fired to a high temperature for maximum body strength and surface durability.

Appearance

Matters of color and layout pattern depend on your taste and the character of your home. The tile you select can make the entry feel formal or casual; it can set the tone for the entire house.

If your entryway is a true hallway, you may choose to lay a continuous pattern right up to the walls, without a border. If your entrance door opens directly into a large room, you may want to define an entry area by laying a field of tiles inside a contrasting border.

When you consider color, remember that tiles are laid with seams between them that are filled with grout. You can choose grout in a color that matches or harmonizes with the tile, or in a decidedly contrasting color. There are no rules to follow, but the following principles apply in most cases.

▲ Dark colors make a room look smaller, while light colors tend to open up a space and make it feel larger and brighter.

▲ Using dark-colored grout with light tiles—or light grout with dark tiles—tends to emphasize the geometry of the individual tiles rather than their pattern or arrangement.

▲ Laying tile in a simple pattern, such as alternating light and dark squares, can add visual interest with little extra work or expense.

Purchasing tile

To evaluate various possibilities, sketch layouts on graph paper—one square per tile. Use colored pencils to help you visualize the possibilities. When you have decided on a layout, you can use the graph-paper plan to count the number of tiles of each type you need, if you are buying tiles by the piece rather than by the box.

If you are buying tiles by the square foot or in boxes (so many square feet per box), figure the total area by measuring the floor:

Length x Width = Area in square feet.

When you buy the tile, also buy thin-set adhesive. It is available in both powdered and premixed forms; get the type the tile dealer recommends. Be sure to explain that you will be putting down a cement board underlayment for the tile (see next page).

You'll need two more items from the tile dealer—grout, the material that fills the seams, and grout sealer. Grout is available in powdered and premixed forms. However, premixed grout comes in a limited number of colors; you may need a powdered grout to get the color you want.

Tools and Materials You Need

Pry bar

Hammer

Fine-tooth saw

Tape measure

Carpenter's square

Chalk line

Utility knife with scoring blades

Metal straightedge

Notched trowel

Rubber grout float

Tile cutter

Tile nipper

Rubber mallet

Small brush

Sponges

Cement backer board

Thin-set adhesive

Fiberglass mesh tape

Tile

Grout

Grout sealer

PREPARING A BASE

Your tile floor will be only as solid as the surface beneath it. The best do-it-yourself choice for a tile base is a double layer—wood subfloor topped with cement backer board as underlayment for the tile—with a total thickness of 1-1/8 inches or more. Your goal is to provide a floor sturdy and thick enough to support the tile under heavy use, yet thin enough so it doesn't stand taller than the adjacent coverings. The box below, Tile Installations, shows how to deal with a good subfloor and a poor subfloor.

Think ahead as you prepare the base for the tile. The final thickness, including the tile, should maintain the height of the existing entryway floor. Any great increase in floor height can make the first step of an adjoining stairway too low for convenience or safety.

Also consider the door. If the threshold of the exterior door needs to be raised to accommodate the tile, the door must be shortened or raised. You'll need to do that before laying the tile permanently in place.

Dealing with the subfloor

Depending on the age of your house, the floor is constructed in either two layers or just one. Pull up the rug or other existing floor covering and investigate. You'll have to remove any interior doors and the baseboard to do any work, so you might as well do that now also. Remove the baseboard carefully so you can reinstall it later. Use a block of scrap wood to protect the wall from damage by your pry bar.

A two-layer floor will contain plywood, particleboard, or planks, both layers the same or in some combination. If you have a two-layer floor, remove the uppermost layer (Figure 1) and replace it with cement backer board. The old underlayment was most likely secured in place after the interior walls were built, so pulling it up rarely involves major problems.

A single-layer floor may be made of boards or tongue-and-groove plywood 5/8 inch or 3/4 inch thick. If the floor is in good condition, fasten the cement board directly to it. If it is in poor condition, cover it with 1/4-inch thick plywood panels secured by construction adhesive. Then put cement board over the plywood.

You cannot get a good tile installation if the subfloor is bouncy, or if it is slanted or has significant variations in level. A bouncy floor can be beefed up by nailing additional joists alongside the existing ones, provided you have access to the joists from below. A slanted or uneven floor can be leveled by laying a mortar bed. You'll need to hire a professional to do that.

Putting down underlayment

Tile experts recommend using cement backer board rather than plywood for underlayment. Plywood can expand and contract with the seasons and will delaminate when wet. Cement board costs twice as much as plywood but is stable and provides a superior bonding surface. It is widely available in easy-to-manage 4- x 4-foot or 3- x 5-foot sheets in three thicknesses. Choose the thickness you need as follows.

▲ Use 1/2-inch cement board over a sound 5/8-inch-thick subfloor, and 5/16-inch board over a sound 3/4-inch floor. If you covered the subfloor with 1/4-inch plywood, use 7/16-inch cement board over that.

▲ Cut and place the sheets of cement board over the subfloor (Figure 2), making sure the seams don't line up with any below. Leave a 1/8-inch gap between the edges of the boards. Stagger the joints so that four corners of the cement board do not come together at the same point. To cut cement board, use a utility knife with a special scoring blade; an ordinary cutting blade will not do the job. Score the board along a straightedge, then snap the pieces apart. You can cut the board with a circular saw and carbide blade but this raises a whirlwind of dust.

TILE INSTALLATIONS

The condition of your subfloor will dictate how to prepare the base for your tile installation.

Solid subfloor: Lay cement board directly on the subfloor as underlayment for the tile (Figure A).

Subfloor in poor condition: Put down 1/4-in. plywood before laying cement backer board (Figure B).

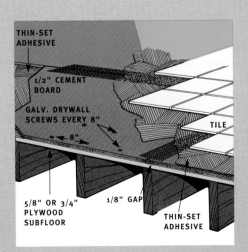

Figure A

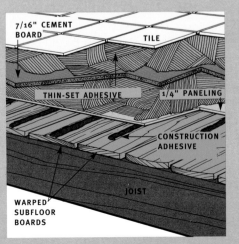

Figure B

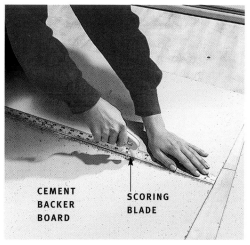

Figure 1. Pull up existing underlayment after removing interior doors and baseboard moldings. Old underlayment can be cut into smaller pieces with a circular saw for easy removal.

Figure 2. Cut and fit cement backer board over the subfloor. Score cement board with a utility knife, then snap along the line. Lay all sheets with a 1/8-in. gap between them.

Figure 3. Mix thin-set adhesive by adding powder to water while stirring continuously. When well mixed, let it sit for a few minutes before use so the powder can thoroughly absorb the liquid.

▲ When the cement board has been placed, mix up thin-set adhesive with water as specified on the package (Figure 3). Let the mixture sit for a few minutes so the powder can thoroughly absorb the liquid. Then lift the cement board, one piece at a time, spread thin-set adhesive with a notched trowel (Figure 4), and set the board back in place. Secure it with galvanized threaded nails or drywall screws. Be sure to maintain the 1/8-inch gap between boards. The thin-set will help bond the cement board to the subfloor, and will fill and span small dips in the floor.

▲ Finally, fill each seam with thin-set adhesive, and spread a 4- to 6-inch wide line of adhesive along the surface. Press fiberglass mesh tape into the adhesive across the seam and smooth a second layer of adhesive over it (Figure 5). This treatment will bond the pieces of cement backer board into one piece.

Figure 4. Spread adhesive on the subfloor with a 1/4-in. notched trowel and lay precut cement board on it. Secure the cement board every 8 in. with galvanized screws or threaded nails.

Figure 5. Bond cement board sheets to one another by filling seams with thin-set adhesive, then covering with special fiberglass mesh tape. Finish by smoothing on a second layer of adhesive.

MARKING GUIDELINES AND CUTTING TRIM

You will need guidelines to keep the tiles straight and equally spaced. And you need to undercut trim for tile to fit around doorways.

Make a trial layout

Begin by roughly laying out loose tiles across the area in both directions to determine the best placement (Figure 6). Space the tiles according to the manufacturer's instructions, or choose a spacing that is visually pleasing within practical limits: A 1/8-inch seam in floor tile is too narrow to grout uniformly; grout may work out of seams wider than 1/2 inch. Rarely will an area lay out with full tiles in every direction. Strive for full, or nearly full, tiles along the most noticeable walls and corners, and where the tile abuts thresholds and other floor surfaces. Small pieces look skimpy and are more likely to crack. You can't avoid them completely, but you can try to minimize them.

Mark a guideline grid

When you have a suitable layout, snap a pair of chalk lines perpendicular to each other (Figure 7). Check with a carpenter's square to make sure they cross at a 90-degree angle. Use these lines as reference points to mark the rest of the floor with a grid of lines spaced about 2 feet apart. These 2-foot squares are optimum-size areas to tile one at a time.

Adapt the grid spacing to the size of your tiles and grout joints. For example, the tiles shown in the photos were 7-3/4 inches square. A grout space of 1/4 inch gave a unit size of 8 inches. A grid of chalk lines every 24 inches accommodated three tiles and three grout lines each way, or a total of nine tiles per square.

Undercut the trim

As a final step, cut off door trim so the tile can slide beneath it (Figure 8). Lay a fine-tooth saw flat on a piece of tile to cut off the trim at the right height for a tile to slip under.

LAYING THE TILE

Mix a small amount of thin-set adhesive initially, so you can work slowly without fear that it will harden before use. Place a small blob of adhesive in a grid section. Distribute it evenly with the smooth side of the trowel, then comb it with the notched side held at a 45-degree angle or greater (Figure 9).

⚠ Lay the first tile at the corner where two guidelines intersect. Continue placing the others, keeping the proper spacing between tiles (Figure 10). Use a small plastic spacer or a thin piece of wood for consistency. Set each tile down with a slight twisting motion, then tap it with a rubber mallet to ensure full contact with the adhesive. Work one grid at a time and make minor adjustments as you go. Remove adhesive that oozes up between tiles.

Use a long, straight board to check that the rows are running straight. Cut and install partial tiles. Straight cuts are most easily made with a tile cutter, which you can rent. Don't try to use a saw or improvise with a glass cutter.

Mark the tile with a pencil, position it in the cutter, and lift up on the handle of the cutting arm to bring the cutter wheel in contact with the surface of the tile. Pull the handle toward you, applying just enough pressure to lightly score the tile. Don't try to cut through the tile, just make a nice even line.

Next, move the arm to about the center of the tile and push down on it to snap the tile apart along the scored line.

Use a tile nipper to make irregular cuts to fit around pipes or other obstructions. The nipper has two sharp jaws, like an end-cutting nail cutter. Mark the shape on the surface of the tile and nibble away little bits at a time, working up to the mark. You cannot take large bites without danger of cracking the tile. If you have a great many irregular cuts, mark the tiles and take them to a tile shop that offers on-site cutting.

MARKING GUIDELINES AND CUTTING TRIM

Figure 6. Lay out loose tiles in both directions on floor, with spaces for grout lines. Adjust the layout to avoid having to cut small tiles, especially along prominent walls and at doorways.

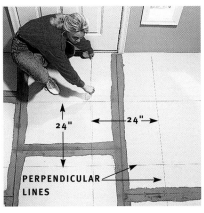

Figure 7. Snap perpendicular lines along the trial-laid tiles. Then mark a grid based on those lines. Make the grid sections about 24 in. square, depending on your tile size, for easy working areas.

Figure 8. Undercut door trim so tile will be able to slide beneath it. Make the horizontal cut with a fine-tooth saw resting on a piece of tile. The tile acts as a support and a thickness guide.

Figure 9. Spread adhesive for the tile first with the flat side of the trowel, then with the notched side. Work in one grid section at a time, taking care not to cover the chalk guidelines.

Figure 10. Position the tiles, setting each one with a slight twisting motion. Tap with a rubber mallet to set the tile firmly in the adhesive. Use a plastic or wood spacer to get equal gaps between tiles.

HOW TO CUT TILE

STRAIGHT CUTS

Use a tile cutter for clean, easy cuts. Position the marked tile with the cutter wheel at the far edge. Lift up on the handle and pull it toward you, scoring the surface (Figure A). A single, firm stroke is sufficient.

Complete the cut by positioning the cutter arm about halfway along the face of the tile. Press down firmly on the handle to snap the two pieces apart along the scored line (Figure B).

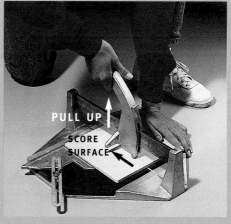

Figure A

Figure B

IRREGULAR CUTS

Use a tile nipper for irregular cuts. Rest the tile on your knee or some other support for stability and nibble away in small 1/4-inch bites (Figure C). Taking too big a bite will crack the tile.

Make nipper cuts to fit tiles around doorways, pipes, built-in features, and other obstructions (Figure D). For difficult shapes, cut a cardboard template and use that to mark the tile.

Figure C

Figure D

GROUTING TILE JOINTS

The package for your thin-set adhesive should tell when you can begin grouting—usually 24 to 48 hours after the tile has been laid. If you use a powdered grout, use a latex additive in place of the water. The latex will help accentuate the grout's color, make it more water resistant, and allow for movement of the tile.

▲ Mix grout properly. The biggest error is to mix the grout to the wrong consistency. Too soupy and the grout can shrink as the water evaporates. Too thick and it's difficult to work into the seams. Mix it about the consistency of toothpaste (Figure 11). Start with a small batch until you get a feel for the proper mix.

▲ To apply the grout, place a small blob in one corner and spread it over the surface of the tiles. Use a rubber grout float held at a fairly low angle (Figure 12). Pack the grout firmly into the joints. When the grout begins to firm up—5 to 10 minutes after application—run the float diagonally across the tile at a steep angle to remove the excess (Figure 13). Complete all these steps in one 5 x 5-foot area before moving on to the next area.

▲ Give the tiles a final cleaning while the grout is soft enough to be washed from the surface of the tiles, yet firm enough not to be pulled out of the joints. This could be anywhere from 10 minutes to an hour, depending on the temperature and humidity in your room, as well as the additives in the grout. Use cool, clear water and a sponge (Figure 14). Rinse and wring out the sponge frequently. If grout has hardened on the face of the tiles, use a nonmetallic scouring pad to loosen it. You'll need to wash the tiles at least twice, until only a light haze remains.

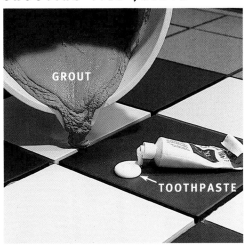

Figure 11. Mix grout to the consistency of toothpaste. A too-watery mix will shrink and crack; a too-thick mix will be difficult to spread and work firmly into the joints, and hard to clean up.

Figure 12. Push grout into the joints with a rubber float. Hold the float at a low angle to spread the grout along the joint lines. Pack the grout firmly to avoid hollow spaces below the surface.

Figure 13. Remove excess grout from the surface of the tiles by pulling the rubber float at a steep angle toward you. Work diagonally across the tiles so grout isn't scraped out of the joints.

Figure 14. Clean off grout by washing the tile with plain water. Wring out the sponge thoroughly and often. Repeat until only a light haze remains on the face of the tile, then buff with a coarse cloth.

▲ Buff the surface of the tiles with a coarse, dry cloth to remove any haze. If you waited too long, use a "grout haze remover," which is available from your tile dealer.

▲ When the grout is dry, protect it and un-glazed tile from dirt and stains by coating them with a sealant. Water-based sealers can be applied 24 hours after grouting; silicone-based sealers can't be applied until the grout has fully cured—usually two to three weeks. Check the grout and sealer instructions. Paint the sealer onto the grout with a narrow brush (Figure 15). If you get any sealer on the face of the tiles wipe it off before it can dry.

▲ When the grout has been sealed, reinstall the baseboard and add a piece of shoe or quarter-round molding to cover any gaps where the baseboard and tile meet.

Figure 15. Seal and protect grout lines with a penetrating sealer. With glazed tiles, use a small brush to seal the grout lines only. Wipe any excess from the face of the tiles immediately.

MAKING TRANSITIONS

As a final step, install threshold or transition pieces where the tile meets another kind of flooring. This will protect the tile edge and will prevent tripping if there is any difference in the levels of the two floors.

Typical transitions are shown here. You can buy metal transition strips and wood, synthetic marble, or synthetic stone thresholds. You can also make a wood threshold from matching hardwood.

Nail a metal strip into the adjacent wood flooring. Set a synthetic threshold piece in adhesive, and caulk the seam with the adjacent flooring; grout applied there would crack. Nail a wood threshold in place. Carpet can be trimmed with metal edging, but turning the edge under presents a much better appearance.

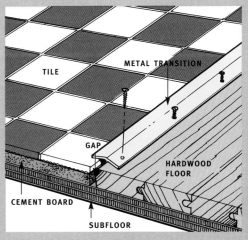

Transition to wood floor

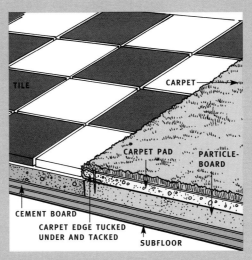

Transition to carpet

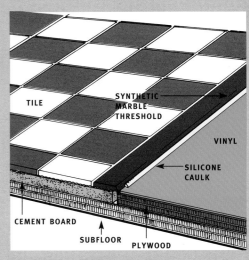

Transition to vinyl flooring

Ceilings

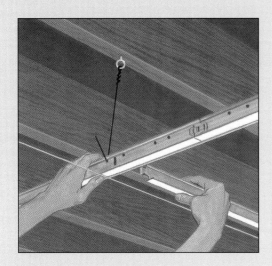

Hang a Suspended Ceiling

A suspended ceiling has large acoustical panels laid in a lightweight grid. It can hide pipes, wires, and a drab old ceiling.

122

Painted Wood Ceiling

Wood ceilings—a heritage from colonial times—fit well in many modern rooms. You can paint them to match any decor.

126

Making Crown Molding Fit

Few improvements enhance a room as impressively as crown molding. Here are professional techniques for installing it.

133

Hang a Suspended Ceiling

Need a new ceiling? Want a finished ceiling in a basement or attic room? There's no faster or easier answer than a suspended ceiling.

The components are all standard sizes, no carpentry is required, and nothing is more economical.

If you can draw a line with a level, bend wire with pliers, use metal snips to cut aluminum strips, and hammer a nail, you can hang a suspended ceiling.

Here's how.

CEILING CONSTRUCTION

A suspended ceiling is both simple and ingenious, consisting of a gridwork of thin metal strips hung on wires, with lightweight, sound-absorbing panels that fit neatly into the grid.

The gridwork strips are shaped like an upside down T. Main tees run the length of the room; they are supplied in 12-foot lengths and you cut them to fit. Cross tees run at right angles to the main tees and fit into slots in them. They are supplied in 4-foot lengths; you use them full length in the center of the ceiling, and cut them to size for partial-width border panels around the perimeter of the room.

The grid structure hangs on short wires fastened to the joists above. At the walls, the ends of all tees are supported by a continuous L-shaped molding nailed in place. The lightweight ceiling panels drop into place in each section. Their edges are supported by the lips of the upside-down tees.

The instructions here show you how to install a basic ceiling. You can hang it from exposed joists, or below the surface of an existing ceiling. If you have ductwork or windows to work around, or want to include lighting fixtures, ask your ceiling supplier for information about how to deal with those elements.

LAYING OUT THE CEILING

Measure the room length and make a scale drawing of your ceiling on graph paper. Lay out the arrangement of panels that best fits the room, and figure out the width of the border panels around the edges of the room. Adjust the arrangement to get equal-size borders on opposite sides of the room.

INSTALLING WALL MOLDING

A suspended ceiling should have at least 3 inches clearance above it, or 6 inches if any light fixtures are to be included. So find the lowest point of your ceiling—whether joist, pipe, or duct—and measure down 3 (or 6) inches from that height along the nearest wall (Figure 1). Using a 4- or 6-foot level (or a water level; see Water Levels, page 123), continue this line around the room (Figure 2).

Use a stud finder to locate the studs or furring strips behind the walls, and mark their positions on the walls just above the level line. Mark both edges of the studs to guide you in joining molding pieces.

Strips of wall molding must meet over a stud, so cut the first piece to start at a corner and end in the middle of a stud. Use metal snips or a hacksaw to cut it. Nail the molding in place using one nail per stud. Keep the top edge level with the line on the wall (Figure 3). Continue all the way around the room. Overlap the molding ends at inside corners. At an outside corner cut a slit in the bottom flange and bend the molding to fit around the corner.

Figure 1. Mark the height of the ceiling at least 3 in. below any pipe, duct, or joist. Leave 6 in. clearance if there will be light fixtures in the ceiling.

Figure 2. Continue the ceiling line around the room. Use a level to keep it straight and level. Then locate and mark the wall stud positions.

Figure 3. Nail wall molding with its top edge aligned with the level line. Use one nail per stud. Join pieces only over a stud.

Tools You Need

Measuring tape

4' or 6' level

Framing square

Hammer

Metal snips or hacksaw

Stud finder

Wire-cutting pliers

Drill

Utility knife

Stepladder

PUTTING UP GUIDE STRINGS

Refer to your scale drawing to stretch strings where the inside edges of the border panels fall across the width and along the length of the room. Tie one end of the string to a finishing nail and slip it under the wall molding (Figure 4). Fasten the other end in the same way at the opposite wall.

Now stretch strings in the same way spaced every 4 feet both ways, to mark where the edges of the full-size panels will go. Use a framing square to adjust the strings so they cross at right angles at each point. These strings will help you locate the border tees and keep the gridwork level.

PUTTING UP GUIDE STRINGS

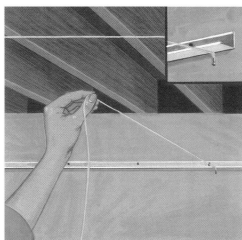

Figure 4. Stretch guide strings across the room where the main and cross tees will run. Pull them tight and get them square to each other. Use the strings to align the grid.

WATER LEVELS

The easiest way to mark a level line around a room is with a water level—a long piece of clear hose, open at the ends and filled almost completely with water.

Mark a starting point on the wall and have a helper hold one end of the level so the water is aligned with the mark. Carry the other end to each corner of the room, hold it in position, and mark the wall at the water height. Then snap the chalk lines between the corner marks.

Hanging Tip

You can use ordinary screw eyes to anchor the wires, but for faster, easier work buy acoustical ceiling lag bolts from a ceiling supplier. They have eyes for the wires and heads that can be driven by an electric drill.

HANGING THE GRIDWORK

Hang the gridwork of tees as shown in Figures 5 through 11. Do the main tees first. Be sure to cut them so that the slots for the cross tees are in the right position (Figures 5, 6).

Drive screw eyes into the joists above to hold wires for hanging the tees. If you are working below an existing ceiling, use a stud finder to locate the joists. Space the screw eyes no more than 4 feet apart. Insert a wire in a screw eye and wrap it around itself three times (Figure 7). Insert the other end of the wire into a hole in the tee and bend it into a V to hold the tee at the right level (Figure 8).

Hang all the main tees, joining them as you go. The ends snap or butt together, depending on the design. Then put the full-length cross tees in place; their ends snap into slots in the main tees (Figure 9). Do not add the border cross tees at this time.

Check the gridwork and adjust the hanging wires so that all the tees are level. Then wrap the lower ends of the wires around the hanging portions (Figure 10).

Now put up the cross tees for the border panels. Hold each one in place, mark it for length, and cut it. Instead of marking the tee with a pencil, you can make a light cut with metal snips, for less chance of error (Figure 11).

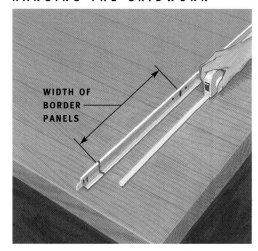

Figure 5. Cut each main tee so a slot to hold the first cross tees is properly located, the width of a border panel from the end.

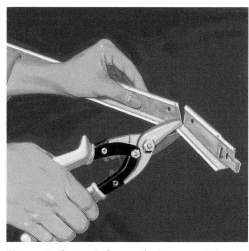

Figure 6. Cut each flange of a tee separately. Snips are fastest, but a hacksaw is also suitable. Watch out for the cut edges—they're sharp.

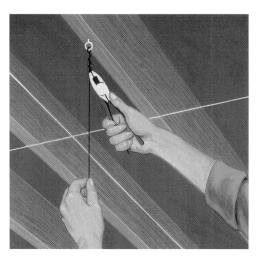

Figure 7. Attach hanging wires to screw eyes spaced no more than 4 ft. apart, by building code. Wrap the wire around itself three or more times.

Figure 8. Hold a tee in position and insert the wire at the top of a hole; use the guide string to set the height. Bend the wire up, but don't wrap it yet.

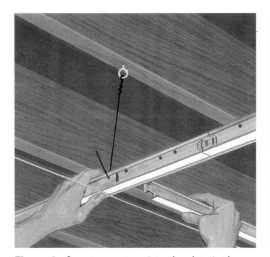

Figure 9. Insert cross tees into the slots in the main tees. The guide strings will show you where the cross tees should be placed.

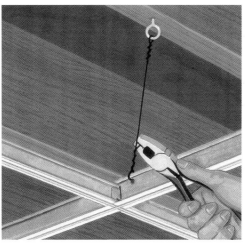

Figure 10. Wrap the hanging wires after the gridwork is up. Make adjustments to get things level before wrapping each wire.

Figure 11. Cut the border cross tees to length after the grid has been leveled. Hold each tee in place to mark it for an exact fit.

Handling Tip

Wash your hands before handling the panels to keep the pieces clean. For even more protection, dust your hands with cornstarch. Remove minor smudges with an art gum eraser.

INSTALLING THE PANELS

The border panels must be cut to size. Measure the spaces and cut the panels individually. Use a sharp utility knife, and a scrap of main tee for a straightedge (Figure 12). To put a panel in place, lift it up through the grid opening at an angle, then lower it so that its edges rest on the lips of the tees.

After all the border panels are in place, install the full-size panels to fill in and complete the ceiling (Figure 13).

INSTALLING THE PANELS

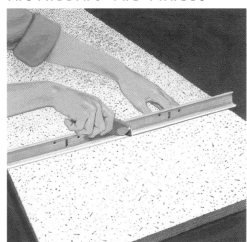

Figure 12. Cut border panels with a utility knife. A scrap piece of main tee makes a good straightedge. Be sure your hands are clean.

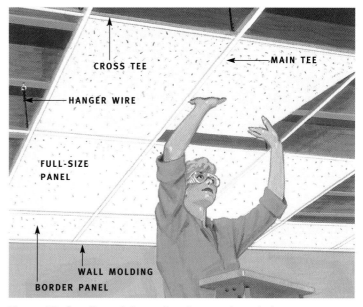

CROSS TEE

MAIN TEE

HANGER WIRE

FULL-SIZE PANEL

WALL MOLDING

BORDER PANEL

Figure 13. Install panels by angling them up through the grid and lowering them into place. Do the border panels first, then the full-size panels.

Wood ceilings were traditional long before plaster or drywall.

Painted Wood Ceiling

In a modern house, a painted wood ceiling can add color and completely change the feeling of a kitchen, family room, or bedroom.

Putting up a wood ceiling like the one shown here requires careful attention to detail, but does not involve any tricky carpentry skills. Even a beginner can do the job in a couple of weekends, with beautiful results.

A painted wood ceiling can give a room a unique appearance. Boards with V-groove edges subtly emphasize a room's length or width, depending on which way they run. Painting the ceiling lighter than the walls gives an impression of greater height.

CHOOSING WOOD FOR A CEILING

The ceiling in this project is built of 1x6 solid wood paneling with tongue-and-groove edges milled to form V joints that emphasize the parallel pattern of the installation. The wood is clear (knot-free) fir. Clear boards cost more than lower, knottier grades, but require far less time to fill, sand, and seal for a perfect paint job.

When you select wood for your ceiling, be sure it is kiln-dried and has been stored indoors, out of the rain. Putting up damp or high-moisture-content wood will only lead to shrinkage and finish problems as the wood dries to interior humidity conditions.

Try to buy boards long enough to span the ceiling, so you won't have to make splices. If the grade of wood you want does not have V grooves at the joints, you can have the edges milled to your specifications for an extra charge—probably $50 to $100.

PREPARING THE WOOD

A smooth, painted surface on wood is just about the most difficult finish to achieve. Proper preparation of the wood is essential.

▲ When the wood for your ceiling is delivered, stack it inside, so it can adjust to the indoor humidity. Separate the boards with spacers to allow the air to circulate (Figure 1). This preconditioning will take about a week; if the indoor humidity is very high—that is, above 70 percent—delay further preparation until the humidity drops.

▲ Prepare the surface of the wood on the side that will show. Fill all gaps and cracks with a nonshrinking wood filler and sand the entire side with 100-grit paper (Figure 2). Sand each board even though it may seem smooth as it comes from the lumberyard. Any slight indentations left from the planing process will show up clearly as ripples under paint or a clear finish unless they're sanded off.

▲ After sanding, vacuum the dust away and wipe the wood clean with a tack cloth. Then brush on a coat of solvent-base primer. When that is dry, follow up with a thin coat of paint. A glossy-surface enamel will create too much glaring surface reflection when dry. You will like the sheen of a semigloss surface much more. You can use either an alkyd (solvent-base) or latex (water-base) paint.

▲ To make painting the first two coats easy, lay out the boards on sawhorses. Because you're almost sure to scuff the surfaces somewhat when you put up the boards, you'll apply a final coat after you finish the installation.

▲ Be sure to paint the tongue of each ceiling board (Figure 3). The boards will contract and separate slightly during periods of very low humidity. The exposed tongues will be much less noticeable if they're painted.

▲ Prepaint the trim boards or molding with a primer and first finish coat also.

Materials You Need

1x6 clear fir or pine tongue-and-groove paneling

Shims

1x2 furring strips, if needed

Wood filler

100- and 120-grit sandpaper

10d finish nails

Drywall screws for furring

Primer

Semigloss finish paint

PREPARING THE WOOD

Figure 1. Stack the ceiling boards, separated with spacers, to let them adjust to indoor humidity. Give them about a week.

Figure 2. Fill all voids, cracks, and knot holes with wood filler. Sand smooth with a sanding block or an orbital finish sander.

Figure 3. Paint the visible side with a coat of primer, then add a thin coat of paint. Be sure to paint the tongue, too.

MARKING OUT THE PROJECT

To make the work go smoothly, first you'll need to mark the existing joist positions and places where shims may be needed. Then mark a gridline for the first board.

Mark joist positions

For the least amount of mess, use an inexpensive electronic stud finder to locate the joists above the existing ceiling. If you don't have a stud finder, use a drill to make probe holes, or drive 16d nails through the ceiling until you hit solid ceiling joists. Since you will be covering the ceiling, these holes won't matter.

When you have located two adjacent joists, measure the spacing between them. In most houses, the ceiling joists are spaced 16 inches on center. If that is the case, you can easily measure and make additional marks every 16 inches. Be sure that you are marking the centers of the joists, not the outside edges, so nails will not miss them. Make a series of accurately positioned marks on the ceiling along one side of the room, and then along the opposite side of the room. Snap a chalk line on the ceiling between each pair of marks (Figure 4).

Mark shim positions

Each time you pull the chalk line taut, before you snap it, take a moment to identify any places where the ceiling surface does not touch the string. You may need to insert shims at these points to keep the ceiling boards level. Have a helper mark these spots now, to guide you later. The helper can either move a stepladder around, or use a pencil or a piece of chalk that has been taped to a long stick or handle to reach the ceiling.

If the existing ceiling surface is quite irregular—say with dips of 3/4 inch or more—or if you want the new ceiling boards to run parallel to the joists instead of across them at right angles, put up 1x2 furring strips (see box, The Furring Strip Method). Then nail the ceiling boards to them.

THE FURRING STRIP METHOD

If you want to run paneling in the same direction as the joists, you'll have to install 1x2 furring strips at right angles to the joists (Figure A). Screw them into the ceiling at 16-inch intervals.

You can level and flatten an irregular ceiling with this system, too. Simply shove shims (available from home centers) or other wood spacers under low spots to eliminate the dips and waves and bring all the furring strips to the same level (Figure B). To flatten a severely sagging ceiling, you can shim furring strips an inch or more, if necessary.

Use screws long enough to pass through the furring strip, shim, and drywall, and penetrate into the joists at least 3/4 inch.

Check frequently for a uniform surface by laying a 6-foot or longer straightedge across several adjacent furring strips, as well as along the individual strips. You can also stretch a string taut to check for surface evenness.

Figure A. Install furring strips

Figure B. Insert shims

MARKING GUIDELINES

Figure 4. Mark the ceiling joist locations with chalk lines. Use an electronic stud finder to help you locate the studs.

Mark the first board guideline

Whichever way the new ceiling boards will run (across or parallel with the joists), identify the side wall that the grooved edge of the first board will lie against. Measure out from that wall the width of one ceiling board at each end and mark the ceiling at those points.

Snap a chalk line between the two marks. Then measure the distance from this line to the wall at several points. If the distance is less than a full board width in some places, snap a new guideline farther from the wall—probably no more than 1/4 inch—so that the first board will fit without trimming. Don't worry about the small gaps this will create at other points; they will be covered with trim molding. Do take care, however, to make this starting guideline parallel to the side wall, because it establishes how all the joints in the ceiling will run.

PREPARING FOR LIGHTING

If you plan to use the existing ceiling lighting, turn off the circuit at the breaker box or fuse panel. Disconnect and remove any hanging fixtures; make a diagram of all wiring connections as a guide for putting the fixture up after the ceiling is finished. Get a 3/4-inch extension collar for each ceiling box and attach it, so the box will extend down to the surface of the new ceiling.

If you have existing recessed lights, you may be able to adjust the cylinder or "can" portion of each fixture to the new depth without cutting into the ceiling. If not, cut an access hole and lower the entire fixture the required amount. The hole will be covered by the new ceiling. Work with the power turned off, of course.

You may want to take the opportunity to replace the existing lighting with new recessed fixtures. If so, follow the instructions in the box Providing Ceiling Lighting, at right.

If you have some experience with wiring lighting fixtures, you can proceed as described here. If you do not have experience, read the material here and follow the instructions in the article Recessed Lights, on pages 160–167.

Knock holes in the ceiling with your hammer at fixture locations, then cut the required opening to size (Figure A). Turn off the power to the room at the main panel while you work—wires to wall outlets and switches commonly run through ceiling space, as well as wiring to ceiling light fixtures.

Break other holes to provide access for running the wires to the new fixture locations. The new ceiling will conceal these access holes. When the wires have been run, connect the fixtures and mount them to the joists with screws, not nails (Figure B). A properly installed recessed fixture is shown in Figure C.

Keep these four guidelines in mind when you install recessed fixtures and choose the trim that fits over them:

1. Buy thermally protected fixtures that are able to dissipate heat. This feature should be written on the can (the cylindrical portion of the fixture).

2. Follow the instructions on the label inside the can that lists maximum bulb size and type and the appropriate finish trim pieces permitted (Figure C). Don't buy a fixture unless it contains this label.

3. Maintain a 1/2-inch minimum clearance between the fixture and anything that is combustible, especially where the wooden ceiling surrounds the can.

4. Never insulate around or above a fixture unless it's labeled "UL Listed" or is "CSA" approved for Canada and "Suitable for direct contact with thermal insulation" or "I.C.T."

Figure A. Break holes in the ceiling to check for existing wires. With the power off, saw cutouts and run wires for recessed lights.

Figure B. Screw the recessed fixtures to the joists after connecting the new wires to them. Use only thermally protected fixtures.

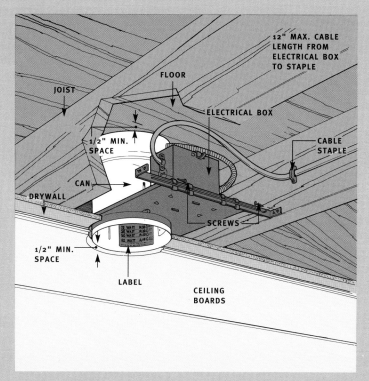

Figure C. Typical proper installation of a recessed lighting fixture.

Stepladder Safety

■ Be sure the ladder is fully opened and all four feet are flat on the floor before climbing it.

■ Never stand higher than on the second step from the top of the ladder.

■ Never rest a foot on the fold-down shelf.

■ Do not reach out to the side so far that your hip is outside the line of the ladder. It takes only a moment to get down and move the ladder to a position where you can reach the work safely and easily.

■ Before moving a ladder, make sure there are no tools on the steps or shelf. A falling tool can damage the floor, or your foot.

PUTTING UP THE CEILING

The ceiling boards are secured by angle-nailing through the tongues, a technique called blind-nailing (see Blind-Nailing, below). The first and last boards are also face-nailed at the edges that will be covered by the trim molding. Use finish nails long enough to pass through the boards and ceiling and penetrate the joists or furring strips 3/4 inch or more. To fasten 1x6 panels through a 1/2-inch thick drywall ceiling, use 10d nails for blind-nailing and 8d nails for face-nailing.

Nail the first board

You'll need a helper to hold the long boards in position as you put them up. Since you will both be standing on stepladders—be careful.

▲ Lift the first board into position and align its tongue exactly with the starting guideline on the ceiling (Figure 5). Drill small holes through the face of the board along the edge nearest the wall—the grooved edge—and drive an 8d nail straight up into each joist or furring strip to secure this edge (Figure 6).

▲ To fasten the front edge of the board, pre-drill an angled hole in the tongue at each joist (Figure 7) and drive in a 10d nail. Hammer the nail until about 1/2 inch is protruding, then use a nail set to drive it the rest of the way (Figure 8), to avoid damaging the edge of the board. Set the nailhead just below the surface. Face-nail boards in the same way.

Put up the remaining boards

After the first board is in place, simply slip the next board in position with its groove fitting over the tongue of the first board. Make sure it fits snugly, then drill holes in the tongue and blind-nail it at each joist. Do not drive any nails through the face of the board.

▲ Put up each succeeding board in the same way (Figure 9). Some boards will be slightly warped, of course, and difficult to fit snugly. Force them into place with a hammer and a scrap block of tongue-and-groove material (Figure 10). The block protects the tongue of the workpiece from being smashed or dented. If you do accidentally damage the tongue, cut away the broken edges with a utility knife, so the next piece will fit over it easily.

▲ If a hammer and block won't close the gap, you can increase the pressure by temporarily screwing a scrap block to two joists and prying against it with a pry bar (Figure 11). Maintain the pressure on the 1x6 panel while you nail it.

▲ When you reach the other side of the ceiling, you must cut the last board to fit. Measure the required width, set it on sawhorses, and cut it lengthwise with your power saw. Trim off the tongue edge, so you get a board with a groove to mate with the next to last board already in place. The cut doesn't have to be precise; you'll cover the edge when you put up the trim. Put the trimmed board in position and face-nail it along the edge next to the wall.

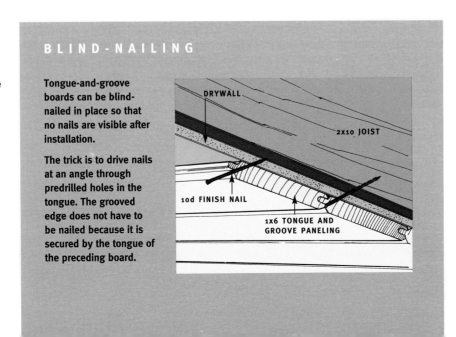

BLIND-NAILING

Tongue-and-groove boards can be blind-nailed in place so that no nails are visible after installation.

The trick is to drive nails at an angle through predrilled holes in the tongue. The grooved edge does not have to be nailed because it is secured by the tongue of the preceding board.

DRYWALL

2X10 JOIST

10d FINISH NAIL

1x6 TONGUE AND GROOVE PANELING

Figure 5. Align the first board with a chalk line snapped 5-1/2 in. from the wall to make sure you nail it up perfectly straight.

Figure 6. Drive 8d finish nails through the face of the first board near the wall. They will be covered by the trim.

Figure 7. Predrill holes to blind-nail the tongue of the first board. Do the same in all subsequent boards.

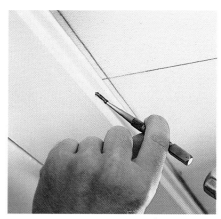

Figure 8. Blind-nail with 10d finish nails. Use a nail set to drive the last 1/2 in. and sink the head just below the surface.

Figure 9. Slide the groove of each new board over the tongue of the previous one. Blind-nail it through the tongue only.

Figure 10. Tap against a scrap block of material to close gaps between panels before you nail them.

Figure 11. Force a warped board into place with a pry bar wedged against a board temporarily screwed to the joists.

DEALING WITH SPLICES AND LIGHT FIXTURES

If your room is especially large, you may not be able to buy single boards long enough to span the ceiling. In that case, you must make splices. Be sure to space them randomly.

To make a splice, cut the ends of the two pieces perfectly square and simply butt them together. The tongue of the board behind them and the groove of the next board will keep the splice locked in place and aligned.

Wherever boards must fit around light fixtures, hold them in position on the ceiling to mark the required cutouts (Figure 12). Mark the edges for 1/2 inch clearance around a recessed fixture or electrical box. Cut the openings with a saber saw (Figure 13). Turn the board face down when cutting, to reduce splintering.

FINISHING THE CEILING

Nail up the trim around the edges of the ceiling (Figure 14). Use 8d nails and set the heads. If you use flat trim boards, cut the ends square for butt joints at inside corners, and make mitered joints at outside corners.

If you use profile (shaped) molding, make coped joints at inside corners and mitered joints at outside corners. For more information about putting up molding, see Install Chair Rail Molding, pages 67–74, and Making Crown Molding Fit, pages 133–143.

Now inspect the entire ceiling, filling any accidental dents and the nail holes in the first and last boards and the trim with wood filler. Sand and spot-prime any large areas.

Finally, apply a finish coat of paint to the entire ceiling and trim.

DEALING WITH LIGHT FIXTURES

Figure 12. Mark the cutouts for recessed lights or electrical boxes directly onto the board as you hold the board in position.

Figure 13. Cut the openings in the board with a saber saw. Work with the board's back side up to reduce splintering on the face.

FINISHING THE CEILING

Figure 14. Fasten trim with 8d finish nails. Fill and sand dents and nail holes, then carefully apply the final coat of paint.

Crown molding provides a graceful, elegant transition from walls to ceiling. It is one of the finest finishing touches you can add to a room.

Making Crown Molding Fit

However, installation can be difficult. The basic cuts are easy, but details of making the molding fit can be troublesome.

Here are instructions, advice, and tips from professionals to help you put up crown molding without mistakes, and with results that will make you proud.

Crown molding, which joins the walls and ceiling, gives a room an impressive and formal finished appearance. The style and finish of the other woodwork and the character of the wallcovering will determine whether the molding should have a natural or stained finish, or should be painted.

Tools You Need

Measuring tape

Framing square

Miter box and saw

Hammer

Nail set

Wood file

Caulking gun

Crown molding is "sprung"—sits at an angle—between wall and ceiling. Its top edge is flat against the ceiling, the back of its bottom edge is flat against the wall. Pieces of crown molding are joined with basic joints: mitered, coped, butt, and scarf, all of which are explained here. Cutting the joints is easy, but it's tough to make the corners fit tightly, to keep the molding straight, and to find solid nailing spots.

The project illustrated on these pages includes solutions to the problems you're most likely to encounter in putting up crown molding: unsquare corners, an uneven ceiling, and walls with bumps and hollows. The working techniques for solving these problems and getting a professional-looking installation have been gathered from several expert finish carpenters. The information is presented in the order in which you will use it, with some additional working tips at the end:

▲ Choosing a miter box
▲ Measuring and planning
▲ Purchasing the molding
▲ Marking the molding position
▲ Cutting and fitting outside corners
▲ Cutting and fitting inside corners
▲ Fastening molding securely
▲ Working with uneven walls and ceilings

CHOOSING A MITER BOX

By far the most important tool for a molding project is the miter box and saw you use to cut the molding for precise, tight joints. There are three kinds of miter boxes: (1) a fixed-cut manual miter box, (2) an adjustable manual miter box, and (3) a power miter box. Your choice depends primarily on the kind of installation you want to make. You must also be sure that the miter box has the capacity to hold the size of molding you want to use.

Fixed-cut manual miter box

A fixed-cut manual miter box is a U-shaped wood or metal box with slots in the front and back walls (fences) to guide a handsaw. All boxes have slots to make cuts at 90 degrees and at 45 degrees right and left. Some boxes also have slots for a 60-degree cut at one side and a 30-degree cut at the other side.

A fixed-cut miter box and a sharp handsaw—a backsaw is best—will let you make the basic cuts you need in putting up crown molding. This kind of miter box is fine if you plan to paint your molding. Painting allows you to use softwood molding, which is easier to cut. Although it cannot be cut as crisply and precisely as hardwood molding, you can fix any gaps at the joints with wood filler. The filler can be sanded to shape when it is dry and will be invisible under two or three coats of paint.

Adjustable manual miter box

An adjustable manual miter box (Figure 1) is far more versatile than a fixed-cut box. It is an L-shaped metal stand with guides that hold a long backsaw above the work and permit it to be lowered for cutting. The guides pivot so the saw can swing left or right and lock in position to make cuts between 90 and 30 degrees.

An adjustable manual miter box can be used for either softwood or hardwood molding with very good results. Its only disadvantages are that cuts take longer than in a power miter box, and it cannot shave molding as precisely for making fine adjustments in the cuts.

Power miter box

A power miter box (Figure 2) is the best choice for working with hardwood moldings that are going to be stained. With that kind of installation every cut must be extremely clean, precise, and crisp. You can't use wood filler, because it would show through the stain and finish.

Also called a power miter saw, a power miter box consists of an L-shaped metal table and a portable circular saw on a pivot mount. The saw can be swung right or left, for cuts between 90 and 45 degrees. When equipped with a carbide-tooth finish blade, no tool is better for making crisp, clean cuts in all kinds of molding in just seconds. Cuts are equally precise whether you are removing several

Figure 1. An adjustable manual miter box permits angled cuts from the left or right. It is equipped with an extra-long backsaw.

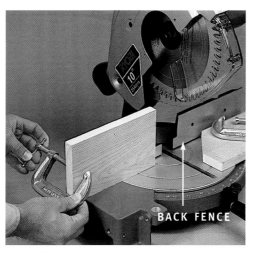

Figure 2. A power miter box is superior for cutting all kinds of molding precisely. Clamp on a taller fence to hold large moldings.

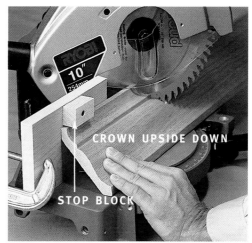

Figure 3. Screw a stop block to the fence to hold the molding. Insert crown molding into the miter box upside down for all miter cuts.

More about Moldings

For additional information about working with molding, see Install Chair Rail Molding, pages 67–74.

inches of molding or shaving off a fraction of an inch to fine-tune a fit. A power miter box is considerably more expensive to buy than an adjustable manual miter box, but you can rent one for about $20 a day.

Miter box capacity

A miter box must be large enough to hold the size of molding you want to use. With crown molding, this is a matter of the height of the rear fence as well as the depth of the base or table from front to back.

The fences of fixed-cut miter boxes are seldom tall enough for the 4-5/8 inch crown molding used in this project, and the base may not be deep enough to permit inserting the molding at the proper angle. Fence height cannot easily be increased in a fixed-cut box, and base depth cannot be changed at all.

The rear fence height in an adjustable manual miter box or a power miter box can be raised by clamping on a taller piece of wood (Figure 2). For cutting crown molding it helps to add a stop block to the fence, to brace the molding edge (Figure 3). If necessary, you can increase the table depth of a power miter box in the same way. (That is not possible with an adjustable manual miter box, because an extension would interfere with moving the front saw support.)

The other critical dimension in a power miter box is the diameter of the saw blade, because the maximum depth of cut you can make is less than half the blade diameter. For large crown molding, you need a saw with a 10-inch diameter blade or larger.

USING A MITER BOX

A miter box is easy to use if you observe the following tips:

• When making any kind of cut, make sure the molding is square against the rear fence and against the table. Provide support under the length of molding that extends out to the side so the edge stays flat on the miter box table.

• If you clamp a taller fence onto a power miter box, do so on both sides of the blade to keep the molding square against the rear of the miter box.

• When making a miter cut in crown molding, always put the molding in the miter box upside down, as if the table of the box were the ceiling and the fence were the wall of the room.

• When using a handsaw, keep the cutting edge horizontal, so you saw with the edge parallel to the miter box table. Make long, steady strokes.

• When using a power miter box, wear eye protection and keep your fingers well out of the path of the blade.

MEASURING AND PLANNING

The key to economy and ease of working is to minimize the number of joints you have to make. The fewer cuts the better. Begin by measuring the walls and mapping out what kinds of cuts are needed for each joint. Outside corners require mitered cuts; inside corners require one butt (square) and one coped cut. If a straight length of molding must be extended, a scarf joint with two angled cuts is required.

The drawing in the box Crown Molding Plan, below, shows the planning for the project illustrated in the photographs. You don't need to make a drawing; just plan the layout on graph paper. Mark down the length along each section of wall and label the cuts at each joint.

When the joints have been identified, you can number the sequence in which you will install the individual molding pieces. It's best to cut the pieces that meet at outside corners first, because they're the hardest to fit and most obvious when you're finished.

In the project shown in the box below, molding No. 2 over the fireplace had to be precisely mitered on both ends, making it the most difficult piece to fit. In a situation like this, it helps to work with another person. After molding No. 1 is in place, your helper can align the miter at one end of No. 2 with it while you mark the exact miter location on the other end where it will join molding No. 3.

PURCHASING THE MOLDING

Use the measurements on your plan to purchase the molding, but remember to add several inches to allow extra material for miters at the ends. As far as possible, buy lengths that will completely span each run. It's hard to find molding in lengths over 16 feet, so you may have to plan for a splice or two. For example, in this project it was necessary to splice two pieces together on the 19-foot side of the room. As the sequence numbers in the planning drawing show, those two pieces, Nos. 8 and 9, were put up last. After coping one end of each piece, it was fairly easy to accurately cut the angle for the final scarf splice.

MARKING THE MOLDING POSITION

A large-size crown molding must be nailed to the wall studs, and to the ceiling joists where possible. To do that, you must mark the stud and joist locations. To keep the molding properly aligned, you must also mark its edge position on the walls and ceiling.

Mark nailing points

Use a stud finder to locate the studs and ceiling joists. Mark the center of each piece (Figure 4). The marks in the photographs were made with a black pen for visibility; you should use a pencil and mark lightly, so you can erase marks easily at the end of the job.

Ceiling and wall framing are shown in the diagram in the box Ceiling and Framing, on page 137. Studs and joists usually fall every 16 inches, or occasionally every 24 inches. Joists are often, but not necessarily always located directly above the studs, so don't be confused if one set of marks does not line up with the other set. Where the ceiling joists run parallel to a wall, you won't have any ceiling nailing. The stud finder will indicate this, so you can plan to use one of the alternatives shown on page 142.

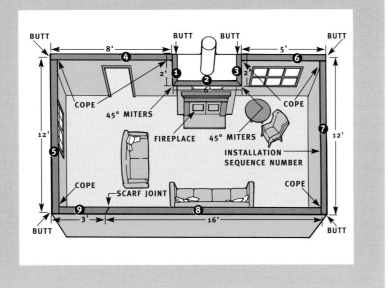

CROWN MOLDING PLAN

Mark all wall lengths on a plan of the room. For simplicity, make a graph-paper sketch rather than a perspective drawing like this. Label the cuts required for each joint. Then number the order in which the pieces will be installed.

Start numbering with the sections that have outside miters; finish with the shortest piece.

Mark the edge positions

It's hard to keep crown molding straight as you put it up, especially at corners where the walls and ceiling tend to be uneven. The molding bears on two points a few inches out from the corner along the ceiling and down the wall. It helps to mark these bearing points on the wall and ceiling along with the stud and joist positions, so you can keep the molding straight as you nail it in place.

Make a template to use as a marking guide. First measure the bearing points by positioning the crown on a framing square (Figure 5). Measure the ceiling bearing point at the front edge of the top. Measure the wall bearing point at the rear bottom edge of the molding.

Nail together two pieces of wood to duplicate those lengths (Figure 6). Then hold this template in the corner and mark the molding edge positions at all nailing points on the walls and ceiling (Figure 7). Where there are no joist marks on the ceiling, use the template to mark the ceiling edge position of the molding about every 24 inches.

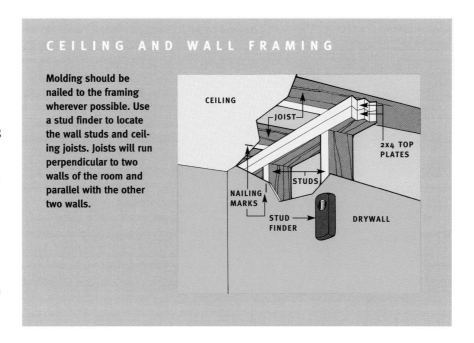

CEILING AND WALL FRAMING

Molding should be nailed to the framing wherever possible. Use a stud finder to locate the wall studs and ceiling joists. Joists will run perpendicular to two walls of the room and parallel with the other two walls.

CEILING

JOIST

2x4 TOP PLATES

STUDS

NAILING MARKS

STUD FINDER

DRYWALL

MARKING THE MOLDING POSITION

Figure 4. Use an inexpensive electronic stud finder to locate wall studs and ceiling joists. Mark them lightly with a pencil.

CEILING BEARING POINT

WALL BEARING POINT

Figure 5. Place the molding on a framing square as if it were mounted on the wall and measure its bearing points.

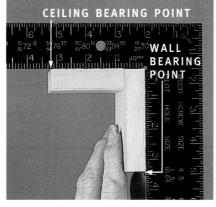

CEILING BEARING POINT

WALL BEARING POINT

Figure 6. Nail together two blocks to make a template that extends to the two bearing points of the crown molding.

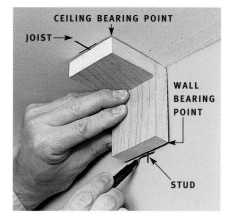

CEILING BEARING POINT

JOIST

WALL BEARING POINT

STUD

Figure 7. Use the template to mark the correct position for the molding edges on the walls and ceiling at each nailing point.

CUTTING AND FITTING OUTSIDE CORNERS

At outside corners, molding meets in a mitered joint. Perhaps it comes as no surprise that most drywall or plaster corners aren't precisely square. In fact, sometimes they aren't even close. It's a good idea to check them with a framing square right away so you'll have some idea in what way you'll have to adjust your miter cuts to make a tight joint, either slightly more or less than 45 degrees. A power miter box is essential when you have to shave small amounts on mitered corners.

Cutting the corner joint

Begin by mitering the ends of both pieces of molding. Make each cut just a bit more than 45 degrees. The slight extra angle will let you put the front edges together and have a 1-degree gap at the rear to adjust for corner unsquareness. The gap will face the wall, so it will not be seen.

Cut the two pieces as described below. Remember that crown molding must be upside down when you make miter cuts, as if the table of the box were the ceiling and the fence were the wall.

▲ For the piece on the lefthand side of the corner, set the saw for a 46 degree cut from the left. Insert the upside-down molding piece into the miter box from the right.

▲ For the righthand piece, set the saw for a 46-degree cut from the right and insert the upside-down molding from the left.

Fitting the joint

Set the two molding pieces with their bottom edges on a flat surface and their mitered edges together. Align them with a framing square (Figure 8) and drill a pilot hole for a 4d nail through the edge of one piece into the other.

▲ Now hold the pieces in place, aligned with the position marks on the wall and ceiling, and check the joint. If the front edges do not fit together tightly, return to the miter box and shave a bit more off each piece, increasing the angle. Then retry the pieces in position.

▲ When the fit is tight, drill pilot holes for 6d finish nails along the bottom and top edges at each nailing point (Figure 9). Nail up the first piece, keeping it precisely in position (Figure 10). Then fit the second piece against it and nail it in place. Finally, drive a 4d nail through the predrilled hole at the top of the corner, to tighten the miter (Figure 11).

It's tempting, but usually counterproductive, to use nails to close all the gaps between the crown molding and the walls and ceiling. You can easily knock the joints askew this way. Instead, simply let the molding run straight and caulk the gaps later (see page 143). If the problem is caused by obvious bumps or a textured ceiling, you can scrape off the highest obstacles with a chisel before nailing.

EXTENDING MOLDING WITH A SCARF JOINT

When you need a straight run of molding that is longer than any individual piece, join two pieces with an overlapping scarf joint.

• To cut the pieces, set the miter saw for a cut of about 22 degrees (the precise angle does not matter). Insert one piece of molding upside down from the left of the miter box and cut its end.

• Without changing the saw position, insert the other piece of molding upside down from the right and cut its end at the same angle.

• When you put up the two pieces of the molding, overlap the angled ends so the finished surface is continuous. The thin edge of the face piece will be barely visible once molding is painted or stained.

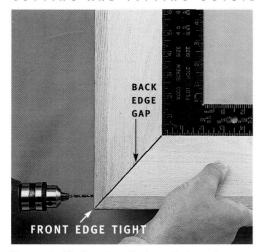

Figure 8. Fit the mitered edges of pieces for an outside corner together and align their bases with a framing square. Drill a pilot hole for a 4d nail to be used when the joint is assembled.

Figure 9. Hold the pieces in position on the wall to check the fit of the joint. Shave the ends more if needed. When the fit is right, drill pilot holes in the bottom and top edges.

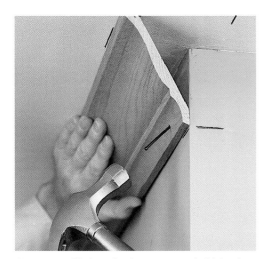

Figure 10. Nail up the first piece with 6d finish nails. Align the joint precisely with the marks on the wall and ceiling. Then fit and nail the second section of molding.

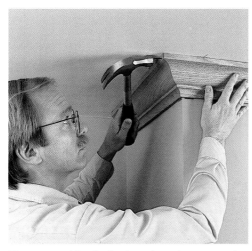

Figure 11. After both pieces have been securely nailed in position, drive a 4d finish nail into the predrilled hole at the top. This will tighten the outside corner miter joint.

OTHER CHOICES

If genuine oak molding is not suitable for your room or if it costs too much for your budget, consider the following possibilities.

Imitation pine molding

Imitation pine molding made of polystyrene is a relatively new product. It looks and feels like clear, sanded pine, but because it is free of knots and other natural imperfections there's less waste. The polystyrene can be nailed, cut, painted, or stained just like wood, but won't warp.

This molding costs about 20% less than clear pine wood molding, and offers much greater savings compared to the cost of oak molding. It is supplied in 19 or more profiles. You can use them alone, or combine them to form more elaborate moldings. If the crown profile is not large enough for your ceiling, you can extend it visually by adding smaller moldings at the edges on the wall or ceiling, or both.

Crown molding

Crown molding has two or three classic profiles. A more elaborate cornice molding is suitable for some rooms. Traditionally such a molding was either made from molded plaster sections or built up with a complex of wood parts.

Today, lightweight cornice moldings with dentils, friezes, acanthus leaf motifs, and a great variety of decorative details are available in lightweight plastic materials that look just like plaster and can be painted to match any decor.

This kind of molding can be cut and shaped with ordinary tools more easily than wood. Joints are made with a cement that fuses the plastic faces together. The molding can be installed on the walls and ceiling with mastic, finish nails, or both.

CUTTING AND FITTING INSIDE CORNERS

Inside corners are likely to be even less square than outside corners, because drywall joint compound or plaster builds up there when the walls are finished (Figure 12). It's almost impossible to cut accurate miters for these corners, particularly because a gap almost always opens up between the moldings when you nail them.

The solution is to use a coped joint at each inside corner. In a coped joint, the end of the first piece is cut square to butt against one wall in the corner. The end of the other piece is coped—cut to the exact outline of the molding—so it fits snugly against the first one.

Coping crown molding, especially large pieces of hardwood, isn't easy, but you can do a nice job if you work carefully. It will take longer than you expect, but don't rush. Professional finish carpenters often plan the lengths of the molding they need in advance and do the coping work in the shop, rather than at the job site. It's not unusual for an experienced pro to spend 20 minutes on a coped joint, so be patient.

Making preliminary cuts

Set the saw at 90 degrees and cut the end of the first piece of molding square. Then set the saw for a 45-degree cut and trim the end of the second piece, the one that is to be coped. Leave this piece a few inches long in case you have to recut this end for a second try.

There is a difference in making this cut from making a miter cut for an outside corner. In the outside-corner cut, the back of the molding is shorter than the front, so that when you look at the molding from the face you do not see any wood at the end. A mitered cut for coping is angled the other way, so you do see raw cut wood. Here's how to do it:

▲ If the coped piece is to be on the lefthand side of the corner (as in Figure 13), set the saw for a 45-degree cut from the right and insert the molding into the miter box from the right side. Remember, the molding must be inserted upside down and angled between the rear fence and the table of the miter box (Figure 3).

▲ If the coped piece is to be on the righthand side of the joint, set the saw for a 45-degree cut from the left and insert the upside-down molding into the miter box from the left.

Coping the molding end

Use a coping saw to cut the angled end to the molding profile. Clamp the molding to a work surface and cut away the exposed wood along the line of the smooth surface (Figure 14). A coping saw cuts on the pull stroke, so it can follow the curved line of the molding profile quite easily. Hold the saw at an angle to undercut the finished molding face about 30 degrees. As with a mitered joint, remember that it's the front edge that counts, not the back.

Fitting the coped joint

Nail the square-cut piece of molding in position, but leave the last 18 inches unnailed. Put the coped piece in position to check the fit (Figure 15). If there are any gaps, use a file to make adjustments (Figure 16). In most cases, fine-tuning the pattern requires shaving wood off the back of the coped end so that the front edge fits snugly against the adjoining piece.

When the fit is exact, nail the coped piece into position. The coped end should clamp the unnailed edge of the other molding tightly and force it into proper alignment.

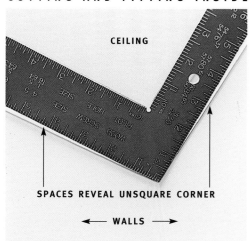

Figure 12. Use a framing square to check each corner. An inside corner like this may be out of square because of wall alignment or the buildup of taping compound at the joint.

Figure 13. For a coped end on the lefthand piece at an inside corner, the 45-degree first cut must leave unfinished wood exposed to the right. It will be removed by the coping cut.

Figure 14. Make the coping cut along the line of the finished surface. Work from below, because the saw cuts on the downstroke. Angle the saw to undercut the face.

Figure 15. Put up the square-cut piece first, then position the coped piece against it to check the fit. When finally installed, the coped end will hold the other piece firmly in place.

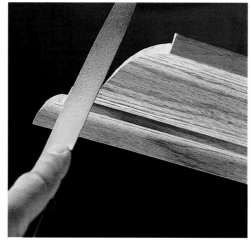

Figure 16. Use a wood file to refine the coped cut. The most common problem is excess wood on the back that prevents the front edge from fitting tightly against the other piece.

WIDER CROWN MOLDING

If the crown molding you want to use is not wide enough, nail 1x2 or 1x3 boards on the ceiling and walls, positioned to extend 1/4 to 1/2 inch beyond the edges of the crown along its entire length. Nail the crown to these boards. Their thickness will set the crown lower on the wall and extending farther out on the ceiling. Add cove or quarter-round molding to finish the edges of the board and visually extend the molding even farther.

FASTENING MOLDING SECURELY

Use finish nails to fasten the crown molding at each nailing point marked on the walls and ceiling. Predrill small holes in the molding to avoid splitting. As in all trim work, drive the nails up to the last 3/4 inch with a hammer. Then, to avoid denting the wood, use a nail set to drive each nail the rest of the way and set the head just below the surface of the wood.

When there is no stud or joist to nail into, there are three alternatives you can use:

▲ Glue the edge and drive crossed nails into the wall to hold the molding in place.

▲ Put up wooden cant strips in the corner and drive nails into them.

▲ Use extra-long nails to reach into the top plate of the wall.

Gluing and nailing

This is a good solution for securing the ceiling edge of the molding (Figure 17). You will seldom need to use it along the wall edge, except perhaps close to a mitered corner. For best results use a construction adhesive. It ensures a good bond because it's thick and fills gaps. Its main weakness is that it must set before you can put much pressure on it, so you can't finish a corner right away. Use 4d finish nails, angled into the drywall or plaster, to hold the molding tight while the adhesive sets.

Cant strips

A cant strip is an angled piece of wood nailed into the corner where the wall and ceiling meet (Figure 18). You can run either a continuous strip or regularly spaced 6-inch blocks to provide a nailing base for the molding. Be sure the strip is small enough to fit behind the molding, so it doesn't force the molding out of position.

Use 16d common nails to put up the cant strips, and 6d finish nails for the molding. Nailing to a cant strip is usually the best alternative to use near joints, to make fine adjustments in the position of the molding.

Extra-long nails

A 10d finish nail will normally be long enough to reach through the center of the molding and penetrate the top plate of the wall about 3/4 inch (Figure 19). This should hold the crown solidly. Using long nails is most effective in the middle of long molding sections, and faster than putting up cant blocks there. Be sure to predrill for the nail, and countersink the large head carefully. Because there is no direct support behind the molding, hammering too forcefully may create a split in the wood. The filled hole will be less visible if you nail through a darker grain line in the molding.

FASTENING MOLDING SECURELY

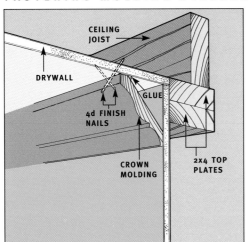

Figure 17. Use construction adhesive when you need to glue up a molding edge. Drive crossed 4d nails to hold the edge in place.

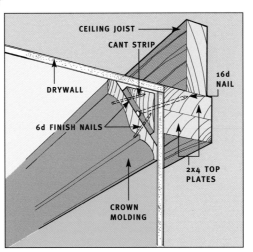

Figure 18. Fasten cant strips in place with long common nails. Nail the crown molding to the strips with two finish nails every 16 in.

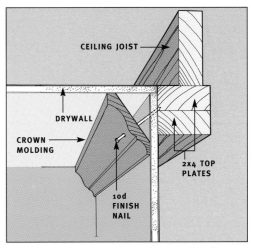

Figure 19. Where feasible, drive 10d (3 in.) finish nails into the wall plate. Be sure to keep the molding in position when nailing like this.

WORKING WITH UNEVEN WALLS AND CEILINGS

Walls and ceilings that look smooth and uniform often reveal bulges, dips, and sags when crown molding is put in place. A large molding doesn't flex easily to follow these contours, so gaps along the edges are inevitable.

In some cases you can scrape minor bumps off the wall or ceiling surface, but that may require touching up with paint before putting up the molding. In other cases you may be able to sand or plane the molding edge to conform to the irregularities. That's a limited solution, however: The top and bottom faces of crown molding are quite narrow and will readily show small variations in thickness.

Here are three other possible solutions:
- ▲ Caulk the gaps along the molding edges.
- ▲ Create a shadow line below the molding.
- ▲ Add a small molding on the wall below the crown molding.

Caulk the gaps

For gaps of up to about 1/4 inch, a good solution is to squeeze caulk into them (Figure 20) and wipe it smooth along the edge of the molding. Some caulks can be wiped with a moistened finger; others are shaped better with a bit of solvent. Wear a rubber glove in either case. Be sure to use a paintable caulk, so that when it has set you can paint it with a fine brush to blend with the ceiling or wall.

Create a shadow line

Gaps make uneven shadows. One way to hide them is to make a definite shadow line by setting the molding a slight distance out from an uneven wall (Figure 21). This solution really creates an optical illusion. You're less likely to notice unevenness if there's at least a 1/4-inch gap along the entire length of the molding.

To create the shadow line, rip 1/4-inch thick strips from the edge of a 1x6 or 1x8 to use as spacers. Nail the strips in a continuous line on the wall a constant 1/4 inch above the molding position marks you made with your L-shaped template (Figure 6). Since this will push the molding farther out on the ceiling, use a scrap of 1/4-inch spacer to make new position marks on the ceiling as well. Then nail the molding to the ceiling joists and through the spacers into the wall studs.

Add a small molding

You also can hide the gaps along the walls or ceiling by running a line of small molding 1/2 inch away from the edge of the crown molding (Figure 22). A small molding bends to the uneven contours more easily than the crown. It blocks the view of the gaps along the crown and adds a decorative feature. The molding shown is a small base cap, but you can use any molding that you think looks suitable.

Finishing Tip

If you plan to paint the crown molding, sand it and apply a coat of primer and one finish coat before cutting and installing it. For stained molding, stain it and give it one finish coat before installation.

After the molding is up, fill all the nail holes with wood putty. Spot-prime the filled holes and any nicks, or touch them up with stain and a tiny brush. Then apply the final coat.

WORKING WITH UNEVEN WALLS AND CEILINGS

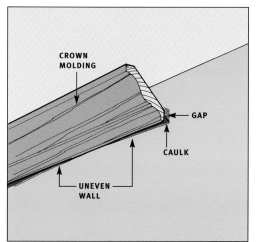

Figure 20. Fill cracks up to about 1/4 in. wide with a paintable caulk. Wipe it even with the molding edge and paint it to match the wall.

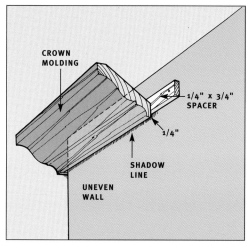

Figure 21. Nail a 1/4-in. spacer to the wall to create a shadow line at the bottom edge of the molding. Shift the ceiling position marks accordingly.

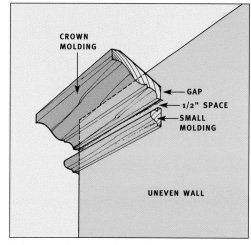

Figure 22. Run a small molding about 1/2 in. from the crown edge to mask gaps. This works on the ceiling as well as the walls.

Lighting and Electrical

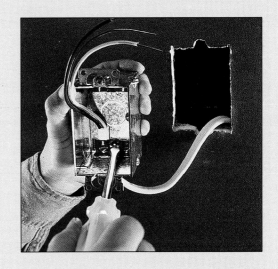

Install an Interior Electrical Outlet

Here's the easy way to add an outlet in any room of the house—no difficult carpentry, and no complex wiring.

146

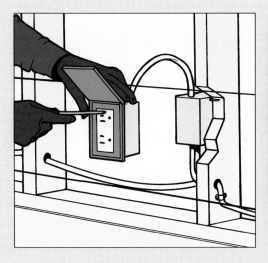

Install an Outdoor Electrical Outlet

Get rid of extension cords out the window. Install a safe, weatherproof outlet whenever you need it in an exterior wall.

152

Putting In Dimmer Switches

To control light intensity for mood or best working conditions, replace an existing light switch with a dimmer. It's easy.

157

Recessed Lights

Recessed ceiling lights can provide specific, general, or accent lighting. Here's how to install them properly and safely.

160

Need an electrical outlet where
there is none?

Install an Interior Electrical Outlet

An extension cord is a temporary,
unattractive, and possibly unsafe solution.
It's far better to add a permanent outlet.
That's easy to do, even if you've never
done any electrical work before.
In addition to a few basic tools you need
only a circuit tester and a wire stripper;
both are inexpensive.
With the tools and materials at hand,
the whole job should take just
one to two hours.

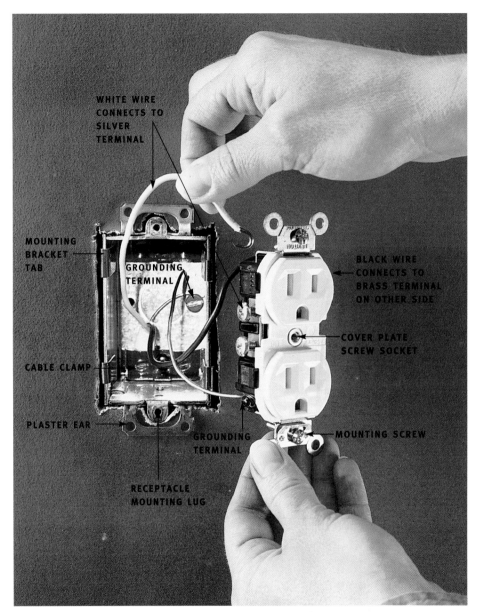

WHITE WIRE
CONNECTS TO
SILVER
TERMINAL

MOUNTING
BRACKET
TAB

GROUNDING
TERMINAL

BLACK WIRE
CONNECTS TO
BRASS TERMINAL
ON OTHER SIDE

CABLE CLAMP

COVER PLATE
SCREW SOCKET

PLASTER EAR

GROUNDING
TERMINAL

MOUNTING SCREW

RECEPTACLE
MOUNTING LUG

A duplex receptacle mounts in an electrical box fastened in a hole
cut in the wall. Refer to this photograph to identify details
mentioned in the text.

PROJECT STEPS

The project explained here is very basic: how to install an outlet in a first-floor interior wall and tie it in to an existing electrical line in the basement below. The job can be broken down into a series of simple steps.

▲ Find a junction box where the wiring for the new outlet can be connected.

▲ Gather the materials required for the job.

▲ Cut and drill holes for the electrical outlet box and the receptacle cable.

▲ Run the cable between the tie-in point and the outlet location.

▲ Install the electrical box in the wall.

▲ Connect the receptacle to the cable and mount it in the box.

▲ Turn off the power to the tie-in point.

▲ Connect the wires in the receptacle cable to those at the tie-in point.

FINDING A TIE-IN POINT

Locate the nearest basement junction box (like the one in Figure 8, page 150) that you can tie in to. It may be behind or part of a light fixture. If so, there will be a few additional wires in the box, but the basic wiring procedure will be the same as explained here.

▲ Make sure the junction box you plan to tie in to has accommodation in one side to accept an additional cable. Also, try to choose one that you can reach without the trouble of drilling through a lot of floor joists in order to run the cable across the basement ceiling to a point below the outlet.

▲ Trace the cable that presently runs from the junction box to the main service panel and switch off the circuit breaker or remove the fuse that activates it. Note whether the breaker or fuse is rated at 15 amps or 20 amps. Also note whether the cable to your tie-in point contains 14- or 12-gauge wires: Look on the cable insulation for the designation 14-2 or 12-2. You will need this information to buy the proper cable for your new receptacle.

▲ With the circuit turned off, determine which lights and outlets throughout the house have been affected. You can do that by trying light switches and plugging a lamp or a circuit tester into the outlets (see page 151).

The reason for doing this is to count the number of items on the circuit. The rule of thumb is there should be no more than a total of eight outlets and/or lights on a 15-amp circuit, and no more than 10 on a 20-amp circuit. If adding the outlet you want to install will exceed these limits, or if the circuit powers a major appliance, find a junction box on a different circuit.

When you have gotten this information you can turn the circuit back on until you are ready to connect the cable at the junction box.

GATHERING MATERIALS

All the materials you need are readily available at home centers, electrical suppliers, and many large hardware stores. They are:

▲ NM-B plastic-sheathed cable (Romex is the best-known brand). Get cable with the same size (diameter) wires as those that come into the tie-in junction box, either 14- or 12-gauge. The cable will be marked 14-2G (or 12-2G), indicating that it contains two wires—one black and one white—of the indicated gauge, and a bare or green ground wire. To determine how much cable you need, measure the distance across the basement, add the vertical distance up to the outlet position, add 2 feet for working slack, and a little extra for making connections at the two boxes.

▲ Twist-on (screw-cap) wire connectors, to join wires without soldering (Wire Nut is the best-known brand). Be sure to get the proper size for the wire gauge in the cable and number of wires to be joined.

▲ Cable staples.

▲ An outlet box of the proper size for a duplex (two-plug) receptacle, with an internal cable clamp and drywall/plaster ears for mounting. A metal box is easier to mount by the method shown in the photographs, but you could easily use a plastic box instead.

▲ Mounting brackets, sometimes called drywall brackets or clamps (Figure 6, page 149).

▲ A duplex receptacle. Choose brown, white, or ivory plastic to match the other receptacles around the walls of the room.

▲ A two-hole cover plate for the duplex receptacle. Choose a decorator plate or a matching plastic plate which you can use as is, paint, or cover to match the wallcovering.

Tools and Materials You Need

Tape measure

Drill and 3/4" bit

Hammer

Drywall saw

Wire stripper

Long-nose pliers

Screwdriver

Circuit tester

NM-B plastic-sheathed cable

Cable staples

Twist-on wire connectors

Electrical box

Drywall mounting brackets for box

Duplex receptacle

Receptacle cover plate

MAKING BOX AND CABLE HOLES

You must cut a hole in the wall for the electrical box, and drill a hole in the sole plate of the wall framing to run the cable into the basement.

Cutting the box hole

When you have identified the spot for the new outlet, make sure that there is no wall stud directly behind. Use an electronic stud finder, or rap on the wall with your knuckles. The rapping will sound hollow between studs, less resonant directly over a stud. Check with a small finishing nail if in doubt.

▲ Trace around the electrical box to mark the cutout (Figure 1). Standard height for an outlet is 12 inches from the floor to the center of the box, but if other outlets in the room are a different height, match them. Trace around the small receptacle mounting lugs at the top and bottom, not the larger plaster ears.

▲ Use a drywall saw to cut the hole. Saw on the marked lines at the top and bottom, and just outside the lines on the sides, to provide space for inserting the mounting brackets.

Drilling the cable hole

You will drill a hole for the cable from the basement, up through the subfloor and the sole plate of the wall framing, into the space between studs where the outlet will be located. To do that you need a reference point in the basement.

Figure 1. Trace the outline of the electrical box on the wall after determining that there's no stud directly behind that point. Match the height of any other outlets in the room in most cases.

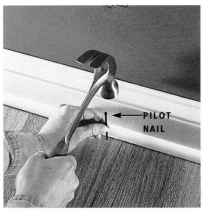

Figure 2. Drive a nail through the floor or drill a hole and poke a wire through the hole as a pilot marker. Position the marker directly under the box location and close to the baseboard.

Figure 3. Locate the pilot marker in the basement and measure back 3 in. to mark a spot under the sole plate of the wall. Drill a 3/4-in. hole for the cable at that point; see illustration in the box below.

▲ In the room where the outlet will be located, drive a finish nail through the floor as close to the baseboard as you can (Figure 2), or drill a tiny hole and push a wire through. Make sure this pilot marker is centered below the hole you have cut in the wall. Be careful not to damage the baseboard or shoe molding as you hammer or drill. You can fill the hole later with wood filler.

▲ Go into the basement and locate the pilot nail or wire. Measure back 3 inches and mark a point directly under the center of the wall (Figure 3). Use a 3/4-inch spade bit to drill straight up through the subfloor and sole plate into the wall cavity, as shown at right.

DRILLING UP FROM THE BASEMENT

Drill from the basement up through the subfloor and wall sole plate. If there is something in the way in the basement, the cable hole can be off-center under the outlet location, as long as it goes into the right wall cavity. A 3/4-inch hole lets the cable be pulled without binding or damaging the outer sheath.

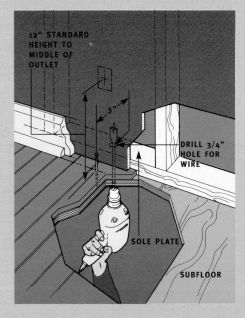

RUNNING THE CABLE

Starting at the tie-in junction box, lay out the cable across the basement ceiling. If it runs across joists, drill a 3/4-inch hole midway between the top and bottom of each joist and feed the cable through.

▲ If the cable runs along the length of a joist, drive staples into the side of the joist, about 3 inches above the bottom edge. Again, leave them loose enough to adjust the cable. The maximum allowable distance between staples is 4 feet 6 inches, and there must be a staple within 12 inches of the junction box.

▲ When you reach the hole you drilled in the subfloor, poke the cable up into the wall cavity (Figure 4). Then go upstairs and pull it out through the hole in the wall.

INSTALLING THE OUTLET BOX

Before putting the box in the wall, fasten the cable to it. Insert the cable end into the box and pull enough through so you can easily cut off about 11 inches of the plastic outer sheath. Then pull the cable back until only about 1/2 inch of the sheath is visible above the top of the clamp and tighten the clamp (Figure 5).

▲ Clip about 2 inches from the ends of the wires and strip 3/4 inch of insulation from the white and black wires. If the grounding wire is also insulated (green), strip the insulation all the way back to the cable jacket.

▲ Insert the box into the hole in the wall, pushing the extra cable into the wall cavity ahead of it. Work a metal box support bracket into the wall along one side of the box. Insert the long arm of the bracket first, toward the top (Figure 6). Push the bracket in and up until the bottom arm enters the hole, then pull it forward by one of the tabs until the arms push against the back of the drywall.

▲ Hold the box with the plaster ears tight against the wall and fold the tabs of the bracket into the box. Squeeze them flat or crimp them with long-nose pliers. Do the same thing on the other side of the box with a second bracket. The box is now effectively clamped in place by the bracket arms, which prevent it from pulling out of the opening, and the plaster ears, which prevent it from sliding in.

RUNNING THE CABLE

INSTALLING THE OUTLET BOX

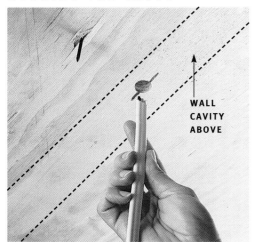

Figure 4. Feed the end of the cable up through the hole into the wall cavity. The rest of the cable runs across the basement to the tie-in junction box but is not yet connected.

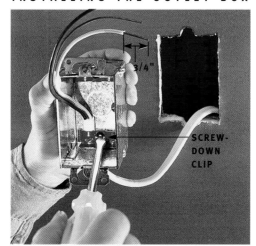

Figure 5. Secure the cable in the box by tightening the built-in clamp, after removing the outer sheath. Also strip 3/4 in. of insulation from the black and white wires.

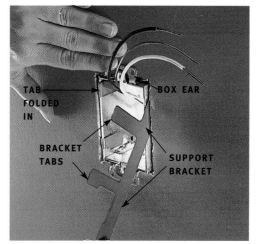

Figure 6. Mount the box in the wall opening with metal box support brackets. Insert brackets one at a time on either side and fold the bracket tabs into the box in order to secure it.

CONNECTING THE RECEPTACLE

With long-nose pliers bend the end of the white wire to hook clockwise—the same direction that a screw tightens (Figure 7). Do the same with the black wire. Connect the black wire to a brass screw terminal on one side of the receptacle. Connect the white wire to a silver screw terminal on the other side.

▲ If you have a metal box, loop the middle of the grounding wire around the screw at the back of the box and tighten the screw. Then connect the end of the wire to the receptacle grounding screw. In a plastic box, connect the grounding wire only to the receptacle screw.

▲ Fold the wires neatly into the box as you fit the receptacle into position. Drive the receptacle mounting screws into the lugs of the box. Then put on the receptacle cover plate; it is held by a center screw.

CONNECTING THE CABLE

At the service panel, turn off the breaker or remove the fuse that controls the circuit running to the junction box where you will tie in the receptacle wiring. Remove the cover plate from the box and use a circuit tester to double-check that the circuit is dead; see page 151, Is the Power Really Off?

▲ Run the wire to the junction box, trim the cable jacket and wire insulation, and secure it with the built-in plastic clamp-downs in the box sides (or with screw-in connectors if you're using a metal box).

▲ Twist the white wire to the other white wires in the box; black to blacks (or other color if they're not black); and green to other green or bare wires. Screw wire connectors onto the exposed ends (Figure 8).

▲ If the junction box is metal, check to make sure that it is grounded to a green or bare wire, and then tie in the grounding wire from the receptacle to that terminal.

▲ Fold the wires neatly into the box and replace the cover. Where the cable is held by staples, tap them in far enough to secure it without pinching the cable.

▲ Turn on the circuit at the service panel. Your new outlet is ready for use.

CONNECTING THE RECEPTACLE

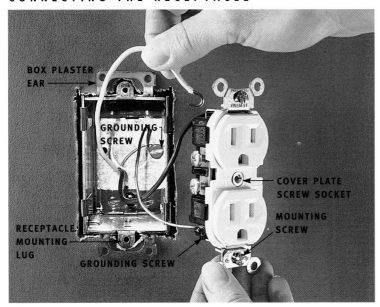

Figure 7. Attach the wires to the outlet with the ends hooked in the same direction that the screw tightens. See text above for instructions on connecting the receptacle.

CONNECTING THE CABLE

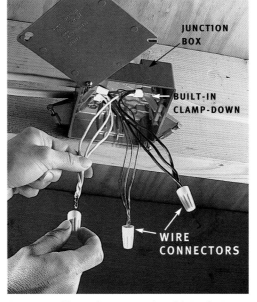

Figure 8. Clamp the receptacle cable in the junction box and connect it with twist-on caps. Match the circuit wire colors.

Before opening any outlet or switch or removing the connectors from any existing wires, you must turn off the power. Plug a radio into the outlet and turn the volume up loud, then flick off circuit breakers or unscrew fuses until the radio goes off. For lights you can do the same thing, but have a helper tell you when the bulb goes off.

To check whether the power is really off in receptacles, switches, and the circuit wires, use a circuit tester, also called a voltage tester. This useful device is widely available in variety and hardware stores, home centers, and other outlets for less than $2.00. It consists of a tiny neon bulb sealed in plastic, with two metal-tipped test leads. It is no bigger than a pocket pen. When the leads are connected to a "hot" circuit the tester bulb lights up; otherwise it stays off.

Testing a Receptacle

Insert one test lead into each receptacle slot where the plug normally goes. If the tester bulb lights up, the circuit is on; if not, the power is probably off.

"Probably," because the tips on some tester leads may be too short or thick to be inserted far enough into receptacle slots to make electrical contact. If you have any reason to suspect that is the case with your tester, go a step farther.

Remove the screws in the face plate and the mounting ears at the top and bottom of the receptacle. Take hold of the mounting ears of the receptacle and pull it straight out of its box. Be careful not to let the terminal screws on either side of the receptacle touch a metal box.

Touch the tip of one tester lead to a brass screw terminal where a black or red wire is connected. Hold it there while you touch the other lead to a silver screw where a white wire is connected. If the power is off, the tester bulb will not light up.

Make two other checks: (1) between the brass/black (or red)-wire terminal and the terminal where the bare or green-insulated grounding wire is connected; (2) between the silver/white-wire terminal and the grounding-wire terminal. If the tester light comes on in either case, the power is not off.

Testing a Switch

After turning off the circuit breaker or fuse, remove the cover plate and the screws in the mounting ears. Pull the switch straight out of its box, being careful not to let the screw terminals on the sides of the switch touch a metal box.

Touch the tester leads to the switch terminals. Also test between each terminal and the grounding-wire terminal. If the power is off the tester will not light in any of these positions.

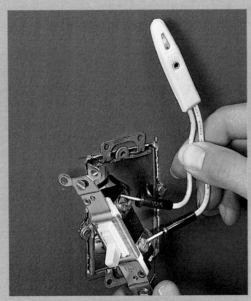

A circuit tester lights up when power is present. Test a switch this way. Test receptacles and circuit wires as explained in text.

Testing a Cable

Remove the twist connectors from the ends of the circuit wires as follows:

• Hold the wires only by the insulated portions. Don't remove the wire connector for the ground wires until after testing and verifying that the power is off.

• Do not touch the bare wires before you have made sure the power is off.

• Do not allow the ends of the wires to touch.

Touch the tip of one tester lead to the bare end of the white-insulated wire in the cable and touch the tip of the other lead to the end of the black-insulated wire in the cable. Also test between each of these wires and the bare or green-insulated grounding wire. If the tester bulb lights up in any of these positions, the electricity is still on and the wires are "hot." In that case, turn off other breakers or fuses until the tester shows that the power in that line is off.

Note: When a cable has three circuit wires—white, black, and red—check with the tester (1) between the white and black wires, (2) between the white and red wires, and (3) between each of these and the bare/green grounding wire. Do not connect the tester between the black and red wires. If they are both hot, the tester will cause a short circuit.

Install an Outdoor Electrical Outlet

Outdoor electrical conveniences—weed trimmer, low voltage lights, power tools, and the like—aren't really convenient unless there's an outdoor outlet at hand.

A safe outdoor outlet is much better than running an extension cord out a door or window every time you want to do some work.

Installing an outdoor outlet is not much more difficult than adding an interior outlet. Follow the instructions given here and you can do the job in an afternoon.

FIRST CONSIDERATIONS

There are two fundamental considerations when you install an outdoor outlet:

- ▲ Using the right kind of receptacle
- ▲ Making a legal installation

Kind of receptacle

By electrical code throughout the country, you can install only a GFCI (ground fault circuit interrrupter) receptacle in an exterior outlet. The greater exposure to dampness outdoors—rain, moist earth, sprinkler water, condensation—poses a significant shock hazard. A GFCI outlet provides protection because it breaks the circuit instantly in case of a short circuit or accidental grounding from any cause. Ordinary circuit breakers or fuses react more slowly, so you can receive a severe shock before they cut off power to the circuit.

GFCI receptacles are widely available. They mount in standard electrical boxes and are wired in the same way as ordinary receptacles. You'll need a weatherproof cover for the box, which is also a standard item and is often included with the GFCI outlet.

Legal installation

In many communities you must have a permit to add an outdoor outlet. Check with your building department and get the proper permit if needed; there may be a small fee. It may also be necessary for the finished installation to be checked by a licensed electrician or an electrical inspector. Do not neglect these requirements; they are intended to ensure your safety. The fine for a violation could make your new outlet an expensive project.

BACK-TO-BACK INSTALLATION

The procedure for marking the exterior position so you can cut a hole for the outlet box differs a bit depending upon whether you plan to connect to an existing interior outlet on the first floor—called back-to-back installation—or to a junction box in the basement.

Back-to-back installation is the method shown here. In this kind of installation the interior and exterior outlet boxes are mounted in the same wall cavity—the space between two studs (Figure 1). They are offset because the cavity is not deep enough for them to be directly behind each other. You need to take this into account in making measurements and marking the outlet position.

BACK-TO-BACK INSTALLATION

NEW CABLE

EXISTING INTERIOR OUTLET

NEW EXTERIOR OUTLET

Figure 1. Back-to-back installation lets you power the new exterior outlet by connecting to an existing interior outlet in the same wall cavity.

Marking for back-to-back installation

Start at the interior outlet. Use a stud finder or rap on the wall to locate the studs on either side of the outlet. You need to know whether it is mounted on the left or the right stud, or someplace in between.

▲ Measure horizontally from the outlet to the center of a window or exterior door in the room. Mark the center point of the window sill or threshold with a piece of tape. Also measure the height of the sill above the floor.

▲ Go outside and measure the same horizontal distance from the tape back toward the interior outlet location. Use a level to make a truly horizontal measurement. This will allow you to find the common wall cavity.

▲ If you measured from a window, subtract 8 inches from the floor-to-sill height and measure down that distance. If you measured from a doorway, measure up 8 inches. This ensures that your position will be above the sole plate of the interior wall.

▲ Now move the position about 6 inches left or right, so the exterior location is not directly behind the interior outlet but is still in the same stud cavity. Mark this point on the siding.

Basement connection

If you plan to connect to wiring in the basement, you must locate the appropriate wall cavity so that you can drill a cable hole into the cavity from below.

▲ Start outside and select the place where you want the new outlet. Run a horizontal line from a window sill or doorway and measure up or down, as described above, to establish the height of the outlet position. Mark this position on the siding with a piece of tape for the moment, in case you have to move it to avoid an interior stud.

▲ Measure along the horizontal line to get the distance to the center of the door or window. Go inside and measure back along the wall to end up opposite the exterior point.

▲ Use a stud finder to locate the studs on each side of that point. Drive a finishing nail through the floor at one stud position, as close to the baseboard as possible, or drill a small hole and poke a wire through (see page 154). This will be a pilot marker to guide your work when you are in the basement.

▲ If the stud finder indicates that there is a stud directly behind the intended outlet location, put a pilot marker through into the basement at that point. Then go outside and mark a new box location 6 inches to the left or right of the tape, so the outlet will be between two studs in a wall cavity.

CUTTING A HOLE FOR THE BOX

Before cutting into the wall from the outside, turn off the power to the interior outlet or any other circuit wires that might be running through the wall cavity where you will be working. Turn off the circuit breaker or remove the fuse at the service panel. Test the outlet to make sure it is off (see page 151).

▲ Hold the electrical box in position on the outside wall with its mouth against the siding and trace its outline. Drill starter holes at the four corners, and at the center top and bottom.

▲ Cut the hole for the box with a saber saw or reciprocating saw (Figure 2). Check the depth of the siding and sheathing behind it through one of the starter holes and use as short a blade as possible, to reduce the chance of nicking any wires or pipes in the wall. Cut precisely along the marked outline. The closer the fit with the box, the better you can seal the edges against weather infiltration.

CUTTING A HOLE FOR THE BOX

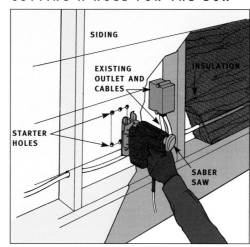

Figure 2. Cut along the marked outline to cut a hole for the exterior outlet box. Starter holes make cutting easier. Turn off power to existing wires before cutting into the wall.

Tools You Need

Measuring tape

Level

Circuit tester

Drill

Saber saw or reciprocating saw

Screwdriver

Wire stripper

Long-nose pliers

Caulking gun

RUNNING CABLE FOR THE OUTLET

You must use cable with wires the same size — 14- or 12-gauge—as those running to the outlet or junction box you will tie in to (see page 156 for more about cable). Procedures differ for back-to-back and basement cabling.

Back-to-back cabling

Be sure the power to the interior outlet is turned off. Remove the wall plate and the receptacle mounting screws, pull the receptacle out of its box, and disconnect the wires. Make a diagram of the connections as you work. If possible, open one of the cable entrance holes (knock-out holes) at the rear top or bottom of the box.

▲ From the outside, cut and push aside the insulation in the wall cavity so you can reach the interior box. If you couldn't open a cable knock-out hole from inside, pry one open with a short screwdriver now. If you have to pull out any insulation, save it so you can put it back before installing the outlet box.

▲ Insert a cable through the hole in the exterior wall (or feed it up from the basement; see below) into the knock-out hole in the interior box (Figure 3).

Basement cabling

In the basement, locate the nail or wire you inserted through the floor as a pilot marker earlier. It is in front of a wall stud. Measure left or right 14 inches and mark the position of the other stud in the outlet wall cavity.

▲ Compare the wall stud positions with those of the joists in the basement ceiling; they may not be aligned (Figure 4). You need to make sure that when you drill a hole for the cable, it goes up into the proper wall cavity.

▲ The center of the wall sole plate is approximately 3 inches back from a pilot marker driven just in front of the baseboard shoe molding, or 2 inches back from the interior wall surface. Don't go any farther than that toward the outside to start drilling or the bit may hit the sheathing in the wall cavity. The rim joist in the basement will limit the starting point.

With a short 5/8- or 3/4-inch diameter bit, drill a hole up into the wall cavity. If you don't have a right-angle drill attachment, angle the drill between the sill on the top of the basement wall and the subfloor above (Figure 5). The reason for using a short drill bit is to minimize the danger of hitting the back of the exterior sheathing in the cavity.

▲ Poke the end of a straightened coat hanger or similar stiff wire up through the hole. If you can't push it through into the cavity there may be a double sole plate in the wall. Try drilling the hole again with a longer bit. Then push 12 to 18 inches of the hanger up into the cavity, and tape the electrical cable to the other end.

▲ Go outside, reach into the hole and find the end of the hanger. Pull it up and out of the exterior hole, bringing the end of the cable with it.

Choosing a Tie-in Circuit and Outlet

Electrical codes limit the maximum load on a 15- or 20-amp circuit. For information about mapping a circuit to determine if you can add to it, see Finding a Tie-in Point, page 147. If you have any doubts, consult an electrician or electrical inspector.

Electrical codes also specify the minimum size of outlet boxes for various installations. In this project, the interior box must have a volume of at least 20 cubic in. (2 x 3 x 3-1/2 in.). If the box is too small, replace it with a larger "remodeling" box.

RUNNING CABLE FOR THE OUTLET

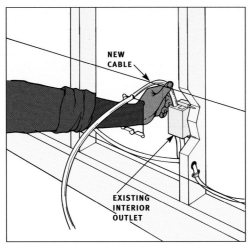

Figure 3. After disconnecting the interior outlet, feed a cable from the outside into a knock-out hole in the interior box. Remove insulation in the wall if necessary; replace it later.

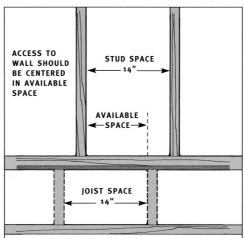

Figure 4. Before drilling up from the basement, compare the positions of the wall studs and the joists below the floor. You must be sure to drill up into the proper wall cavity.

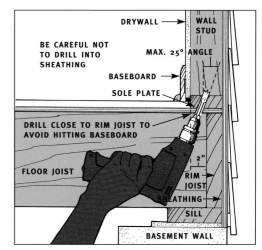

Figure 5. Angle the drill as nearly vertical as possible to make a 5/8- or 3/4-in. hole through the sole plate in the wall cavity. A right-angle drill attachment may help.

MOUNTING THE NEW OUTLET BOX

Use a 2-1/2 inch deep metal electrical box with an internal clamp for nonmetallic cable and mounting ears or brackets at the top and bottom, around the receptacle mounting lugs. Prepare the box by opening one of the cable holes and removing 1/4 inch from the center of the mounting ears (Figure 6).

▲ Insert the end of the cable into the knock-out hole in the box and pull it out through the front. Cut away about 11 inches of the outer sheath without nicking the cable wires. Pull the cable back into the box until about 1/2 inch of the sheath is visible above the cable clamp in the box, then tighten the clamp.

▲ Replace or rearrange the insulation in the wall, leaving room for the box. Insert the box in the hole and drive No. 4 1-inch flathead sheet metal screws through the holes in the mounting ears to secure it. Caulk between the box edges and the siding.

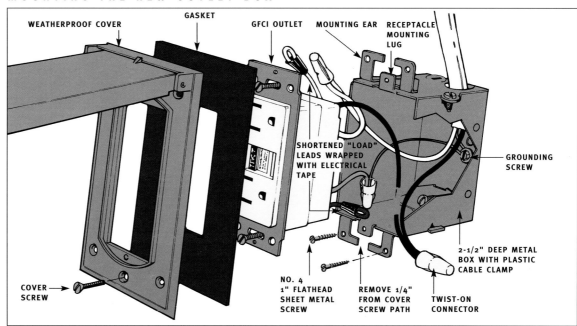

Figure 6. Prepare the mounting ears on the exterior box as shown, clamp in the cable, and install the box. Then connect and install the GFCI receptacle as shown.

WIRING AND INSTALLING THE GFCI RECEPTACLE

Wiring connections to the exterior receptacles are shown in Figure 6. Proceed as follows:

▲ Clip about 2 inches off the ends of the white and black wires in the cable, and then strip 3/4 inch of insulation from each wire. If the grounding wire is insulated (green), strip the insulation all the way back to within about 1 inch of the cable clamp.

▲ Examine the leads on the GFCI receptacle. You will not use the two leads labeled "Load." Clip them off short, double the ends back, and tape them to themselves.

▲ The black and white "Line" leads and the green grounding lead of the receptacle should have 3/4 inch of bare wire at the ends; strip them to 3/4 inch if necessary.

▲ Connect the black and white cable wires to the matching GFCI "Line" leads. Use twist-on connectors. Lay the two bare wire ends side by side and screw on a connector.

▲ Loop the bare grounding wire around the grounding screw at the back of the outlet box and tighten the screw. Then connect the end of this wire to the GFCI green grounding wire with a twist-on connector.

▲ Fold the wires into the box behind the receptacle as you insert it into the box. Fasten it to the mounting lugs on the outlet box using the screws supplied with the receptacle.

▲ The weatherproof cover has a gasket. Position the gasket over the receptacle, then mount the cover with screws into the siding. Follow the directions supplied with the cover.

Grounding in a Metal Interior Box

If the existing interior box is metal rather than plastic, you will need two grounding pigtails.

Connect them together with all the cable grounding wires. Then connect one pigtail to the receptacle and the other to the grounding screw in the box.

CONNECTING THE CABLE TO AN ELECTRICAL CIRCUIT

As with locating and cabling, there are differences between back-to-back and basement wiring procedures.

Back-to-back wiring

Pull the end of the new cable out of the front of the existing outlet box. Trim the jacket, secure it, and cut and strip the individual wires as for the exterior receptacle.

▲ From a scrap length of cable, cut pigtails—6-inch lengths—of black, white, and grounding wire. Strip 3/4 inch of insulation at each end. With long-nose pliers, bend one end of each pigtail into a hook to go around the terminal screws on the receptacle.

▲ Connect the wires and the straight ends of the pigtails as shown in Figure 7, using twist-

on connectors. Connect all of the black cable wires and the black pigtail together. Connect all of the white cable wires and the white pigtail together. Connect all of the bare or green cable grounding wires and the grounding pigtail together.

▲ Now connect the hooked ends of the pigtails to the receptacle. The hook of each wire should go clockwise around the screw, so it is pulled farther around the shaft as the screw is tightened. Connect the black pigtail to a brass terminal on one side of the receptacle. Connect the white pigtail to a silver terminal on the other side. Connect the grounding pigtail to the green or dark-colored terminal near the bottom of the receptacle.

▲ Fold the wires into the box as you insert the receptacle. Replace its mounting screws, then replace the cover plate.

Basement wiring

With power to the existing junction box turned off, trim, secure, and strip the cable wires as described for back-to-back wiring.

▲ If you have an existing junction box with only a single cable running to it, connect the cable as shown in Figure 8 below.

▲ If the junction box is part of a fixture or has other wires running to it, connect the cable as shown in Figure 8 on page 150.

When all wiring is completed, the outlet is ready to have the circuit turned on at the electrical supply panel. If an inspection is required, have that done first.

CONNECTING THE CABLE TO AN ELECTRICAL CIRCUIT

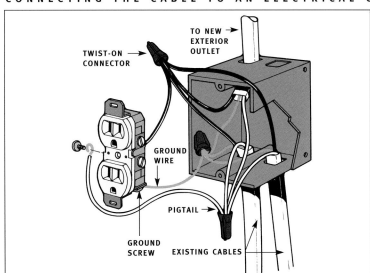

Figure 7. In the interior outlet box, connect like-colored cable wires together. Include pigtails of matching color to make connections to the receptacle.

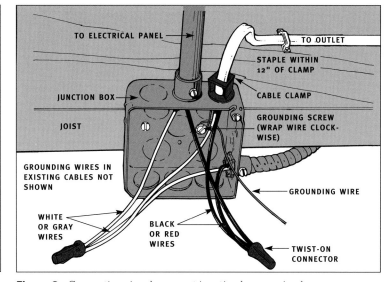

Figure 8. Connections in a basement junction box are simple. The black wire from the exterior outlet can connect to red or black wires in the junction box.

Sometimes plenty of light is simply too much light.

Putting in Dimmer Switches

There are many places in a home where you want full light at times, and softer, less intense light at other times. Wherever you want fingertip control over the light—to change the mood, or to adjust it for comfort or convenience—install a dimmer switch. It takes only minutes, and no previous experience is needed.

USES AND FEATURES OF DIMMER SWITCHES

Most people think first of a dining room, living room, or den as a spot for a dimmer switch. But those aren't the only places to consider. Adjustable hall lights are a useful feature for nighttime, or outside a child's room. A dimmer-controlled bathroom light can reduce the wake-up shock of bright light in the middle of the night. Outdoor lights can be adjusted for nighttime lawn or patio activities, for welcoming guests, and for providing security.

Economy

As well as affecting mood, comfort, and convenience, dimmer switches for incandescent lights have at least three economic advantages:

▲ The most widely used types are inexpensive.

▲ They can greatly extend the life of your bulbs. The filament of a dimmed bulb doesn't burn as hot as one at full intensity, so it lasts longer. Dimming a bulb by only 10 percent can more than double its life span; dimming it to half intensity can increase longevity 30 fold or more—a nice feature, especially with bulbs in places that are hard to reach.

▲ They can lower your electric bills. A dimmed bulb uses less electricity. In one year, a single 100-watt bulb dimmed to half capacity during the hours of normal use will save $7 to $10, paying for the switch in short order.

Screwdriver

Circuit tester

Long-nose pliers

Wire stripper

Types of dimmer switches

The basic and most widely used devices, shown below, are adjustable toggle and rotary dimmer switches for controlling incandescent bulbs. They permit you to turn the light fully on or off, or select any level in between. You can install any one of them in place of an ordinary single-pole light switch.

If you have a light controlled by two separate switches—called three-way switches—you can buy three-way dimmers to use in place of one or both of the switches.

Other types of dimmers for incandescent bulbs include touch-sensitive models, combination dimmer/timers, and dimmers designed to snap on to the power cord of a lamp.

Dimmer Dont's

Dimmer switches can be installed in most—but not all—lighting situations. Beware of these important exceptions:

▲ Don't try to jam a dimmer in a box that is too shallow or overcrowded with wires. Most dimmers have deeper backs than switches, and two more connectors are added to the box when a dimmer is installed.

Before purchasing a dimmer switch, check the interior of the box where you intend to install it. Turn off the power, loosen the mounting screws on the old switch, then check the box's depth and capacity. A thin-profile switch will ease crowding in some situations, but in some cases a dimmer switch just won't fit.

▲ Don't try to use a standard dimmer on fluorescent lights. Fluorescent tubes require a special dimming ballast inside the fixture as well as a special switch.

▲ Don't use standard light dimmers for fans or for controlling outlets where appliances, power tools, computers, or transformer-powered lights (like a high-intensity desk lamp or low-voltage outdoor lighting) might be plugged in.

▲ Don't change bulbs with the dimmer switch on. Unscrewing a bulb can cause a short, ruining the dimming mechanism.

▲ Don't exceed the recommended wattage listed on the dimmer. One rated at 600 watts (the standard) can safely control up to six 100-watt bulbs, but no more than that.

TYPES OF DIMMER SWITCHES

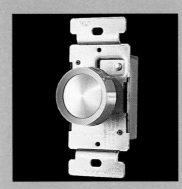

Rotary dimmers ($4–$6) raise the light level when turned clockwise, lower it when turned the opposite way. Some turn on and off by rotating; others are pressed.

Preset slide dimmers ($10–$15) let you adjust light level with a big slide switch, and turn the fixture on and off with a small rocker switch at the bottom.

Toggle-switch dimmers ($5–$10) have a handle that clicks off at the bottom, and increases the light as it is moved upward. This dimmer has a thin profile and works well in shallow or crowded boxes.

INSTALLING A DIMMER SWITCH

Putting in a dimmer switch is an electrical project you can do, even if you've never done anything more complex than change a light bulb. Before buying anything, however, make sure you can install a dimmer in place of a given switch. When you're sure you can go ahead, follow these steps:

▲ Turn off the power to the switch at the fuse box or circuit breaker panel. Remove the switch cover plate and mounting screws and carefully pull the switch straight out of the box on the wall. If it is a metal switch box, be careful not to let the screw heads of the wire connections touch the sides of the box. Use a circuit tester to make sure that the circuit is dead; see Is the Power Really Off? (page 151).

▲ Remove the wires from the screw terminals on the switch (Figure 1). If the wires are connected to back-entry, push-in contacts, cut them next to the switch.

▲ Use long-nose pliers to straighten out the hooked ends of the wires (Figure 2). Cut the ends if necessary so that only 5/8 inch of bare wire extends past the insulation. If you had to cut the wires at the switch, strip 5/8 inch of insulation from each one. This is enough to connect with the dimmer switch without leaving any of the wire exposed.

▲ Attach one wire to each of the leads on the dimmers. Lay the bare ends side by side and use a twist-on connector to fasten them together securely (Figure 3).

▲ Fold the wires into the box, behind the dimmer, as you push it into place (Figure 4). Secure it to the mounting lugs in the box with the two screws supplied with the dimmer, or use the mounting screws from the old switch.

▲ Replace the cover plate or install a new one, then turn on the power to the circuit at the fuse box or circuit breaker panel.

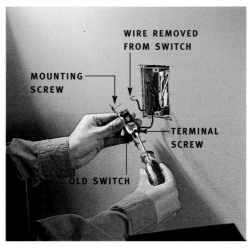

Figure 1. With the power off, remove the old switch from its box. Use a circuit tester to double-check that the power is off before you begin to disconnect the wires.

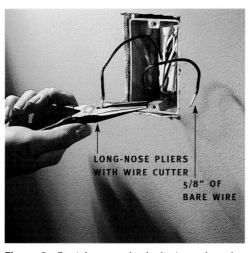

Figure 2. Straighten any hooked wire ends and cut or strip them so that only 5/8 in. of bare wire remains. This way, no bare wire will be exposed past the connector.

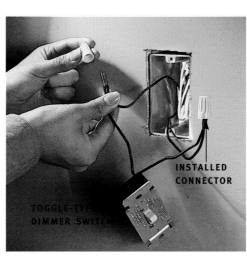

Figure 3. Connect the circuit wires from the box to the leads on the dimmer. Use twist-on wire connectors. They screw on in a clockwise direction over the ends of the wires.

Figure 4. Fold the wires neatly into the switch box in order to fit the dimmer in place. Secure the dimmer with two long screws, then mount the wall plate and turn on the power.

For versatile, unobtrusive, and useful

illumination, you can't beat

recessed lights.

Recessed Lights

Whether you want better lighting for work

or reading, or directed light for display,

decoration, or accent purposes, there are

recessed light fixtures to fill the bill.

You can install one or more recessed

lights in place of an ordinary ceiling

fixture without any major remodeling.

That's what makes this project so appealing.

Recessed lights are manufactured in a wide array of shapes and sizes. Once an oddity known primarily to designers and architects, they are now available at home centers and lighting stores everywhere.

Standard recessed lights are designed to be fastened to the open joists or ceiling supports of new construction. Remodeling-type recessed lights are designed for installation in rooms that already have finished ceilings.

The instructions on these pages show you how to install remodeling-type recessed lights, and how to keep the work and mess to a minimum using an existing switch and ceiling box and a few wire-fishing tricks.

RECESSED VS. SURFACE-MOUNTED LIGHTS

Recessed and surface-mounted lighting fixtures give very different kinds of illumination, as shown in the illustration below.

▲ Surface-mounted ceiling fixtures emit light in all directions. They spread the light for general illumination, but useful light intensity is reduced everywhere except on the ceiling. In fact, the ceiling is the brightest-lighted area in the room. Surface-mounted fixtures also

extend into the room space, so they are directly visible and often are impractical in a room that has a low ceiling.

▲ Recessed fixtures provide "sourceless illumination"—they direct light toward the area or objects below them while drawing very little attention to themselves or the ceiling. Since their light is concentrated in an area of coverage, the illumination there is brighter. This makes them an excellent choice for areas where you want plenty of light without the cluttered look of lots of light fixtures.

Because they are housed above the ceiling surface, recessed fixtures are virtually invisible. In addition, they solve the problem of good lighting in low-ceilinged areas. The three major types of recessed lights are shown on the opposite page. In addition to choosing a particular type, you can vary the lighting by using standard, flood, or spot bulbs and by connecting the lights to a dimmer switch (see "Putting in Dimmer Switches," pages 157–159).

Recessed lights often can be used where other fixtures won't fit or aren't allowed by electrical code—inside closets, bookcases, and kitchen cabinets, for example. Specially designed types can even be installed in damp locations such as showers, saunas, and outside eaves.

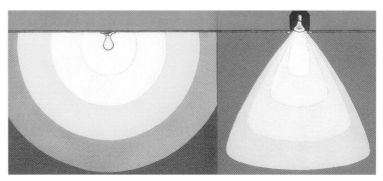

A surface-mounted fixture (left) spreads light over a large area; the ceiling is brightest. A recessed light (right) directs all light to a given area, with virtually no loss in intensity.

Home lighting falls into three broad categories; recessed fixtures can provide all three kinds of light. The three categories are:

• General lighting—the overall illumination that spreads throughout a room.

• Task lighting—the small area light required for cooking, reading, or other close activities.

• Accent lighting—the light concentrated on illuminating a particular object, such as a picture, or area of the home, or light that helps to set a mood.

The types of recessed fixtures that can provide these kinds of light are shown at the right. Whatever type you choose, always buy fixtures that are thermally protected. These contain a safety device that automatically shuts off the light in case it overheats because too large a bulb has been used or the fixture itself is improperly installed.

Wall Washers

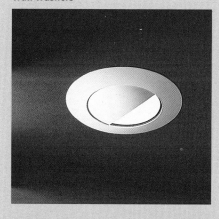

Wall washers are used mainly for accent or mood lighting. Like eyeball fixtures (shown below), they can highlight some of your favorite objects. They are not readily adjustable, but because they don't bulge below the ceiling they are virtually unnoticeable.

Wall-washing fixtures should be spaced 1–3 feet from the wall and 3–5 feet from one another.

Downlights

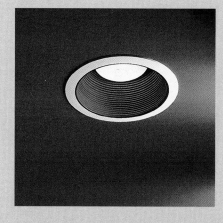

Simple, fixed downlights can be used for general, task, and accent lighting. When using them for general lighting, be sure to install an adequate number. A 100-watt light will illuminate an area about as large as the ceiling height at which it's installed; that is, a 100-watt fixture in an 8-foot ceiling will cast an 8-foot diameter circle on the floor.

Downlights can be either baffled or open style. Baffles, which are black coils surrounding the interior of the fixture, eliminate glare and de-emphasize the fixture. They have a crisp, clean look. Open lights have either reflector bulbs or reflector rings, which tend to highlight the fixture itself.

Eyeballs

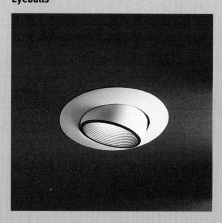

Eyeballs can rotate up to 350 degrees and tilt 30 to 40 degrees. They are used mainly for accent lighting—highlighting artwork or a fireplace mantel—but can be used for task lighting and other purposes as well. Because their adjustable collars extend below the ceiling, eyeballs are the most obtrusive of recessed lights but are also the most versatile.

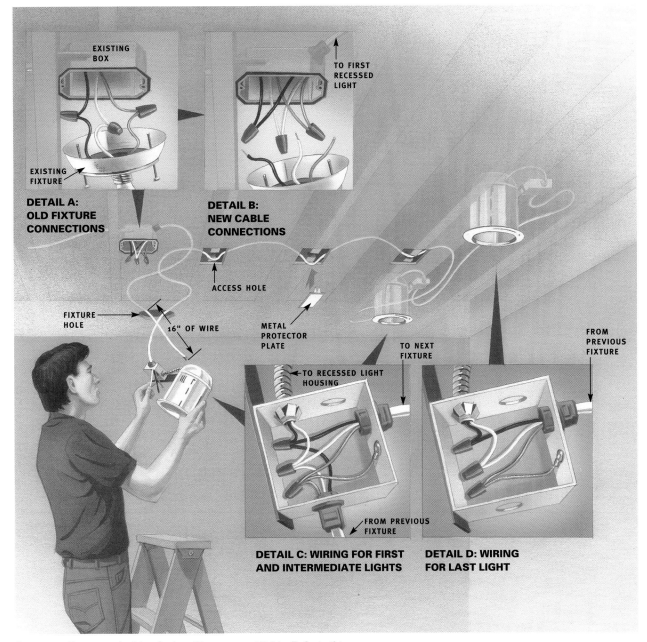

Tools You Need

Drywall saw

Screwdriver

Circuit tester

Long-nose pliers

Wire stripper

Hammer

Chisel

EXISTING BOX

EXISTING FIXTURE

DETAIL A: OLD FIXTURE CONNECTIONS

TO FIRST RECESSED LIGHT

DETAIL B: NEW CABLE CONNECTIONS

ACCESS HOLE

FIXTURE HOLE

16" OF WIRE

METAL PROTECTOR PLATE

TO NEXT FIXTURE

FROM PREVIOUS FIXTURE

TO RECESSED LIGHT HOUSING

FROM PREVIOUS FIXTURE

DETAIL C: WIRING FOR FIRST AND INTERMEDIATE LIGHTS

DETAIL D: WIRING FOR LAST LIGHT

Overview of layout and wiring for installing recessed lights. Refer to this figure when planning your overall layout, and to the details when making wiring connections to the fixtures.

INSTALLING REMODELING-TYPE RECESSED LIGHTS

Before starting to install recessed lights you need to consider a few factors that might limit your work. You also need to get a clear idea of what work the project requires, so you can decide where you may need help.

Limitations

The following three things may limit where or how you install recessed lights:

Space. A ceiling cavity that's very shallow or narrow can prohibit installing recessed fixtures, but this is rare. Most recessed lights require 7 to 8 inches of headroom. The framework above the ceiling, whether floor joists or ceiling rafters, can usually accommodate this height. If not, there are specially designed fixtures that fit into a 5-1/2 inch space.

Circuit capacity. Since you'll be using an existing switch and power supply, you are limited as to the number of lights you can safely install. The total wattage of the new fixtures cannot be more than the old one. If the old fixture had three 100-watt bulbs, you can safely install four 75-watt recessed lights. But you must not overtax the existing circuit—other outlets and appliances are being powered through that same circuit. If you don't know what fixtures and outlets are on the circuit you want to use, see page 147 for a way to find out. Consult an electrician if you are unsure of whether you'll be overloading the circuit.

Insulation. You probably won't encounter insulation in a basement or first-floor ceiling, but it is likely to be present in upper-floor ceilings. To choose fixtures for safe installation in an insulated ceiling, see Dealing with Insulation in the box at right.

Work involved

Installing a recessed light involves fitting the fixture housing through a hole you have cut in the ceiling and installing the trim that covers the rim of the housing and the ceiling edges around it. To run cable for wiring the fixtures you'll need simple carpentry and drywall patching skills. The work is not difficult, but this should not be your very first electrical or do-it-yourself project. Read through the instructions to see what is required. Pick and choose the tasks you feel comfortable doing, and hire a professional for the others.

You can install recessed lighting fixtures in five basic steps:

▲ Remove the old fixture.
▲ Mark the cutting holes for the fixtures.
▲ Run cable for the recessed fixtures.
▲ Wire the fixtures.
▲ Install the fixtures.

The overview on the opposite page shows what has to be done. Here's how to do it.

If the ceiling space where you want to install recessed lights is filled with insulation, you have two options:

• The first, and simplest, choice is to install recessed light housings that are rated as safe for direct contact with insulation (Figure A). Their special design allows them to be completely buried in insulation. The main drawbacks to these housings are that they cost slightly more than standard housings, and that fewer trim styles are available.

• The second option is to create a safe area in the insulated space. You must provide at least 3 inches clearance between all parts of the housing, including the junction box, and any insulation (Figure B). To hold insulation 3 inches away from the top of the fixture, fasten wire mesh to the ceiling framing and put the insulation above it. Box off the sides of the fixture space with fiberglass batts cut to fit.

You must space either type of housing at least 1/2 inch from combustibles, including rafters or joists and the subfloor of the room directly above.

Heat must also be able to make its way out through the insulation, which means that no plastic or airtight enclosures can surround either type of fixture.

Figure A. Housing rated for direct contact with insulation.

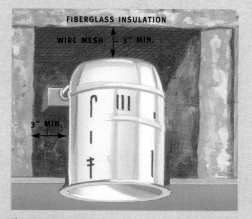

Figure B. Housing not rated for contact with insulation.

REMOVING AN OLD FIXTURE

Before you do anything else, go to the electrical service panel and remove the fuse for that circuit or turn the circuit breaker off and tape it in the off position.

▲ Remove the dome or cover from the fixture and undo the mounting screws so that it can be lowered, pulling the wires out of the outlet box above (See Detail A, page 162).

▲ Unscrew the connectors from the white and black cable wires and touch the leads of a circuit tester to them. If the tester does not light up, the circuit is dead and you can proceed. If the tester does light up, find the fuse or breaker that controls this circuit and cut the power off. (Also see Is the Circuit Really Off? on page 151.)

▲ Disconnect the fixture from the cable wires and remove it entirely. Later you will connect the cable for the recessed lights at this spot.

MARKING AND CUTTING HOLES FOR THE FIXTURES

Select where you would ideally like to place the lights. At each location, drill a small hole and probe with a bent coat hanger in every direction to determine if there are any obstructions. If you find a joist or rafter in the way, shift away from it, drill another hole and probe again (you can fill and touch up the first hole later). You need enough space for the fixture plus the minimum 1/2-inch (or manufacturer's specified) clearance on all sides.

▲ Use the template included with the fixtures to trace the required hole outline at each position (Figure 1). It will be a circle or a square, depending on the style of your fixtures.

▲ Cut the holes with a drywall saw (Figure 2); it will create much less mess than a saber saw. If you have trouble getting the saw started, drill a 3/4-inch hole inside the opening outline to insert the tip of the saw blade. Cut neatly along the marked outline.

MARKING AND CUTTING HOLES FOR THE FIXTURES

TEMPLATE →

Figure 1. Mark the opening by tracing around the template included with the fixture. Probe with a coat hanger through a small hole first, to locate the ceiling framing or other obstructions.

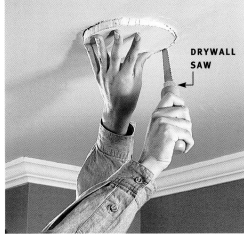

DRYWALL SAW ←

Figure 2. Cut and remove the ceiling material using a drywall saw. The edges of the ceiling hole will be covered by the trim piece when the recessed fixture is installed.

RUNNING CABLE FOR THE RECESSED FIXTURES

Use cable of the same type and with wires the same size as in the existing cable. The most common type is 14-2G: a cable with 14-gauge black- and white-insulated circuit wires and a bare or green-insulated ground wire.

▲ Starting at either the first or last fixture hole, feed cable up into the hole and across the ceiling toward the next hole. When you can, reach up through the second hole, grasp the cable and pull it along. Running the cable goes faster with two people, one to feed cable up into the ceiling, the other to pull the cable along from hole to hole.

  If the fixture holes all lie between the same two joists, running the cable is easy. But if they are in different joist or rafter bays, you must run the cable across the ceiling framing.

▲ To get across the framing, cut a neat 6-inch hole under each joist or rafter to give you access (Figure 3); save the cut-out pieces of ceiling. Make the access holes at least 1 foot away from the line of the fixture holes, so the wire has room to accordion out of the way.

▲ Cut a 1/2-inch deep notch in each exposed joist edge with a sharp chisel and run the cable through the notches. Protect it by nailing a 1/16-inch thick metal plate across the notches (Figure 4). Patch the access holes with the pieces of drywall you originally removed. Use drywall backing at the edges.

▲ At each fixture hole, pull a loop of cable at least 16 inches long down through the ceiling and let it hang. You will need it to make connections with the fixtures.

▲ At the outlet box where the old fixture was mounted, open one of the unused knock-out cable holes. You usually can pry out the knock-out filler piece by inserting a screwdriver blade into the slot in its center. Your job now is to get the cable into the box.

▲ Push a straightened coat hanger or other stiff wire through the knock-out hole until you can reach it through the first fixture hole. Tie on a piece of strong string and pull one end back into the outlet box. Tie the other end of the string to the cable and wrap it with tape so the cable end won't snag. Then pull the string to draw the end of the cable into the outlet box. Pull about 12 inches through, slip on an internal cable clamp, and secure the cable in the box.

RUNNING CABLE FOR THE RECESSED FIXTURES

Figure 3. Run a cable continuously from one fixture location to another. To run cable across the framing, remove a small section of ceiling at each joist or rafter for access.

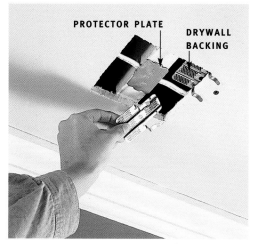

Figure 4. Notch the framing for the cable and cover it with a metal protector plate. Use drywall backing plates to replace the cutout piece; patch with tape and compound.

WIRING THE FIXTURES

At the outlet box, cut back the plastic sheath of the new cable, clip 2 to 3 inches off each wire, and strip about 5/8 inch of insulation from the ends. Connect them with the existing cable wires (as shown in Detail B of the overview, page 162). Use twist-on wire connectors to secure. Connect only to the full-size wires that were connected to the old fixture leads and to the grounding wire. There may be wires from other circuits in the box; don't disturb them. Fold the wires up into the outlet box and place a blank cover plate over it, so that the wiring is accessible.

At each light position, cut the cable loop hanging out of the fixture hole in half. Secure the ends inside the built-in junction box of the fixture and connect them with the fixture leads (Figure 5). For all except the last fixture, make the connections as shown in Detail C of the overview. At the last fixture, make the connections as shown in Detail D.

INSTALLING THE FIXTURES

Fit the fixture through the hole in the ceiling and fasten it in place according to the manufacturer's instructions for the unit.

▲ Manufacturers have different methods for securing their particular remodeling lights in the ceiling. Some have clips that pinch the drywall once the light is in position (Figure 6). Others fasten the housing to a small frame that you slip into position in the ceiling.

▲ When the housing is in place, add the trim (Figure 7) and the correct size and shape of bulb. Most housings can accommodate a variety of types of trim—downlight, wall washer, or eyeball. That means you could change the function of an installed light at a later time if you wish. In some units you must install the bulb before putting the trim in place. Finally, turn the circuit power on again.

WIRING THE FIXTURES

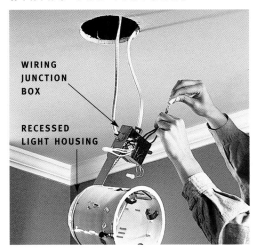

Figure 5. Connect the fixture leads to the cable wires. Secure each connection firmly with a twist-on wire connector. Then fold the wires into the fixture junction box.

INSTALLING THE FIXTURES

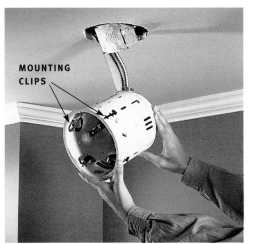

Figure 6. Push the light housing into the ceiling opening. The fixture shown here is secured with built-in clips that pinch the drywall. Other models may mount somewhat differently.

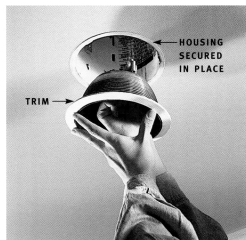

Figure 7. Install the trim—this is a downlight—and the proper bulb. The trim usually snaps into place, but check the fixture instructions for any special procedures or attachments.

WIRING OPTIONS

The preceding instructions assume that you could remove a switch-operated ceiling light and tie the recessed lights into the existing fixture box and switch. There are three other possibilities, for which you will need the aid of a licensed electrician.

1. Add a recessed fixture at the ceiling box location

Replace the existing ceiling box with a recessed light. This will eliminate the blank cover plate over the old box. You can use the built-in junction box in the recessed fixture to make the connections with the power supply and switch, and with the cable going to the other recessed fixtures. This addition involves removing and reconnecting all the wires now located in the ceiling box—a task that requires a great deal of care.

2. Install an additional switch for the recessed lights

You may not have an existing switched ceiling fixture to replace where you want to install recessed lights. Or if you do, you may want to keep it while adding recessed lighting to the room. To deal with either situation, either add a completely new circuit from your service panel, or run power from an outlet in the room to a new switch. An electrician can handle this sort of work easily.

3. Power the recessed lights directly from the switch

In many cases, power to the recessed lights can be routed through the switch, instead of the ceiling box. If there is no other wiring in the ceiling box, this would allow you to remove it and patch over the ceiling where it was located.

LIGHTING OPTIONS

In addition to the standard installation with incandescent recessed light fixtures described on the preceding pages, the following possibilities are worth considering.

1. Fluorescent lights

Fluorescent lights cast a soft, diffused light that is excellent for general illumination, especially if the light is on continuously. The initial cost is much higher than conventional lights, but operating and bulb replacement costs are low.

2. Low-voltage lights

Low-voltage lights cast a very pure light in a specific pattern, making them ideal for accent lighting. Some have adjustable lenses that can change the size and shape of the light beam. They operate on 12 volts, so a small transformer is required.

3. Valance installation

If it is impossible or impractical to cut into the existing ceiling, you can install a valance that boxes in the ceiling–wall corner. Locate it 15 or more inches from the wall, extending downward an equal distance, and returning to the wall. Frame it with a 2x4 ceiling plate attached to the joists, and a 2x4 plate on the wall attached to the studs. Run 2x2 or 2x3 struts down from the ceiling plate and out from the wall plate to support a 2x3 for the lower outside corner. Space the struts to make it easy to attach recessed fixtures where you want them. Cover the face and bottom of the valance with drywall.

4. False-beam installation

If the ceiling is particularly high, it may be desirable to install recessed lights in one or more false beams built on the ceiling surface, to bring them a bit closer to the area being illuminated. Construct the beams similar to the valance (option 3) but with two ceiling plates, and struts down to and between 2x4's at the lower edges. Make it wide enough and deep enough to provide good ventilation around the fixtures, and cover it with drywall.

5. Luminous panel

To spread soft illumination over a very wide area, build a luminous panel with recessed flourescent fixtures. Cut an opening in the ceiling surface as long as the fixtures and two, three, or four joist bays wide. Install flourescent fixtures side by side across the width of each bay. Cover the entire opening with white diffusing plastic, held by a wood frame screwed to the ceiling joists. To eliminate shadow lines of the joists between pairs of fixtures, mount the plastic about two inches below the ceiling surface, so the light from one bay can spread out and overlap the light from the adjacent bay.

Storage

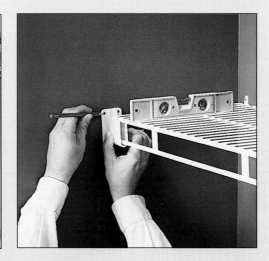

Bathroom Vanity and Medicine Cabinet

New cabinets will virtually make over a bathroom, and increase storage space at the same time. Installation is simple.

170

Build a Simple Closet

Create storage space where you need it— build a closet in the corner of any room. Here's the easiest way to do it.

175

Closet Systems

Get the most into and out of your closets. Use modular units to organize the interior storage space with maximum efficiency.

184

Storage space is scant in most bathrooms, especially for families of three or more.

Bathroom Vanity and Medicine Cabinet

Few bathrooms feature closets; some provide undersink storage, but a great many have only a medicine cabinet. For the convenience of more storage space in your bathroom, put in new vanity and medicine cabinets.

It's a project you can do in one weekend. It will improve the looks of the bathroom immediately and will make life easier for years to come.

A new vanity and medicine cabinet can provide an almost instant redo of a bathroom. You may want to recover the wall or floor at the same time, for a complete transformation.

CHOOSING NEW BATHROOM CABINETS

The vanity cabinet that houses the bathroom sink and the medicine cabinet above it get heavy use. Stock units are manufactured in many different grades of quality as well as style, so look carefully at both the construction and the appearance of these items before you buy. Check drawers to make sure they're smooth edged and well built, and that they slide open and closed easily. Make sure that doors are square and sturdily hinged. Check mirrors for smoothly finished edges. Here are some additional points to consider.

Vanity cabinets

Stock vanities come in two depths—18 and 21 inches—and in lengths from 10 to 72 inches. These are the actual cabinet sizes; a countertop will extend 1 inch more in the front and at each end. Your choice of cabinet will depend in part on personal preference, but mainly on how much space is available in your bathroom. You'll probably want to get as much counter space as possible, but don't crowd the vanity closer than 2 inches from the toilet tank, or 3 inches from the side of the tub.

The longer the vanity, the more storage space it will provide; you can never have too much. Usually there is a hinged door in front of the compartment where the sink, drain, and water lines are located. There is always space there for tall items. Adjacent compartments may have shelves or drawers. If you choose a vanity with shelves, make sure they are adjustable. A vanity that has both shelves and drawers is ideal for most situations.

Tops for vanities are often priced separately from the cabinets, with or without a sink. Stock depths are 19 and 22 inches. The most common types are either cultured—that is, synthetic—marble, or chipboard (or equivalent material) covered with plastic laminate. Check the underside of whatever unit you buy to make sure that there are no cracks or unusual irregularities in the material. This is a good time to get a new sink and faucets, too. But if you choose to use your old sink and hardware, make sure you get a top with cutouts that match their sizes and spacing, to make reinstallation easy.

Medicine cabinets

There are two styles of medicine cabinet, surface-mounted and recessed.

Surface-mounted cabinet. This type is the easiest to install: you simply drive screws through the back into wall studs. It also brings the mirror a few inches closer, which can be helpful to a nearsighted family member who prefers not to wear glasses when shaving, coiffing, or putting on makeup.

Recessed cabinet. A cabinet set into the wall saves space in a small bathroom and gives the wall a sleek, modern look. Installing a recessed cabinet requires cutting into the wall. Units that fit between two studs are available, but they dictate the location of the sink, which must be centered under the cabinet. Also, you will probably want more space than their 14-inch interior width. Wider units require removing part of one or two studs to install. Never install a recessed cabinet in an exterior wall or cut through studs of a load-bearing wall.

Whichever style you choose, make sure the cabinet has adjustable shelves and a mirrored door or doors. Some units have a built-in light or lights, and many more are available with matching or harmonizing light units.

PLANNING AHEAD

The new vanity and medicine cabinet will replace the old ones, but plan carefully to avoid unnecessary work, especially if the new units are larger than the old.

▲ To save time and plumbing work, plan to center the new sink within a few inches of the old sink centerline. Both the drain and water lines will be a lot easier to reconnect.

▲ If you're going to install a recessed medicine cabinet, check whether a plumbing vent pipe runs up through the space where the cabinet is to go; if so, you may have to use a surface-mounted cabinet instead. If you can use a recessed unit, install it first, so you have plenty of room to work without danger of damaging the vanity cabinet.

▲ Also check about wiring a lighting fixture. Can you use existing wiring, or do you need to pull wire for a new circuit? The best location for a light is on the wall above the medicine cabinet, so that it illuminates your face and the sink. A ceiling light directly overhead or a bit behind you cannot illuminate your face evenly and will cast shadows across the sink.

▲ Examine the condition of the walls and the floor. If you want to improve them, plan to do it after removing the old vanity and cabinet, before installing the new. That way you won't have to do any special cutting or fitting around the cabinets. For information about upgrading the walls, see Hanging Wallcoverings (pages 60–66). Be sure to choose a vinyl or plastic-coated covering for bathroom walls, to avoid moisture problems. For information about laying a new floor covering, see Vinyl Floor Tile (pages 99–105), or Ceramic Tile Entryway (pages 112–119). You can use the same techniques to redo the bathroom floor.

Tools You Need

Measuring tape

Level

Wrench or large-jaw pliers

Saber saw

Stud finder

Drywall saw

Drill

Screwdriver

Caulking gun

PREPARING THE AREA

Turn off the water at the stops in the supply lines under the sink. Disconnect the faucets and the drain. Remove the old sink and its cabinet or other support.

▲ Take out the old medicine cabinet. If it has an integral light fixture, or if you are going to change the fixture above it, turn off the power to that circuit at the fuse or circuit breaker panel and remove the fixture.

▲ Relocate the cable for the light fixture if necessary. Then do any repair or remodeling work on the walls and floor.

▲ Measure and mark the location of the medicine cabinet. The top of the mirror should be about 6 feet above the floor, or high enough so the tallest member of the family can see his or her image, plus about 2 inches. Use pieces of masking tape to mark top and side edge positions of the cabinet.

▲ Mark the side edge positions of the vanity cabinet as you did for the medicine cabinet. Also use a stud finder or tap on the wall to locate any studs you need for fastening the cabinets. Mark the stud positions with tape.

INSTALLING THE VANITY CABINET

Measure and mark the back of the vanity to cut an opening for the water and drain pipes. A single triangular opening (Figure 1) is better than individual holes, because it makes it easy to slip the cabinet into place and adjust its position. Drill a starting hole inside one edge of the marked section and make the cutout with a saber saw. Round the corners of the triangle as you make a single, continuous cut.

▲ Set the vanity against the wall, center it, and check the level from front to back, and side to side across both the front and back edges (Figure 2). If the cabinet is just slightly off level, shim the bottom; otherwise, trim the bottom edges. When it sits level, fasten it with two or three screws driven into studs.

▲ Mount the drain and faucets before you install the sink (Figure 3). This will keep you from having to work on your back inside the cabinet. Turn the sink upside down to tighten the mounting nuts; be sure to protect its surface from scratches. If you are putting in new fittings, follow the instructions supplied with them. Use plumber's putty to seal joints where the fittings join the sink.

▲ Use a caulking gun to apply a bead of construction adhesive to the top edges of the cabinet on all four sides (Figure 4). Then set the vanity top in position.

▲ Adjust the top so there are equal overhangs at each end of the cabinet and it is tight against the wall (Figure 5). It will slide in the adhesive. Scrape off any excess adhesive from the underside before it hardens. If the top is supplied with mounting brackets, fasten them from underneath to hold it in place.

▲ If the sink is not an integral part of the top, install it without knocking the top out of position. Run a thin strand of plumber's putty under the rim of a self-rimming sink before putting it in place (roll the putty between the palms of your hands). For other sinks, follow the supplied instructions for mounting, sealing the rim joint, and installing trim.

▲ Reassemble the drain trap and connect the water lines as they were before. If the sink is no longer in line with the drain stub in the wall, use adjustable plastic drain pipe and fittings to position the trap under the sink drain (Figure 6). If necessary, hang a string with a weight on the end through the center of the drain, like a plumb bob, to mark the position.

If the faucets are in new positions, use easy-to-install tubing or flex fittings to connect them to the water supply stops. The fittings are available with instructions at home centers and plumbing supply shops.

▲ Connect the pop-up stopper in the sink. Turn on the water supply stops and check for any leaks at the fittings. Tighten the connections if necessary, but be careful not to overdo it and crack the couplings.

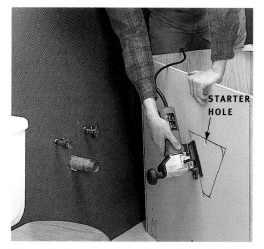

Figure 1. Cut a single opening in the back of the new vanity cabinet for the water and drain lines. Make it 1 to 2 in. wider than the pipes, so you can shift the cabinet right or left to adjust its position.

Figure 2. Level the vanity both front to back and side to side. Shim for a minor adjustment, otherwise trim the bottom edges with a saw. Secure the cabinet with screws driven into the wall studs.

Figure 3. Mount the drain and faucet before installing the sink. Use plumber's putty where the drain and faucets pass through the sink; follow the instructions supplied with the fittings.

Using Plastic Pipe

Pieces of plastic pipe must be joined to their fittings with a liquid cement that fuses them together permanently.

To work with plastic components, first assemble them in place without cement and get them properly aligned. Then make a pencil mark across each joint, that runs from the fitting onto the pipe.

Take the assembly apart and remake the joints one by one. Coat the inside of the fitting and the outside end of the piece of pipe with cement. Immediately insert the pipe into the fitting with the pencil marks a quarter-turn out of line. As soon as the pipe is fully seated, turn it to align the pencil marks and do not disturb it for a minute or two, to give the cement time to fuse the joint together. Then go on to the next joint.

Figure 4. Use construction adhesive to hold the vanity top in place. Apply a thin bead to all four edges of the cabinet with a caulking gun, then put the top in place.

Figure 5. Measure the overhang at each end to center the top, and push it tight against the wall; make sure it is secure on all edges. Scrape off any excess adhesive below before it hardens.

Figure 6. Reassemble the trap and water lines. If the sink position is different than before, use plastic drain fittings, pipe, and trap for easy, flexible assembly; see the sidebar.

INSTALLING THE MEDICINE CABINET

Putting up a surface-mounted cabinet is quite simple. You can do it before or after installing the vanity cabinet. Installing a recessed cabinet is more complex and, as noted earlier, should be done before the vanity cabinet is in place.

Surface-mounted cabinet

Have one or two helpers hold the cabinet in place, aligned with the tape marks on the wall (Figure 7). Place a level across the top and adjust until the cabinet is exactly horizontal. Then drive screws through the back into studs, also marked with tape.

Connect and install the light fixture above the cabinet. If the housing mounts on top of the cabinet (Figure 8), pull the cable into it and fasten it in position before making the wiring connections to the fixture.

Recessed medicine cabinet

Mark the outline of the cabinet on the wall. Be sure that the top is the proper height above the floor and that all of the lines are exactly horizontal and vertical.

⚠ Double-check that the power is off to any electrical lines that run through the wall.

⚠ Cut away the wall precisely along the marked outline. Use a drywall saw rather than a saber saw to minimize the mess. Cut with a utility knife across the edges of studs.

⚠ Cut off the studs running through the opening and install a 2x4 header across the top. If the cabinet trim is wide enough or if a light fixture will provide masking, cut through both the drywall and the studs to remove the 1-1/2 inches needed for the header. Otherwise, cut a split header to go on either side of the center stud.

Screw, don't nail, a full header into the bottom ends of the cutoff studs and to the studs at either side behind the wall. If you can't toe-screw at the ends of the header, screw cleats to the studs beforehand and fasten the header to them. Toe-screw a split header at all points.

Install a "split sill" across the bottom of the opening: Screw cleats on the sides of the studs, 1-1/2 inches below the edge of the opening. Cut pieces of 2x4 to fit between the studs and screw them to the cleats.

⚠ Insert the cabinet in the recess. Lay a level across the bottom on the inside and shim as necessary to get the cabinet horizontal. Then drive screws into the headers at the top and bottom, or secure the cabinet according to any instructions supplied with it.

⚠ Install the light fixture as described for a surface-mounted cabinet. Be sure to pull plenty of cable into the fixture and test its position before cutting the cable to length. Then mount the fixture and make the wiring connections.

INSTALLING THE MEDICINE CABINET

Figure 7. Install a surface-mounted medicine cabinet on the wall with screws driven into studs. Be sure it is level. Have helpers hold it in place so that it is aligned with the pre-positioned tape marks while you work.

Figure 8. Mount a light fixture above the medicine cabinet after you have run the electrical line through from the wall. A light situated directly above the mirror will illuminate your face and body without casting shadows.

When your storage space is stuffed and you need more, try the direct approach. Build a closet.

Build a Simple Closet

Wherever you have a free corner—
bedroom, entry hall, den,
or family room—you can build
this simple closet.
You can make it as long or as deep
as you need, and finish it to match
the style of any room.
Only basic carpentry is required, and
the simplest of drywall work.
Just follow the instructions and your
storage problem will be solved—
at least for a while.

Choose a corner for your new closet so you'll only have to build two walls. Putting up the framework and drywall will take one weekend. Installing doors and trim will take a second weekend. In between, you can tape and finish the drywall seams.

MARKING THE LAYOUT

You need to mark the positions of the sole plates and top plates of the new closet walls on the floor and ceiling. This will help you build the frames to the right size, and align them easily when you put them in place.

▲ Decide on the interior depth and length of the closet. For a clothes closet, the absolute minimum depth is 22 inches, otherwise you can't store clothes on hangers. It is far better to make the inside depth 24 inches or more. The length of the closet can be any dimension that provides sufficient width for the door or doors you plan to install.

▲ From the corner of the room, measure out alongside the existing wall, which will serve as the end of the closet. Make the measurement equal to the interior depth of the closet plus 4 inches—1/2 inch for the thickness of the drywall on the inside and 3-1/2 inches for

the width of the sole plate of the new wall. (If you build the closet with 2x3's instead of 2x4's, add only 3 inches.) Be sure to subtract the thickness of the existing baseboard if you measure from its face, because you will be removing it. Mark the floor at that point.

▲ Now measure the length of the closet from the marked point. Use a carpenter's square to make the measurement at right angles to the existing wall. Again, subtract the baseboard thickness from the interior length and add 4 inches to allow for the interior drywall and sole plate of the new end wall. Mark that point on the floor; it is the outside corner of the closet wall framing. Draw a line from there back to the first marked point (at the end wall). This line shows the position of the outside edge of the sole plate for the front wall of the closet.

▲ At the outside corner point, use a carpenter's square to mark the edge position of the

end wall sole plate (Figure 1). This method ensures that the outside corner of the closet is square and that the front wall will be square to the existing wall at the other end. If the inside room corner is not perfectly square, the only variation will be where the new end wall of the closet meets the room wall, and any variation will not be noticeable.

▲ Now transfer the layout lines up to the ceiling. Use a plumb bob to mark the ceiling point directly above the outside corner, and points close to each wall directly above the sole plate lines (Figures 2, 3). Have a helper align the plumb bob exactly at the floor as you mark the ceiling. Then snap chalk lines between the marked ceiling points.

▲ Finally, either use a level or snap chalk lines between the ceiling and the floor to mark the edges of the framing studs that will be fastened against the existing walls.

Tools You Need

Measuring tape

Level

Carpenter's square

Plumb bob

Stud finder

Pry bar

Hammer

Nail set

Drywall saw

Handsaw

Drill

Screwdriver

Drywall taping tools

MARKING THE LAYOUT

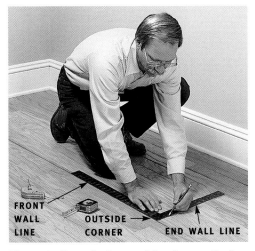

FRONT WALL LINE   OUTSIDE CORNER   END WALL LINE

Figure 1. Draw the layout of the closet wall sole plates on the floor. Measure for the front wall first, then draw the end wall line. Make sure the outside corner is square.

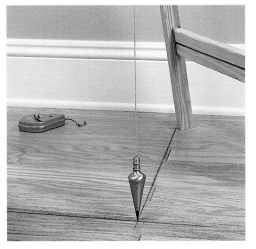

Figure 2. Use a plumb line bob to transfer the marked floor layout up to the ceiling. Ask a helper to reduce its swinging and tell you when it is in position over the outside corner.

Figure 3. Make marks on the ceiling above the outside corner and at the two walls. Snap chalk lines on the ceiling between these points to show where the top sole plates go.

Figure 4. Pry off the baseboard and ceiling trim carefully for reuse. Protect the wall with scrap plywood. Cut trim 1/2 in. beyond the marked stud line, to allow for the drywall on the outside of the closet walls.

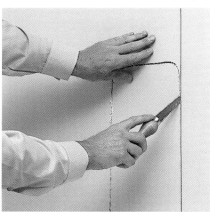

Figure 5. Cut holes in the walls or ceiling to put in support blocks for the wall framing. Cut the outer edges along the marked lines; finishing will conceal the cuts. Shut off electricity before cutting.

Figure 6. Fasten 2x4 support blocks to wall studs or ceiling joists. Toe-screwing avoids potential wall damage caused by hammering nails. Also screw the cut drywall edge to the support block.

Figure 7. Replace the drywall after adding a support block. Screw cleats on the back of the drywall at the top and bottom to support the edges of the cutout. Finish with tape and compound later.

REMOVING TRIM AND INSTALLING SUPPORT BLOCKS

Mark the baseboard and ceiling trim (if any) 1/2 inch outside the vertical layout lines on the wall, to allow for the drywall on the exterior of the closet walls. If there is a corner or natural break in the trim not far from those points, pry off the entire piece (Figure 4). If not, score and saw through the trim at the marked point and remove the closet section. Be careful; you must use this trim on the outside of the new closet walls in order to match the rest of the room. (You can use a plain baseboard inside the closet; it won't be seen.)

▲ Use a stud finder to locate the studs in the existing walls near the marked vertical lines. If a line falls right over a stud, you can fasten the closet wall stud directly to it. But if the line falls between two existing studs, you must add a support block at the center (you can fasten the top and bottom of the closet stud to the top and sole plates of the existing wall).

▲ Cut out a section of the existing wall midway between top and bottom (Figure 5). Cut along the line marked on the wall and back to the stud inside the closet. Remove a piece big enough so you can reach inside the wall cavity with a power screwdriver. Cut neatly and save the piece of drywall for reuse.

▲ Fasten a 2x4 block between this stud and the one at the other side of the wall cavity (Figure 6). Toe-screw the block; hammering could crack seams or pop out drywall fasteners. Also fasten the cut edge of the drywall to the block with a drywall screw.

▲ Screw a 1x4 cleat to the back of the drywall at the top and bottom of the opening (Figure 7). Then replace the cutout piece and screw it to the cleats and the support block.

▲ Follow the same procedure to provide support blocks in the ceiling where necessary. If the line of the top plate of the closet runs parallel to the joists, install a block at the center and at the outside corner (see Closet Framing diagram, page 178). If it runs across the joists, you can fasten the plate to the joists through the existing ceiling, but you may need a block at the outside corner if it does not fall directly under a joist. In the ceiling, and the walls as well, you may be able to screw a support block to the side of a joist or stud rather than running it between two studs.

BUILDING AND INSTALLING THE WALL FRAMES

Build the two wall frames separately on the floor. Put down a drop cloth or sheets of cardboard to protect the floor. Make the short end wall first and install it. Then construct the long front wall with a rough opening for the doors. The instructions assume using 2x4's. If you use 2x3's, remember that they are the same thickness—1-1/2 inches—but only 2-1/2 inches instead of 3-1/2 inches wide.

End wall

To cut the top and sole plates for the end wall, subtract 3-1/2 inches from the measurement between the outside corner and the existing wall, because the plates of the long wall frame go in front of them.

▲ Measure and cut the studs individually, in case the floor and ceiling are not parallel. Remember that the studs will be 3 inches shorter than the floor-to-ceiling measurement, because they fit between the 1-1/2-inch-thick sole and top plates.

▲ Nail the framework together on the floor. Put a stud at the outside end, at the wall, and midway between (see Closet Framing diagram). Drive two 16d nails through the plates into each end of the studs.

▲ Tip the frame up into position and align the sole plate with the line on the floor. Nail the plate in position. Align the end stud with the vertical line on the wall and fasten it to the support block in the middle and to the existing wall top plate. Use 3-inch screws rather than nails, to avoid vibration damage.

▲ At the ceiling, pull or push the outside corner so the top plate aligns with the chalk line there. Check with a level alongside the outside corner stud to make sure the frame is perfectly vertical. When it is, screw through the top plate of the frame into the joists or support blocks. If there is a gap at a fastening point, insert a thin shim and screw through it.

Front wall

Build the front wall frame as shown in the Closet Framing diagram and Figure 9. Measure for the top and sole plates from the outside of the end wall plates back to the existing wall.

▲ Cut and nail the two end studs first. Again, subtract 3 inches from the floor-to-ceiling measurement, because the studs go between the plates, and drive 16d nails through the plates into the ends of the studs. Then construct the outside corner by adding a second stud, separated from the first by 2x4 spacer blocks. This offsets the inner stud to provide a nailing surface for drywall at the corner inside the closet.

▲ Frame the door opening with two full-length king studs and two shorter trimmer studs set next to them. The trimmer studs support a double header that spans the opening between the king studs. Check the specifications for the doors you plan to install to get the dimensions of the rough opening. When you measure the trimmers, subtract 1-1/2 inches from the rough opening height, because the trimmers will stand on top of the sole plate.

CLOSET FRAMING

Build the two wall frames separately. Note construction of the outside corner and the door opening in the front wall frame (also see Figure 8). Install and plumb the end wall first, then the front wall. Fasten the frames to existing wall and ceiling framing where possible; otherwise fasten them to the support blocks (B).

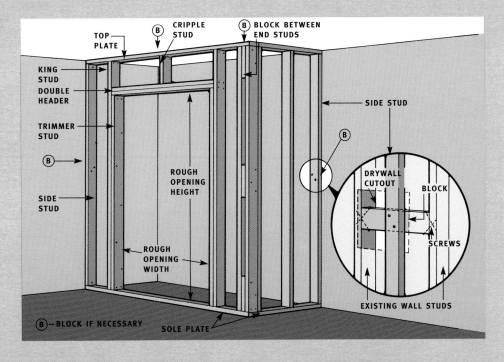

TOP PLATE
Ⓑ CRIPPLE STUD
Ⓑ BLOCK BETWEEN END STUDS
KING STUD
DOUBLE HEADER
TRIMMER STUD
Ⓑ
SIDE STUD
ROUGH OPENING HEIGHT
ROUGH OPENING WIDTH
SIDE STUD
Ⓑ
DRYWALL CUTOUT
BLOCK
SCREWS
EXISTING WALL STUDS
Ⓑ—BLOCK IF NECESSARY
SOLE PLATE

The rough opening width takes into account the door width, plus the thickness of the jamb on each side, plus a small allowance on each side for adjustment and shims. When you measure the headers, add 1-1/2 inches to the rough opening dimension at each end, because they rest on top of the trimmers.

⏶ As with the end wall, assemble the frame on the floor with 16d nails. Insert a short cripple stud between the headers and top plate, over the center of the door opening (Figure 8). If the end studs of the frame are more than 16 inches from the king studs of the doorway, add full-length studs centered between them.

⏶ Before erecting the frame, prop up the sole plate on three or four scraps of 2x4 and, from the bottom, cut about one-third of the way through the plate. Do this in line with the inside face of the trimmer stud at each side of the doorway rough opening. The sole plate is left full length to help keep the frame square and stable while you assemble and erect it. The cuts in the bottom of the sole plate will make it easy to remove the section across the doorway before you install the doors.

⏶ Tip the frame into place, aligning the outside corner with the end wall frame (Figure 9). This is easier with a helper than working alone. Nail the sole plate to the floor, but not across the door opening. Screw or nail the end wall frame to the corner stud and blocks in the front wall frame. Use 3-inch screws to fasten the top plate and the stud at the other end of the front wall to the existing ceiling and wall framing, to avoid damage from hammering vibrations. Shim any gaps in the top plate.

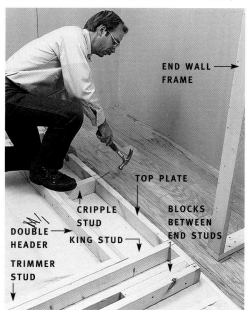

Figure 8. Use 16d nails to assemble the wall frames on the floor before erecting them. This photo shows how the outside corner and the door opening in the front wall are constructed.

Figure 9. Tilt wall sections into place, end wall first, and plumb them before fastening. Use 16d nails into the floor and at the outside corner, but 3-in. screws into the existing walls and ceiling.

COVERING THE FRAMES WITH DRYWALL

Cover the interior first; it's easier to get the pieces of drywall in while the framework is open. Cover the inside of the front wall, then the end wall. This gives you the greatest amount of fastening surface at the inside corner. Use drywall screws or nails.

⏶ On the outside, also do the front wall first, then the end wall (Figure 10). In the front wall, a seam between two pieces of drywall must fall over a stud. If you can place the seam over the cripple stud above the header, you will have the least amount of taping to do.

⏶ To finish the joints, use corner bead on the outside corner and drywall tape at the inside corners, along with taping compound. Finish the corners, seams, and nail or screw heads. Also tape and compound the edges of any cutouts you made to install support blocks.

COVERING THE FRAMES

Figure 10. Fasten drywall to the frames with either nails or screws. Do the inside first, then the outside. Also, do the front wall first. Finish joints with corner bead, tape, and compound.

INSTALLING THE DOORS

The bifold doors shown in the photographs are installed with jambs and face trim (casings) for a rather elegant, formal appearance.

Depending on the style of your home, you might prefer a simple, clean installation that omits the jambs and casing: Wrap the rough opening with 1/2-inch drywall and set the doors directly in the opening. If you plan to use this method, be sure to allow for the thickness of the drywall on each side when you build the rough opening. One difficulty with this method is that you must be sure to get the header absolutely level, because the track for the door will mount directly to it (rather than to a head jamb that can be shimmed level). If you choose to do this, don't cut the trimmers or install the headers until the front wall frame has been erected. Then you can measure the trimmers individually, to ensure that you install the header level even if the floor is not.

▲ Whichever method you use, you must remove the section of sole plate that runs across the doorway. Saw from the top alongside each trimmer stud (Figure 11). The partial cuts you made earlier in the bottom of the plate will help you to do this without damaging the floor, but put down a scrap of hardboard or plywood for protection, just in case.

Installation Tip

You may not want or be able to cut into the walls or ceiling to install support blocks for the end studs and ceiling plates. In that case, run a bead of construction mastic along the studs and plate and glue them to the old wall and ceiling. Shim the new frames up from the bottom to clamp the bond at the ceiling, and nail the sole plates through the shims.

This method isn't as solid as using screws to install the frames, but it will work fine if all the glued surfaces are clean and free of loose wallcovering or flaking paint. It's much quicker, too.

Install the jambs

You can buy specially milled jamb stock 4-5/8 or 4-9/16 inches wide, which exactly fits a 2x4 wall with 1/2-inch drywall on both sides.

▲ The instructions included with the bifold doors will help you to calculate the proper length of the side jambs. There must be sufficient height for the doors to clear the track on the top and the pivot on the bottom. You'll also have to add a little more clearance for carpeting. Cut just one jamb to that length. If the jamb is rabbeted at the top, be sure to measure the finish opening height to the bottom of the rabbet and mark the cut 3/4 inch longer than that, allowing for the thickness of the top jamb.

▲ Next, check the floor level across the doorway opening (Figure 12). If one side is low, measure the difference and cut the other side jamb that much longer.

▲ Cut the top jamb to length and nail the side jambs to it with 8d nails (Figure 13). If the side jambs are rabbeted, cut the top jamb longer to make the finish opening measure correctly.

▲ Set the jamb assembly in the rough opening and shim one side to make it exactly plumb (Figure 14). Tape the level to the jamb to leave both hands free to work. Place pairs of shims near the floor, at the middle, and near the top (see Closet Door Finish diagram, page 182). When the jamb is plumb, fasten it with two 8d nails through each pair of shims.

▲ Shim and fasten the other side jamb in the same way (Figure 15). Leave the shims sticking out from the jambs until you are ready to install the casings. Then score them with a utility knife and snap them off.

Hang the doors

Screw the track to the top jamb (Figure 16). Refer to the door instructions for measurements to set it back far enough from the front edge to install a door stop molding.

Set the doors in the track and make adjustments so they hang parallel to the side jambs. Insert shims above the center of the top jamb to keep it level (Figure 17). Once it is level, secure the jamb with 8d nails.

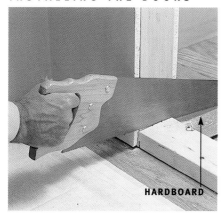

Figure 11. Cut out the sole plate in the doorway, meeting the partial cuts made before the frame was erected. Put down hardboard or plywood to protect the floor surface while sawing.

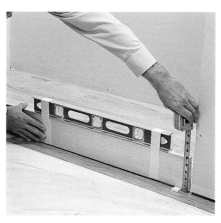

Figure 12. Check the level across the doorway. Tape the level to a straight board cut to the doorway width. Measure the gap at the low side. Cut one side jamb that much longer than the other.

Figure 13. Cut the top jamb to length and nail the side jambs to it with 8d nails. Finish opening dimensions are to the inside surfaces of the jambs. Be sure to allow length for rabbets when cutting the jambs.

Figure 14. Side jambs must be plumb both front to back and side to side, and top jamb level for doors to hang properly. Taping a level to the jamb leaves your hands free to insert shims for adjustments.

Figure 15. Fasten the side jambs in place with 8d finish nails driven through shims at the bottom, middle, and top. Leave the shims sticking out until you are ready to put up the door casing.

Figure 16. Measure carefully for proper setback when screwing door track to top jamb. Upper corner pivots are secured in the track with locking screws. Lower pivots (not shown) screw to jambs and floor.

Figure 17. Hang the doors and check their alignment. Adjust the pivots in the track so the door edges are parallel with the side jambs. Shim and nail the top jamb so there's no sag in the middle.

INSTALLING THE TRIM

Fasten the exterior casings to the edges of the jambs with finish nails. For a more finished look, create a reveal by setting the casings back 1/8 to 1/4 inch from the edges of the jambs. If the casings have decorative corner blocks like those in the photographs, the corners require simple square cuts. If not, make 45-degree cuts for mitered joints.

▲ Install the door stops on the side jambs (Figure 18 and Closet Door Finish box). Align them with the face of the doors and fasten them with finish nails. The stop across the top disguises the metal track without interfering with the operation of the doors.

▲ Add baseboard around the exterior. Use the baseboard you removed in Step 2. To get enough length for a mitered joint at the outside corner, you may have to cut the end piece of baseboard from the original long, back-wall piece. The doors take up enough space for you to get the baseboard for the front wall out of the remaining original pieces. Nail the baseboard into the wall studs with finish nails driven near the baseboard's top edge.

▲ Install ceiling trim, if any, around the top. You can either reuse the original trim or cut new molding. Nail or glue it in place. Also install molding down the exterior wall joints, if you choose not to tape them.

▲ Inside the closet, install simple baseboards and door casings. You will need new lumber for this, because the original trim is now on the exterior. Use clamshell molding or stock 1x4 and 1x6 square-edge boards.

Figure 18. Take great care in cutting and fitting the exterior casing, because it affects the appearance of the closet greatly. Install door stops on the side jambs after the casing is in place.

CLOSET DOOR FINISH

Refer to this diagram to install jamb shims, exterior casing, and door stops. Style of casing can vary widely, but installation is the same.

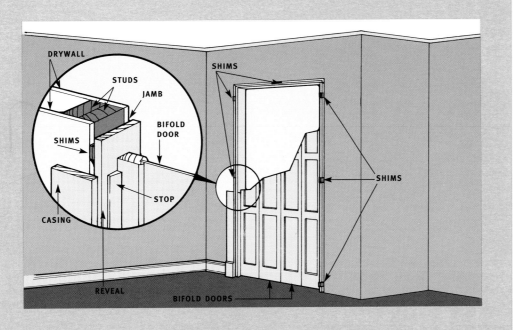

DRYWALL
STUDS
JAMB
SHIMS
BIFOLD DOOR
SHIMS
STOP
CASING
SHIMS
REVEAL
BIFOLD DOORS

INSTALLING INTERIOR FITTINGS

How you equip the closet will depend on the room it is in and its intended use. The simplest arrangement is a rod for hangers, with a shelf above it. Figures 19–22 show you how to finish the interior this way.

Another solution is to use ready-made components. There are many adaptable modular systems available from home centers that combine hanger rods, wire bins, shelves, racks, and drawers. One system is shown in Closet Systems, pages 184–187.

PAINTING THE CLOSET AND TRIM

Use a nail set to drive all the finish nail heads below the surface of the trim; fill them with wood putty. Sand those spots and all patches of drywall compound. Give all new drywall and wood surfaces a coat of primer, and spot-prime other places where needed. Paint a finish coat on the closet walls first, inside and out, then do the trim.

Remove the doors to paint them. If they were supplied unprimed, sand them lightly with medium-grit paper and prime them. Sand the prime coat with fine-grit paper before you apply a finish coat. Hang the doors when dry and install the pulls and alignment hardware that were supplied with them.

Figure 19. To put up a hanger rod and shelf, mark a level line around the inside of the closet 66 in. above the floor. Nail a 1x4 at that height to the studs in the back wall and each end wall.

Figure 20. Use a closet shelf-and-rod bracket as a guide to position a rod holder on the 1x4 at each end of the closet. Fasten the rod holders with screws through their centers.

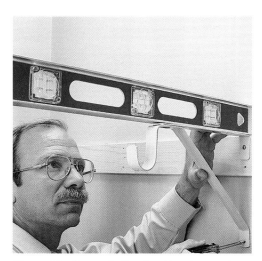

Figure 21. Screw shelf-and-rod brackets to the back-wall 1x4 and studs in the existing wall. Space brackets no more than 48 in. apart. Level each bracket so the shelf will not rock or sag.

Figure 22. Measure, cut, and fit the rod first. Then cut a shelf and check its fit. When you paint the inside of the closet, remove the shelf and rod and paint them separately.

Most closets are full—of wasted space!
Typical closet storage fittings consist of a
rod, a shelf, and the floor.

Closet Systems

When they become overloaded, the closet
becomes "too small."

Using storage fittings that take advantage
of all the available space immediately
makes a closet "bigger," often twice as
big in capacity.

The equipment you need for this
wonderful expansion is available in what
are called closet organizers, storage
systems, or simply closet systems.

Here's what you can get, and how to install
and use them efficiently.

A closet system lets you organize the interior space quickly and easily.
The various components can be installed in any number of ways to get
maximum storage capacity.

CLOSET SYSTEM FEATURES

Closet systems are sold at home centers, space-planning stores, and many large hardware stores. Check the Yellow Pages under "Closet Accessories" for sources in your area.

Most factory-made, ready-to-assemble closet systems use three basic components:
- ▲ Wardrobe shelf
- ▲ Linen shelf/shoe rack
- ▲ Baskets and frame

The components may be enameled or plastic-coated metal, or high-strength plastic.

Wardrobe Shelf. This is a heavy-duty, one-piece rod and shelf unit. A properly installed wardrobe shelf can hold 50 to 75 pounds per linear foot. Shelves are sold in 3-, 4-, 8- and 12-foot lengths, and 12- and 16-inch depths. You can run a shelf from one end wall of the closet to the other, or stop it partway. A very efficient scheme is to put a full-length wardrobe shelf high in the closet and a shorter shelf below it at one end. That gives you a section for hanging long garments, and two for shorter items.

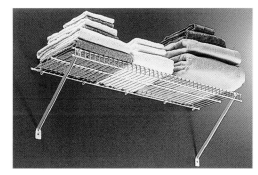

Linen Shelf

Linen Shelf/Shoe Rack. This is a one-piece, double-function unit. When mounted level, it will store towels, pillows, and other items commonly kept on shelves. When the shelf is turned over, to take advantage of the lip at the front edge, and mounted to slope down, away from the wall, it becomes a shoe rack. You can mount two or three of these racks one above another for great capacity in quite limited space. These racks come in 3-, 4-, 8- and 12-foot lengths, and 9-, 12-, 16- or 20-inch depths.

Baskets and Frame. These make up a free-standing unit. The baskets are an open mesh that lets air circulate to help keep clothes fresh and makes it easy to see the contents. They stack vertically in the frame, suspended on runners. Baskets are usually 18 inches wide and 20 inches from front to back; in most systems they come in three or four depths, typically from 4 to 16 inches. Frames are available in various heights, depending on the number and spacing of the basket runners.

Tools You Need

Measuring tape

Pencil

Level

Drill and 1/4" bit

Phillips screwdriver or drill bit

Hacksaw or bolt cutter

Stepladder

Baskets and Frame

Wardrobe Shelf

Shoe Rack

Accessory Items. There are basket liners to keep small items from falling through the gridwork, and frame tops, which give the frame a more finished look and provide additional shelf area. Mounting brackets, support braces, and related hardware are generally sold as accessory packages with the proper items for installing a particular component.

Closet space planning consultants offer these standard measurement rules to aid in your planning. All figures are based on a ceiling height of 8 feet.

Horizontal Hanging Space

• Ordinary-weight clothing: Allow 1 inch of horizontal space for each garment.

• Winter clothing, coats, bulky items: Allow 2 to 3 inches for each article.

• Shoes: Allow 9 inches of width per pair for women's shoes, 10 inches for men's shoes.

Vertical Hanging Space

• Shirts/blouses: Allow between 40 and 42 inches of vertical hanging space.

• Suits/slacks: Allow 42 inches for suits and folded slacks; 48 to 52 inches for slacks hung full-length.

• Dresses: Allow 66 to 70 inches of vertical space.

Shelf Height

• Place a top wardrobe shelf 82 to 84 inches above the floor. With an 8-foot ceiling, this will give 12 to 14 inches of storage space above the shelf and allow adequate space for a second wardrobe shelf directly below shirts, blouses, or other short items.

DESIGNING YOUR CLOSET

The first thing to do is measure your closet's height, width, and depth. Next, sketch your plan to visualize what the system will look like in place. Try a few different layouts.

When planning your closet layout, remember to allow for additions to your wardrobe. Basic spacing requirements are given in the box at the left. Here are some tips on how to make the most efficient use of the space:

▲ Hang shirts and blouses from the bottom of an upper wardrobe shelf.

▲ Hang suits, sport coats, and slacks below the shirts, on a lower wardrobe shelf.

▲ Store shoes 10–12 inches off the floor. Horizontal or slanted racks make it easy to see shoes. Vertical racks—which many space planners feel make better use of space—can be mounted on the back of a hinged door, on a side wall in a walk-in closet, or centered on the back wall in a straight closet.

▲ Position a basket-and-frame unit in the center one-third of the closet. Most people feel it works best in this location. You can pull the baskets out without interference from the doors or racks on the side walls. A basket unit also helps you separate your hanging clothing. For example, put your casual clothes on one side, your dress clothes on the other.

▲ Store the things you don't need to get at every day on upper shelves.

INSTALLING A CLOSET SYSTEM

You can install a complete closet system in just one weekend. The work is easy and goes fast for several reasons.

▲ The units are modular in size.

▲ They are easy to cut to length.

▲ Best of all, most manufacturers provide mounting hardware that does not have to be secured to a wall stud.

Mounting hardware

Each system manufacturer produces recommended fasteners, braces, brackets, and related hardware. These items are usually either packaged with or displayed near the other components wherever closet systems are sold.

The system shown in the accompanying photographs uses specially designed "fin back" clips for studless installation in 1/4-inch holes (Figure 1). As the mounting screw is driven in, the clip's "wings" spread wider than a conventional plastic wall anchor, which eliminates having to secure them into a wall stud. However, if there is a stud, just insert the clip into the hole and drive the screw. The screw bites into the stud to hold the clip in place.

Putting up a shelf or rack

Here are the steps for installing a wardrobe shelf or linen/shoe rack:

▲ Mark a level line on the wall at the desired shelf height. Make the line as long as the shelf.

▲ Drill 1/4-inch diameter holes along the line every 9 to 11 inches—or at the spacing given in the instructions, if different—and insert a mounting clip into each hole (Figure 2). Secure each clip with the screw that comes with it. Hold the clip as you tighten the screw to prevent it from spinning.

▲ If necessary, cut the shelf to length with a hacksaw or bolt cutter. Then put an end mounting bracket on each end at the front.

▲ Insert the rear edge of the shelf in the clips on the wall and lower the shelf into position. Place a short level on the shelf, get it level from front to back, and then mark the holes for the bracket screws on the wall (Figure 3).

▲ Swing the shelf and end bracket up far enough to drill 1/4-inch holes. Insert an expanding plastic wall anchor in each hole (Figure 4). Lower the shelf into place and drive the mounting screws into the anchors.

▲ Attach a support brace to the shelf at least every 36 inches. Clip the brace to the front rail of the shelf, and fasten it with a screw driven into an expanding plastic anchor (Figure 5). For a shelf or rack less than 36 inches long, attach a support brace at each end.

▲ Mount a shoe rack in the same way as a short shelf, but use short angled support brackets that extend to the middle rail rather than the front edge of the rack (Figure 6).

▲ Before hanging up your clothes, slip protective plastic caps over any exposed cut ends of the shelves or racks.

▲ If you wish to move a shelf or rack, it's easy to unmount it, remove the clips, and patch the holes in the wall. The clips and support braces can be reused in a new location.

Installing a basket-and-frame unit

Simply position the frame where you want it and slide the baskets into place. In most units the runners are fixed in place, but spaced so that you can use various sizes of matching baskets without wasted space. Some units provide clips or mounting holes for securing the frame to the floor or to the wall behind.

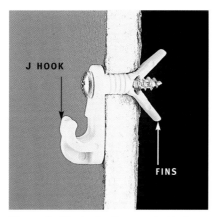

Figure 1. Fin-back clips are plastic J-hooks with ribbed shanks that grip the sides of 1/4-in. mounting holes, and fins that spread wide behind the wall.

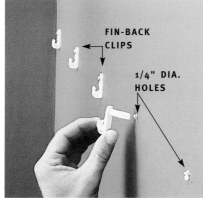

Figure 2. Mount fin-back clips 9 to 11 in. apart along a level line at the desired shelf height. The rear rod of a shelf slips into the row of J-hooks.

Figure 3. Hold a shelf end bracket against the wall with the shelf in place to mark for the anchors. Be sure the shelf is level before marking the hole positions.

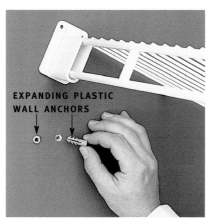

Figure 4. Swing the shelf and end bracket up to drill holes and insert plastic wall anchors. Don't install the bracket separately; if you install it first, you won't be able to get the shelf into position if you do.

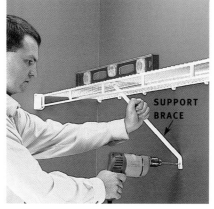

Figure 5. Support shelves and racks with a brace at least every 36 in. It is not absolutely necessary to fasten the bottom end of the brace into a stud; however, it's a good idea if possible.

Figure 6. Use short angled brackets to support a shoe rack. The brackets snap onto the rack. Some simply rest against the wall, while others have a screw in the foot for more secure mounting.

Index

Acknowledgments

Special thanks to these members of The Family Handyman family:

Charles Avoles, Ron Chamberlain, John Emmons, Bill Faber, Roxie Filipkowski, Barb Herrmann, Al Hildenbrand, Shelly Jacobsen, Duane Johnson, Mike Krivit, Phil Leisenheimer, Don Mannes, Doug Oudekerk, Deborah Palmen, Don Prestly, Dave Radtke, Art Rooze, Mike Smith, Dan Stoffel, Eugene Thompson, Mark Thompson, Bob Ungar, Alice Wagner, Gregg Weigand, Gary "Mac" Wentz, Marcia Williston, Donna Wynenbach, Bill Zuehlke.

This book was produced by Roundtable Press, Inc.,
for the Reader's Digest Association
in cooperation with The Family Handyman magazine.

If you have any questions or comments, please feel free to write us at:

The Family Handyman
7900 International Drive
Suite 950
Minneapolis, MN 55425

More Top-Rated How-To Information From Reader's Digest® and The Family Handyman®

THE FAMILY HANDYMAN WOODWORKING ROOM BY ROOM

Furniture, Cabinetry, Built-Ins and Other Projects for the Home

The easiest, most complete guide of over 20 different projects, ranging from straightforward items beginners can easily master to more sophisticated pieces for experienced woodworkers looking for new challenges; includes such projects as a country pine bench, traditional bookcase and Victorian hall stand.

192 pages
10 ¹¹/₁₆ x 8 ³/₈
over 500 color photographs
ISBN #0-89577-686-3
$19.95

THE FAMILY HANDYMAN OUTDOOR PROJECTS

Great Ways to Make the Most of Your Outdoor Living Space

The most popular outdoor projects targeted for all skill levels are found in this easy-to-use volume. There's something for everyone in this comprehensive how-to guide—from a relatively simple garden bench and a children's sandbox to more complex structures—a spectacular gazebo and romantic garden arbor and swing.

192 pages
10 ¹¹/₁₆ x 8 ³/₈
Over 500 color photographs
ISBN #0-89577-623-5
$19.95

THE FAMILY HANDYMAN EASY REPAIR

Over 100 Simple Solutions to the Most Common Household Problems

Designed to help save hundreds, even thousands, of dollars in costly repairs, here is that one book that should be in every household library. It offers simple, step-by-step, quick-and-easy solutions to the most common and costly household problems faced at home, from unclogging a sink to repairing broken shingles to fixing damaged electrical plugs.

192 pages
10 ¹¹/₁₆ x 8 ³/₈
·725 color photographs
ISBN #0-89577-624-3
$19.95

Measuring the Metric Way

Use these guides and table to convert between English and metric measuring systems.

Fasteners

Nails are sold by penny size or penny weight (expressed by the letter *d*). Length is designated by the penny size. Some common lengths are:

2d	(25 mm/1 in.)
6d	(51 mm/2 in.)
10d	(76 mm/3 in.)
20d	(102 mm/4 in.)
40d	(127 mm/5 in.)
60d	(152 mm/6 in.)

Below are metric and imperial equivalents of some common **bolts:**

10 mm	⅜ in.
12 mm	½ in.
16 mm	⅝ in.
20 mm	¾ in.
25 mm	1 in.
50 mm	2 in.
65 mm	2½ in.
70 mm	2¾ in.

Calculating Concrete Requirements

Multiply length by width to get the slab area in square meters. Then read across, under whichever of three thicknesses you prefer, to see how many cubic meters of concrete you will need.

Area in Square Meters (m^2)	Thickness in Millimeters		
(length x width)	100	130	150
	Volume in Cubic Meters (m^3)		
5	0.50	0.65	0.75
10	1.00	1.30	1.50
20	2.00	2.60	3.00
30	3.00	3.90	4.50
40	4.00	5.20	6.00
50	5.00	6.50	7.50

If a greater volume of concrete is required, multiply by the appropriate number. To lay a 100-millimeter-thick patio in an area 6 meters wide and 10 meters long, for example, estimate as follows: 6 meters x 10 meters = 60 meters square = area. Using the chart above, simply double the concrete quantity for a 30-meter-square, 100-millimeter-thick slab (2 x 3 m^3 = 6 m^3) or add the quantities for 10 m^2 and 50 m^2 (1 m^3 + 5 m^3 = 6 m^3).